INVESTIGATING
PSYCHOLOGY

INVESTIGATING PSYCHOLOGY

Sciences of the mind after Wittgenstein

Edited by
John Hyman

London and New York

First published 1991
by Routledge
11 New Fetter Lane, London EC4P 4EE

Simultaneously published in the USA and Canada
by Routledge
a division of Routledge, Chapman and Hall, Inc.
29 West 35th Street, New York, NY 10001

Typeset in 10/12pt Garamond by Selectmove, London
Printed in Great Britain by
Biddles Ltd, Guildford, Surrey

British Library Cataloguing in Publication Data
Investigating psychology: sciences of the mind after Wittgenstein.
1. Man. Mind. Theories of Wittgenstein, Ludwig
I. Hyman, John
128.2092

Library of Congress Cataloging in Publication Data
Investigating psychology: sciences of the mind after Wittgenstein /
edited by John Hyman: contributors, Norman Malcolm . . . [et al.].
p.   cm.
Includes bibliographical references and index.
1. Psychology and philosophy. 2. Wittgenstein, Ludwig,
1889–1951. 3. Psycholinguistics. 4. Visual perception.
5. Cognition. 6. Hyman, John. 7. Malcolm, Norman
BF41.I58   1991
150′.1—dc20   90–47343

ISBN 0–415–01982–6

In memory of Norman Malcolm
Philosopher and Teacher
11.6.1911 – 5.8.1990

CONTENTS

THE CONTRIBUTORS

John Dupré is an Associate Professor of Philosophy at Stanford University. He received his Ph.D. from Cambridge University and was subsequently a Junior Research Fellow at St John's College, Oxford. He is the editor of *The Latest on the Best: Essays on Evolution and Optimality* (Cambridge, Mass.: Bradford Books/MIT, 1987) and has published a number of articles on metaphysics and the philosophy of science.

Bruce Goldberg is an Associate Professor of Philosophy at the University of Maryland, Baltimore. He was formerly an Assistant Professor of Philosophy at Cornell University. His publications include articles on the philosophy of mind and the philosophy of language.

Peter Hacker is Fellow and Tutor in Philosophy at St John's College, Oxford. He is the author of *Insight and Illusion* (Oxford: Oxford University Press, 1972; revised edition 1986), *Appearance and Reality* (Oxford: Basil Blackwell, 1987), and *Wittgenstein: Meaning and Mind* (Oxford: Basil Blackwell, 1990). He is also author of a number of books with Gordon Baker, including *Wittgenstein: Understanding and Meaning* (Oxford: Basil Blackwell, 1980), *Wittgenstein: Rules, Grammar and Necessity* (Oxford: Basil Blackwell, 1985), and *Language, Sense and Nonsense* (Oxford: Basil Blackwell, 1984).

John Hyman is Fellow and Praelector in Philosophy at The Queen's College, Oxford. He was previously a research fellow at the Hebrew University, Jerusalem, and a visiting lecturer at Swarthore College, Pennsylvania. He is the author of *The Imitation of Nature* (Oxford: Basil Blackwell, 1989).

THE CONTRIBUTORS

Anthony Kenny is Warden of Rhodes House, Oxford, and was previously Master of Balliol College, Oxford. His many published works include *Wittgenstein* (Harmondsworth: Penguin, 1973), *The Anatomy of the Soul* (Oxford: Basil Blackwell, 1974), *Freewill and Responsibility* (London: Routledge & Kegan Paul, 1978), *The God of the Philosophers* (Oxford: Oxford University Press, 1979; reissued 1986), and *The Legacy of Wittgenstein* (Oxford: Basil Blackwell, 1984).

Norman Malcolm was Susan Linn Sage Professor of Philosophy at Cornell University, where he taught from 1947 until his retirement in 1978. He was Visiting Professor of Philosophy at King's College, London, from then until his death, and latterly Fellow of King's College. His many publications include *Ludwig Wittgenstein: A Memoir* (Oxford: Oxford University Press, 1958), *Dreaming* (London: Routledge & Kegan Paul, 1959), *Memory and Mind* (Ithaca: Cornell University Press, 1977), *Nothing is Hidden* (Oxford: Basil Blackwell, 1986) and, with D. M. Armstrong, *Consciousness and Causality* (Oxford: Basil Blackwell, 1984). Norman Malcolm died in London on 5 August 1990.

Stuart Shanker is a Full Professor in the Department of Philosophy at York University, Toronto, Canada. He is the editor of *Ludwig Wittgenstein: Critical Assessments* (London: Croom Helm, 1986) and *Godel's Theorem in Focus* (London: Croom Helm, 1988), and author of *Wittgenstein and the Turning-Point in the Philosophy of Mathematics* (London: Croom Helm, 1987).

ACKNOWLEDGEMENTS

Five of the essays in this book are new. For their permission to reproduce the other three, I am grateful to the original publishers.

Bruce Goldberg's 'Mechanism and Meaning' was first published in *Knowledge and Mind*, edited by Carl Ginet and Sydney Shoemaker (New York: Oxford University Press, 1983).

Anthony Kenny's 'The Homunculus Fallacy' was first published in *Interpretations of Life and Mind*, edited by Marjorie Greene, (London: Routledge & Kegan Paul, 1971).

Norman Malcolm's 'The Relation of Language to Instinctive Behaviour' was first published in *Philosophical Investigations* 5/1 (1982).

INTRODUCTION
John Hyman

What can philosophers say to psychologists? What benefit could
somebody engaged in the experimental study of the acquisition and
exercise of human capacities for sensation, perception, memory,
language and problem-solving derive from reading work that belongs
to a discipline which has as much use for measurement and
experiment as theology, and which has generally shown more
interest in the ruminations and speculations of distant intellectual
ancestors than in the theories and hypotheses of contemporary
scientists?

Presumably, a great many British and American philosophers
today believe that the answer is not 'None at all!'; for while they
have much to say about physics and biology, English-speaking
philosophers seem nowadays to have far more to say – or at any
rate they want to say far more – to psychologists and others working
in the human sciences. Why is this so? Is it because philosophers talk
about problems until the means of solving them by experimental
enquiry has been discovered, and then hand over to the scientists?
Is the far greater attention that psychological problems receive
from philosophers due to the fact that experimental psychology,
to borrow a term from political economy, is a *developing* science?
It need not be considered demeaning to philosophers to be hurried
offstage before the drama begins: Socrates was happy to call himself
a midwife to the ideas of young men, and it does philosophy no
discredit to be regarded as midwife to science.

However, this view of philosophy and its relation to psychology
is unsatisfactory, for it combines a careless picture of philosophy
and a misguided conception of science. Greek philosophy, for
example, included a wealth of cosmological speculation, which
is now acknowledged to be beyond the ken of sober-minded

1

philosophy. But this does not show that the range of problems suitable for philosophical study diminishes with the progress of empirical science; it shows what is in any case obvious, that ancient Greek philosophy was a hodgepodge of anecdote, *a priori* theorizing, mythology, taxonomy and much else besides – as well as the sort of enquiry that is still called 'philosophical'.

The misguided view about science which fosters the idea that philosophy ends where incipient science begins is the Whiggish and implausibly refined view that regards the history of science as the paradigm of intellectual progress, the more or less straightforward succession of increasingly powerful, increasingly general theories.

Progress, of sorts, there is: technology bears witness to it. And it may be because progress, like economic growth, is a modern fetish that many enthusiasts about science cleave to the notion that science is purely progressive. Nevertheless, the notion is wrong. As one philosopher of science has put it,

> the history of science ... does not just consist of facts and conclusions drawn from facts. It also contains ideas, interpretations of facts, problems created by conflicting inter-pretations, mistakes and so on ... This being the case, the history of science will be as complex, chaotic, full of mistakes, and entertaining as the ideas it contains, and these ideas in turn will be as complex, chaotic, full of mistakes, and entertaining as are the minds of those who invented them.[1]

This does not mean that science is polluted or compromised: the complexity is an intrinsic part of science and has both good and bad consequences. For example, the idea that seeing is a matter of finding out from images (whether ethereal images emitted from objects, as many Greek philosophers supposed, or retinal images, as contemporary visual theorists believe) what is present in the percipient's visible environment enabled Kepler to describe the geometry of the eye correctly, but it also led visual theorists to puzzle for hundreds of years over the fact that we see the world upright in spite of the inversion of the retinal image, and to regard the explanation of this anomaly as, in George Berkeley's words, 'the principal point of the whole optic theory'.

The view that philosophy is the midwife of science is as mistaken as the view that it is the Queen of the Sciences; and like the latter view it derives from a mistaken conception of science itself. If science were as austere and purely empirical an activity as is sometimes believed, philosophy could have nothing to do with it, at any rate once it is in its stride. But because science is a rich and complex cultural tradition, and not an intellectual engine that turns remorselessly at its own pace, unaffected by what surrounds it, it contains its measure of mythology – not necessarily pernicious, and in many cases fruitful and inspiring – and its measure of confusion too. It is this fact about science that explains one aspect of the need for philosophy to investigate it.

This does not mean that philosophy is necessarily anti-scientific, in the sense that Blake was anti-scientific, and set out to destroy what he regarded as a vicious intellectual tendency which promised only to strangle man's divine faculty of imagination. Scientists and philosophers can participate in the same intellectual project – they may, for example, both contribute to progress in the psychological sciences – but they do so in fundamentally different ways. One must beware of exaggerating the uniformity of the sciences: palaeontology and astrophysics are no more similar in method than they are in subject-matter. By contrast, the distinctive character of the philosopher's contribution to science remains constant. As an example, I shall take the problem already mentioned, the problem of the inversion and reversal of the retinal image.

When Greek philosopher-scientists were first puzzled by the faculty of sight, they sought to discover what invisible connection exists between the eye and what it perceives. In other words, they wanted to know what conveys the visible features of an object to the observer's eye; and many of them thought that they had found the answer in the tiny picture – which as we now know is reflected by the cornea – of the visual field that is visible in anybody's eye. A picture, after all, does enable you to know what its subject looks like; and here was a picture of everything visible to a person actually located in the organ of sight!

The problem and its solution are a fascinating mixture of sharp and muddled thinking; and it is edifying to discover how difficult it is, even with the degree of detachment we can maintain from Greek thought, to unmix the two. But it is certainly muddled to suppose that a picture conveys to the eye the appearance of the visible environment. Indeed, it is the very fact about a picture that recommended it to the Greeks as a mediator between eye and visible object that debars it from this office. A picture, to be sure, reproduces the appearance of what it depicts; and it is therefore the ideal means by which to convey the appearance of some person or thing – of Anne of Cleves to Henry VIII, for example. But this is the case because a picture is the very epitome of the visible: we discover what it depicts precisely by looking at it. Indeed, that is what it means to say that it 'reproduces the appearance of what it depicts', and does not merely suggest or evoke it. But because a picture is something that functions primarily by being seen, it is of necessity a part of the visible environment – something to be presented to the eye, so to speak, and not the thing that does the presenting. And so the sense in which visual theory aims to discover what conveys the appearance of an object to an observer's eye – i.e., how the object acts on the eye so as to enable us to see it – cannot be the sense in which a picture does so: a picture cannot bridge the very gap that it requires in order to function as a picture.

The idea that a picture is sent by an object to the eye was modified in the Middle Ages by the Arab scientist Alhazen, who argued that the picture is sent out in a fragmentary form and reassembled in the eye. Each individual point on the object, he argued, like the individual tesserae of a mosaic, independently emits its own image along every straight line, including the straight line to the eye. The refractive properties of the eye alter the direction of each line that reaches its surface; and finally an image of the entire mosaic – of the object, that is – is properly organized somewhere within the eye. This was an original and important development; but the basic idea of the Greeks, that seeing is rather like learning what a man looks like by inspecting his portrait, was not abandoned.

Johann Kepler, writing at the beginning of the seventeenth century, was the first person to describe the optics of the eye correctly. He explained how to trace the path to and through the eye that is followed by light emitted by a point-source in a person's visual field; and how to identify the point where the light would strike the retina. But Kepler remained captive to the idea that seeing is like learning what a man looks like by inspecting his portrait. So what he believed he had discovered was just where in the eye this picture is to be found, and how it gets there. Now as we all know, the picture that is indeed visible on the retina (albeit with a complicated apparatus) is upside down and left–right reversed. Hence the problem, explicitly posed by Kepler, but anticipated by Alhazen: if seeing is a matter of inspecting the picture, why doesn't the visible environment look upside down and left–right reversed?

In view of what has been said about ancient visual theory, it would clearly have been futile to address this question by postulating a mechanism that reinverts the image, and seeking to establish how this mechanism functions. The solution to the problem is not to be found in physiology; nor for that matter in optics, although many scientists of great stature, such as Leonardo da Vinci, have supposed that it is. In a sense, it cannot be solved: instead, it has to be *dis*solved, by remembering why the very idea of a picture conveying to the eye the appearance of a visible object is confused, and by precipitating the optical theory from this muddled solution. Such a task, despite that metaphor, does not require the appurtenances of a laboratory. If you look back to the paragraph in which I attempted to untangle the original muddle, you will notice that it does not depend upon any physiological fact about the eye or any physical fact about light or the visible environment; and it follows that experimental evidence cannot play a part in assessing its validity.

Perhaps the problem of the inversion and reversal of the retinal image occupied centre-stage in an experimental discipline for a couple of centuries precisely because it was not amenable to experimental solution – in other words, because it is the articulation of a muddle masquerading as a scientific problem. And the masquerade succeeded because the original Greek idea that a picture mediates between the eye and its object exercised such a powerful grip on the scientific imagination. Learning what a man looks like by inspecting his portrait is an entrancing symbol of the faculty of vision: it captures the magic of sight rather as certain mythological stories capture the magic of fire or wine. And mythology, as I have said, has always played its part in science. Nevertheless, to mistake a myth for an empirical hypothesis that can be tested, confirmed or confuted leads only to confusion. The philosopher's job is to identify and describe the mythology, and above all to diagnose and extirpate the confusion.

Alhazen, Leonardo and Kepler were the intellectual equals of the greatest living scientists – at a very modest reckoning! It would therefore be astonishing if contemporary science were not at least as permeated by mythology and confusion as any of theirs. (I say 'at least as permeated ...' because history suggests that it is far easier to cause confusion than to dissipate it. When we muddy the waters they clear themselves: gravity sees to that. But there is no natural force that inclines us to think clearly.) To be sure, we know more than they did. But as we have seen, additions to the store of knowledge – new facts – are of no use at all in the struggle against confusions like the problem of inversion and reversal. For these knots in our understanding are tied not by the facts themselves, but by our manner of representing them. It is not the phenomenon under scrutiny that puzzles us here, although it seems to be; it is the language we employ to describe it. Indeed, the special character of such problems derives from the fact that they impel us to examine the matter itself with all the energy and imagination we can muster – when that is the last thing we should be doing.

Now we can return to the question, why philosophers take such a keen interest in psychology. Human beings are sociable animals, and many of our most absorbing and important activities are social ones. (Science and philosophy are and always have been social activities: 'I'm a lover of learning,' said Socrates 'and trees and open country won't teach me anything, whereas men in the city do.') Language is not only the medium of many of these activities; it is also the most sensitive index of the interests and priorities of its users. As every philosopher knows – the example crops up again and again – the language of the Eskimos has many words to distinguish between different kinds of snow. This is remarkable, although it is not at all surprising. But it is quite unremarkable that English has dozens of words to distinguish between a glance, a glimpse, a gaze, a leer, a look, a stare, a peep and so forth, and thousands of words to distinguish between different sorts of motive, mood and temperament. And far more important than the number of words – a crude measure of linguistic subtlety – is the rich freight of metaphor that even the most mundane expressions or reports of our mental lives must carry. Wittgenstein wrote that

> our language can be seen as an ancient city: a maze of little streets and squares, of old and new houses, and of houses with additions from various periods; and this surrounded by a multitude of new boroughs with straight regular streets and uniform houses.[2]

Electrical engineering is definitely suburban, which makes life relatively simple for electrical engineers; but it is the fascination and the curse of psychology that it lives in the middle of the city – right in the thick of things!

More than its mere complexity, it is the uncanny power of the pictures imbedded in psychological language which breeds confusion: the memory as a storehouse or library, thought as silent soliloquy, feelings as perturbations of a 'glassy essence', hidden from public view, motives as ethereal forces which propel our acts.

Pictures such as these are not merely harmless in ordinary discourse; they are indispensable. But they wreak havoc if, when we theorize about the mind, we take them at face value, for their significance (like the significance of an icon) is not simply what meets the eye, but derives also from their use. These pictures of the mind sound antiquated, and so they are. But it would be a mistake to infer that scientific psychology has outgrown their influence, for they are not comparable to superannuated psychological theories. (It would be a bizarre claim that the theory of the humours, for example, continues to exert an undetected influence on cognitive science.) Their grip on the imagination is not the grip of a tremendous hypothesis, like the big bang, but more like the grip of an entrancing metaphor or myth; and their influence on theory is as permanent as the language in which they are lodged.

Although the psychological theories examined in this book are heterogeneous in subject-matter, they are homogeneous in style, for all are products of the mainstream of British and American psychological research in the post-war period. Certain themes recur. The orthodoxy is now computational, representationalist and methodologically austere: cognitive faculties are deemed to be computational faculties; computational processes are construed as manufacturing and manipulating representations; and the methodological bias is towards laboratory experiments rather than field studies. It is the premiss of this collection that philosophical investigations can contribute to psychological science by extirpating conceptual confusions that have been woven into the fabric of empirical research; and it is a striking fact that emerges from investigations of this sort, that in many cases the conceptual problems raised by psychological theories have an independent, and sometimes extensive history in the philosophical canon. This is most obviously the case with the second theme, representationalism, which is treated in several of the articles collected here. But it is surprising to discover that the same is true of the first theme, the computational analogy, which was inspired by a process of technological innovation that began less than fifty years ago and is far from over.

The computational analogy raises questions that appear both profound and entirely new: whether a suitably programmed digital computer would deserve to be dignified by the use of cognitive predicates – 'thinks', 'calculates', 'believes', 'perceives', and so forth; and whether the fact that human beings and many other animals qualify for this distinction is to be explained in terms of the programmes that would enable a digital computer to behave in an apparently thoughtful way. I shall not propose answers to these questions, but merely introduce the philosophical problems that must be faced if they are to be answered.

Computers are very large systems of switches. A single switch, a light switch for example, has two positions, on and off. It can, so to say, be in two states. A system that comprises two switches has four possible states, a system that comprises three switches has eight possible states, and so forth. The very first digital computers, which were made in Britain and America more than forty years ago, had about $10^{50,000}$ possible states. In the 1940s and 1950s it was widely believed that the brain is also a large system of switches, a complex web of neurons each of which has two states, but this has been shown to be wholly false, and so the putative analogy between brain and computer is now defended only in terms of what computers do, not how they are built.

The design of digital computers was anticipated a hundred years before the first was built; but the scope of computation was understood only in the 1930s. In 1937 the British mathematician Alan Turing published a paper which exploited an analogy between mathematical and mechanical procedures in order to demonstrate that there can be no definite method to determine whether an unproven mathematical statement – 'every even number is the sum of two primes', for example – admits of proof.[3] In fact, Turing devised an imaginary machine capable of transforming strings of mathematical symbols in conformity with definite rules and, in effect, he proceeded to show that no such mechanical device could exist which accepts as its input an arbitrary mathematical proposition, and delivers as its output the correct answer to the question whether the proposition is provable.

In order to serve its purpose, the type of machine defined in Turing's paper had to be, and had to be shown to be, an absolutely general device, capable of executing any definite procedure whatsoever for the manipulation of mathematical symbols: otherwise, the possibility remained that the paper's argument reflected only the limited scope of Turing's concept of mechanism. The type of machine that Turing conceived – it is known as a 'Turing machine' – consists of a scanning device and a tape of unlimited length, divided into squares. The scanner moves back and forth along the tape, one square at a time, and at each square (which may have a symbol printed on it already) it either prints a symbol from a limited repertoire, erases a symbol, leaves the existing symbol unchanged or leaves the square blank. The scanner has a finite number of states (like a light-switch, which has two, and unlike a mercury thermometer) and at each step, the symbol which is being scanned and the state of the machine together determine whether the scanner will print, erase or neither, whether it will remain in the same state or change to another specified state, and whether it will move one step to the left, one step to the right or neither.

Because the number of states and the number of symbols are limited, it is possible to describe the behaviour of a Turing machine in tabular form. For example, the *machine table*, as it is called, for a rudimentary adding machine is shown in Table 1.

The machine specified by this table is designed to receive an input such as '11 + 111' and to produce an output such as '11111'. It starts in state A and moves along the tape from left to right. In effect, it replaces the '+' with a '1', erases the final '1', and then stops. If it encounters a nonsensical formula, such as '+ . . .', '1 + + . . .' or '1+1+ . . .', it stops. This is not a terribly sophisticated example, but it is generally agreed that any routine method for the manipulation of a limited number of symbols can be carried out by a machine of this general sort. As Gödel put it in 1964, 'Turing's work gives an analysis of the concept of "mechanical procedure" (alias "algorithm" or "computation procedure" or "finite combinatorial

Table 1 A machine table for a rudimentary adding machine

	1	+	blank
state A	move R state B	no move state D	move R state A
state B	move R state B	erase no move state B	print 1 move R state C
state C	move R state C	no move state D	move L state D
state D	erase move R state D	no move state D	no move state D

procedure"). This concept is shown to be equivalent with that of a "Turing machine".[4]

With the machine table for such a machine it is obviously possible to calculate the machine's output for any given input. What is less obvious, but nevertheless true, is that a machine table can be devised so that the Turing machine it specifies will accept as part of its input a suitably codified machine table and perform such a calculation automatically. It follows that a single Turing machine of this particular sort – a Universal Turing Machine – can do anything that any Turing machine can do. In the jargon, it can *imitate* any Turing machine – including another Universal Machine. An electronic digital computer is a practical realization of a Universal Turing Machine, an infinitely flexible device for the manipulation of symbols. And when my computer is running, for example, a word-processing programme, it is, in effect, imitating the Universal Machine specified by the so-called *language* in which the programme is written, which is in turn imitating the Turing Machine specified by the programme. Consequently, when I say that my computer has deleted a sentence, or moved a block of text, I am describing its behaviour at a giddy level of abstraction, rather as the rate of inflation describes the economic behaviour of traders in goods and services. And just as two countries with different major industries and different sorts of economic organization may nevertheless have the same rate of inflation, so the same computer programme can be run on computers that are differently built of different materials.

An automatic digital computer, then, can be programmed to simulate the behaviour of a human being computing according to the rules of a formal system. (The significance of the word 'simulate' will emerge in due course.) In the rudimentary example already given, the machine, like the human being, will produce the formula '111111' in response to the formulae '11+1111', '111' in response to '11+1', and so forth. In one sense, such a machine can even be programmed to simulate the behaviour of human beings who are not (ostensibly at least) computing according to the rules of any formal system, so long as the human behaviour can be formally described. And the same goes for the behaviour of a pendulum or a planet. But as we shall see, the word 'simulate' means something rather different when we say that a computer can simulate doing arithmetic, and when we say that a computer can simulate traffic in Naples or a hurricane in the Caribbean.

We can now sharpen the questions raised by the computational analogy, which were: whether a suitably programmed digital computer would deserve to be dignified by the use of cognitive predicates – 'thinks', 'calculates', 'believes', 'perceives' and so forth; and whether the fact that human beings and many other animals qualify for this distinction is to be explained in terms of the programmes that would enable a digital computer to behave in an apparently thoughtful way. We can now construe the first question as asking (1) whether something can be deemed to think, calculate a flight-path or understand Portuguese, simply because it (mechanically) manipulates symbols, defined in purely formal terms, in conformity with the rules of a formal system; and we can construe the second question as asking (2) whether human cognitive capacities are in fact capacities to perform computational operations on formally specified elements, and (3) whether our ordinary descriptions of the mental lives of human beings, ourselves and others, are descriptions of the workings of the brain, albeit at a giddy level of abstraction. (Notice that we cannot consistently answer 'No!' to (1) and 'Yes!' to (2).) Computational psychology is committed to the view that these are empirical questions which will eventually be settled by experiment, and which have at least a sporting chance of being answered – when the experiments have been done – in the affirmative.

Philosophers who presume to dismiss hypotheses such as these on *a priori* grounds infuriate the scientists who advance them. (Witness the splendid torrent of abuse provoked by Hubert Dreyfus's *What Computers Can't Do!*) There are two reason for the fury. First, it seems fabulously arrogant to anticipate the results of decades of experimental enquiry; and second, it seems that this arrogance is compounded, in some cases, with a disdain for the experimental method itself. But as I have said, it is the business of philosophers to extirpate confusions that masquerade as empirical hypotheses; in other words, to examine questions – such as the question, 'How do we see the world upright in spite of the inversion of the retinal image?' – that in fact betray conceptual confusion, whilst appearing to express puzzlement about the causes of natural phenomena. The philosophical challenge that computational psychology must face is the array of arguments – several of them are presented in this collection – which have been thought to demonstrate that the three questions posed in the previous paragraph are questions of this sort. This approach certainly does seek to delimit the boundaries of experimental science; but it does not betray a disdain for experimental enquiry *per se*; and neither does it depend upon anticipating experimental results. In a nutshell: the scientists complain that the philosophers are trying to do *a priori* science, which can't be done; and the philosophers reply that the scientists are trying to do experimental philosophy, which is an absurdity.

Consider now question (1), whether something can be deemed to think, calculate or understand a language simply because it manipulates symbols defined in purely formal terms in conformity with the rules of a formal system. To begin with, the something in question need not be an electronic computer; and in fact it is helpful to suppose that it is a human being. Human beings certainly do think, calculate and understand languages, and so we can pursue question (1) by asking ourselves whether somebody who has learned to manipulate an uninterpreted formal calculus isomorphic with, for example, the rules of arithmetic has acquired the same intellectual capacity, the same mathematical skill as somebody who has been taught arithmetic in the usual way.

I presented above the machine table for a rudimentary adding machine. It is easy to check that the machine specified by this table actually does the job: one need only mimic the behaviour of the machine, consulting the table at each step. Now the table for a Turing machine that can handle arithmetic in binary notation is considerably larger than this one. Suppose nevertheless that a mathematical ignoramus with a prodigious memory managed not merely to mimic the machine – which would be no more difficult than mimicking a twelve-box-table machine – but actually committed the table to memory. Given the written formula '10110 × 1010', perhaps using his finger to mark the place he is supposed to be scanning, and mumbling '. . . now I'm in state B and I'm scanning a circle so I've got to erase it and move left and stay in the same state . . . now I'm still in state B, and I'm scanning a line so I've got to . . .', he is able, eventually, to hand back the written formula '11011100'. But does he know any mathematics?

I think it is obvious that he does not. After all, he does not know what a number or an arithmetical operation is, and he neither understands nor misunderstands the signs that he scans, writes and erases. The most rudimentary understanding of arithmetic involves the abilities to count and to draw simple inferences about the numbers and magnitudes of things observed. For example, I have three counters in my left hand and two in my right, so I have five counters altogether. But the computational skill described in this story does not involve anything of the sort.

If we maintain that the mathematical ignoramus in the story does not understand (or misunderstand) the signs that he scans, what exactly is supposed to be missing? It is easy to misconstrue this proposition, for one might ask just the same question about a person who has learned arithmetic in the normal way. We can see that he is able to add and multiply, count and calculate, but how do we know whether he understands what he is up to? It seems that we cannot have any access to the psychological experiences he has when he calculates; and yet surely the question whether he understands arithmetic is one that could only be answered by studying the character of these experiences. Many writers impressed by the computational analogy are inclined to see the problem in this way. One such wrote that

> if I am asked for the phenomenology of anyone else's under-
> standing, I have, of course, no feelings and immediate assurance
> to fall back on, and I am out in the cold world of watching his
> behaviour for appearances of understanding.[5]

And the upshot is that we cannot really complain that mere computation ignores the problematic but vital ingredient of human mental life – understanding – for 'the existence of subjective understanding is just as much a problem for the human experimental psychologist as it is for the [computer simulation] worker'.[6]

The idea that the difference between calculating or, for that matter, uttering a word, with and without understanding consists in the presence or absence of an ineffable psychological experience which accompanies the calculation or the utterance is confused. It is true that we may have all sorts of experiences when we, say, follow an intricate argument, and understand it. For example, I sometimes feel something like a buoyant fluency which is simply lacking when I creak and judder through an argument which eludes my grasp. But it would be absurd to say that my understanding *is* the experience, or that the description of the experience says what my understanding essentially consists in, for I might have the experience but nevertheless fail to understand the argument, and conversely I might understand the argument without feeling any such thing. The definitive measure of understanding is not an experience, but what I can do. If I understand an argument I can explain it; and if I understand a word, I can use it, show how it is used – whether by means of a dictionary definition or an example – and respond to its use in an appropriate manner. For this is what it means to understand a word, whether it is the name of an architectural style ('Gothic', 'Palladian'), a term which denotes an act or activity ('interrupt', 'swim'), or a numeral ('eleven', 'π').

If we maintain that the mathematical ignoramus in the story does not understand (or misunderstand) the signs he manipulates, this does not mean that he lacks an experience: it means that he lacks the range of abilities without which computation – the manipulation of uninterpreted signs according to definite rules – of whatever kind will not count as doing arithmetic. We may use his esoteric computational skill to fix prices, measure ingredients or cut cloth, but unless *he* understands the nature and purpose of activities such as these he is neither adding nor multiplying, but simply shuffling tokens. The difference between a rain dance and a ballet will not be registered in the notation of its steps.

Since the mathematical ignoramus does not understand arithmetic, must we say that he has multiplied 22 by 10 *unwittingly*? This is about as plausible as the idea that somebody might play poker unwittingly. It would be less misleading to say that he provided the result of a calculation *without calculating*. This is not a paradox. A pianola is not a piano that plays itself, or plays by itself: it is a piano that can make music without being played. A pianola makes unplayed music; a calculating machine, despite its name, provides the result of a calculation without calculating. (Nothing turns on the fact that binary arithmetic was taken as the example. This simply makes it easier to specify the symbols involved in purely formal terms.)

Stories of this sort are often called 'thought experiments'; but this is misleading. The thought experiments conducted by philosophers do not stand to experiments as mental arithmetic stands to arithmetic, but as rhetorical questions stand to questions. An experiment is not merely a demonstration; rather, an experiment will test whether the result deduced from a theory is what actually occurs. A thought experiment is not an experiment at all: it is a demonstration of the use of a concept that is couched in the form of the description of an experiment. In this particular case, the story suggests that a person (or a machine) manipulating formally specified symbols in accordance with a set of rules that can be mapped onto the rules of binary arithmetic is not necessarily exercising any sort of arithmetical skill. It is true, of course, that you or I may decide to perform a calculation in this peculiar (and very time-consuming) fashion. But such a performance would count as a calculation only because we would be able to show that we understand its significance. In other words, our concept of doing arithmetic does not extend to cases like that of the ignoramus or the mechanical device; and if, mesmerized by the fact that calculating machines give us the right answers, we imagine for a moment that it does, the story serves as a useful reminder. Of course we could stipulate that henceforth this too will be called 'doing arithmetic': but if the question, whether a suitably programmed computer could be said to think, perceive, calculate, and understand, will someday be answered by linguistic fiat, then it ceases to be a question worth thinking about; for an answer to it becomes a speculative anticipation of future linguistic habits, a sort of etymological crystal-gazing.

A person (or a machine) manipulating formally specified symbols in accordance with a set of rules isomorphic with the rules of binary arithmetic is not exercising any sort of arithmetical skill. We can mark the difference between the normal child and the mathematical ignoramus by saying that the latter has been taught to simulate doing arithmetic. However, this is not the sense in which a computer simulates the exercise of a cognitive skill, for although in the last paragraph I wrote 'a person (or a machine)', there is a fundamental difference between the two cases. The human computer who memorized the machine table was at least following rules of some sort, even if they are not the rules of arithmetic. What about the computer? Should we say that the computer also follows rules, perhaps not the rules of arithmetic, but rules for the manipulation of formally specified symbols? I think we should not. For the lesson of Turing's paper is precisely that the manipulation of formally specified symbols according to definite rules can be mechanized. It might be objected that to mechanize a normative (rule-governed) task plainly means that the mechanical device *mechanically follows rules*. This objection is confused, and the confusion can be brought out by means of a couple of examples.

Suppose the headmaster of a school decrees that pupils shall not leave the premises during the lunch-break. This rule might be enforced by punishing offenders. Might it also be enforced by locking the school gates before the lunch-break and only unlocking them when the lunch-break is over? It is tempting to say that this is the best possible way of enforcing the rule, but this is certainly a mistake. Locking the school gates does not enforce the rule, it makes the rule superfluous. Similarly, the first clocks that were made to strike the hour automatically were not machines constructed to obey the rules 'Strike once at one o'clock', 'Strike twice at two o'clock', and so forth: they were machines that made these rules, and the business of ensuring that they were followed, otiose. Mechanics replaced disciplinarians; but a mechanic is not a special sort of disciplinarian!

The point is that if I am causally constrained from breaking a rule (or, for that matter, from obeying it), then I can no longer obey or break the rule at all: the rule can no longer apply to me. I am, so to speak, removed from its province. As a contributor to this collection has put it,

> to follow a rule is to *use it* as a guide to conduct (not to be causally necessitated to do something). It is to consult it in evaluating as correct or incorrect those operations which *ought* to conform to it. It is to justify conduct, if challenged, by reference to it, to identify conduct as appropriately normative and to explain or be willing to explain one's normative identifications and descriptions by reference to the rule. But none of these acts, activities, reasons or justifications are involved in the mechanisms which we build to relieve us of tedious normative tasks.[7]

A person may be said to have followed a rule mechanically if he did so unreflectively, without deliberation, without even thinking about what he was doing. By and large, experienced drivers follow (most of) the rules of the Highway Code mechanically, in this sense. But they are nevertheless able to explain their actions by reference to the rules when called upon to do so, and they are not of course causally constrained from following or breaking the rules they follow in this mechanical way.

It is absolutely vital that we appreciate the profound and ineradicable difference between the mathematical ignoramus who commits a machine table to memory, slightly de-humanized as he is, and a machine which is programmed to supply the result of a calculation. The difference is not a sentimental one. Indeed, there is no reason to deny *a priori* that it will ever be possible to manufacture thinking creatures capable of following rules, such as the rules of arithmetic or the rules of chess. But in order to do so, we would have to make a creature capable of using rules – as instruments by means of which to distinguish between correct and incorrect applications and as standards against which success or failure can be measured. Such a creature would have to be capable of the very complex pattern of behaviour which would entitle us to say that it has tried and failed to follow a rule, as opposed to simply malfunctioning, and so it would need to be, in general, capable of setting itself goals and pursuing, modifying or abandoning them, as opposed to merely being (passively) capable of use for certain ends. The comparison between a mathematical ignoramus and a machine is meant to highlight the difference between a pattern of behaviour which qualifies as normative, precisely because it is woven into a behavioural fabric of this sort, and its mechanical counterpart, which does not.

We build machines to relieve us of tedious (or complicated, or expensive) normative tasks – not by assigning the normative task to a mechanical device that cannot complain, but by devising a means to accomplish our ends without any rules being followed. A computer scientist or an engineer who decides that only something capable of following rules can manipulate symbols, or that only something possessing intelligence can pilot an aircraft, designs a machine that manipulates symbols or pilots a plane, and concludes that he has designed a rule-following or an intelligent machine, has been fooled by his own ingenuity. This is not an uncommon mistake. For example, Professor Richard Gregory has written as follows:

> [An automatic pilot] is not worried about missing an appoint-
> ment and it will not be feeling tired or interested in the air
> hostess. But in accepting and acting on navigational and other
> data it *is* a pilot. So in so far as being a pilot requires a mind, it
> must have a mind.[8]

Of course, the fact is that piloting an aeroplane or a ship used to require an expert in the cockpit – a human being, a creature with a mind, and one with a very particular range of skills. But not any more.

As we have seen, an automatic digital computer can be pro-grammed to simulate the exercise of a cognitive skill – calculating in binary arithmetic, for example. We can now see what 'simulate' means here, for the difference between calculating in binary arith-metic and the computer's simulation is the sum of two differences: the difference between a normal child exercising arithmetical skills in the normal way and the mathematical ignoramus, and the difference between the mathematical ignoramus and the machine.

17

As I have said, we also talk about computer simulations of planetary motion and the weather; but it should now be clear that simulation means something quite different in this sort of case.[9] The sense in which a computer simulates the progress of the planets is the sense in which an orrery does. One is made of chips and the other of clockwork, but both a suitably programmed computer and a suitably designed orrery can be used to deduce, and even see, the relative position of the planets at some future date. On the other hand, a computer programmed to produce the results of calculations in binary arithmetic is not a means of predicting the behaviour of a mathematician. If it were, then it would be a defect in the machine (or the program) that it never produced the wrong result or stopped half-way through a calculation and asked for a coffee.

Why then is it so tempting to suppose that the machine calculates, merely because it mechanically manipulates symbols, defined in purely formal terms, in conformity with the rules of a formal system? There are probably many reasons, but I shall mention only two. First, it is easy to suppose that if the inputs and outputs are the same, then there simply cannot be any difference between a machine and an arithmetician, or a language-user. (Particularly so in the case of mathematics, if mathematics is regarded as nothing more than a game with symbols. If formalism in mathematics were correct, then no test of mathematical skills could be appropriate except a test of the ability to manipulate these symbols.) Here we imagine an absurdly austere examination of the capacity, the inputs and outputs apparently pared down to the bare essentials, so as to isolate the mathematical skill from any others.[10] This is deeply misconceived. Our cognitive skills are woven together inextricably: perception, memory, understanding, thought, and so forth, are like so many superimposed patterns on the same piece of cloth; and one cannot hope to lift out a single pattern by pulling the right threads.

This is fundamental, and its importance may be brought out by considering a remark Wittgenstein made in his *Philosophical Investigations*: 'It comes to this: only of a living human being and what resembles (behaves like) a living human being can one say: it has sensations; it sees; hears; is deaf; is conscious or unconscious.'[11] The essential point to notice about this remark is that Wittgenstein does not write 'only of a living human being and what resembles (behaves like) a living human being can one say: it has sensations; it sees; hears; is conscious.' His point is that the affirmations and the negations alike are intelligible only if we are speaking of a living human being or something that resembles a living human being. It makes sense to ask whether a person has fulfilled the terms of a contract or broken them, or whether a person is in contempt of court, only against the background of a complex social institution: the concepts of contract, etc., are only applicable in this context. Similarly, the concepts that we employ when we affirm or deny that a person sees, hears etc. are fixed in terms of the patterns of behaviour which are deemed to be (defeasible) criteria for the application of these linguistic expressions; and these patterns of behaviour are identifiable only against the background of a richly differentiated form of life.

Many Artificial Intelligence (AI) enthusiasts acknowledge the force of this argument to the extent that they allow that AI 'would certainly require robots rather than "bedridden" computers'.[12] But this is hopelessly inadequate, for human beings are living creatures with needs, creatures that can flourish or be hurt; in short, creatures for which things can be categorically good or bad.[13] Things can also be good or bad for a car or a computer: rust and dust, for example. But this is because cars and computers are designed to serve our purposes, and rust and dust will interfere with their capacity to do so. So the sense in which something can be said to be good or bad for a car or a computer is secondary, and essentially parasitic upon the sense in which things can be good or bad for the human beings who make and use them. But only a creature which can flourish or be hurt, a creature for which things can be categorically good or bad, can be capable of suffering or desire. And only a creature that is capable of suffering and desire can be afraid or fearless, pleased, displeased or indifferent; can set itself goals, hope to succeed, or be disappointed at failure; can act with a purpose, as opposed to merely serving a purpose for agents such as us. And the intellectual and cognitive capacities which we are tempted to attribute to computers are inextricably linked to these conative and affective ones, for a creature which can reason, calculate and believe can believe fervently, tentatively or reluctantly, trust his own judgement or another's, plan on the basis of his calculations, and execute these plans with confidence, unwillingly or with regret.

The second reason why we are tempted to confuse a computer's mechanical simulation and actual calculation derives from the profound change, in the twentieth century, in the way we think about the mental life of human beings. Descartes distinguished mental life in terms of its privacy: creatures with minds (i.e. human beings), he believed, are creatures that live in the natural world; but possess in addition what thoughtless creatures lack, an inner world of their own, peopled by their thoughts and imaginings and by the gamut of sensory experience. This view has not been discarded by any means, but no less influence is exerted now by a very different view, which sees mental life as the special possession of language-users, not because, as Descartes believed, the use of language is an outward sign of the invisible traffic of ideas, but because the possession of a language and analogous capacities are, as it were, the vital organs, the heart, lungs and liver of the mind.

In the same period, however, our conception of language itself has been radically altered. The development in the second half of the nineteenth century of logical calculi of unprecedented sophistication and the more recent conception of logic as a study of the structural features of languages, have led philosophers and psychologists alike to regard the capacity to use language as a fundamentally computational skill – that is, a skill whose exercise consists in the transformation of concatenations of formally specified elements, according to the rules of an axiomatic calculus. No wonder the digital computer has been greeted as a *deus ex machina* in the drama of psychological research!

Nevertheless, it is vain to hope that we can extract from the exercise of our cognitive abilities a fundamental computational skill, as if we were extracting precious metal from an ore. As we have seen, the process of computation, far from constituting the very essence of our mental lives, is a thoroughly mindless business. In fact there is no reason to believe that our mental life, and hence what is distinctively human about our lives, has an essence at all. On the contrary: as Mary Midgley put it,

> a triangle without three sides ceases to be a triangle. But a flightless bird, does not cease to be a bird, nor a flying fish a fish. What is special about each creature is not a single, unique quality but a rich and complex arrangement of powers and qualities, some of which it will certainly share with its neighbours.[14]

I have mentioned the discontinuities between Cartesian and modern attitudes to the mind, but the continuities are no less significant. The notion that the essence of mental life is thought, and that thought is an abstract process which organizes, controls and directs human behaviour, whilst remaining essentially distinct from it, is a notion inspired by Cartesian philosophy, even if its chief advocates today are staunch anti-Cartesians. But this notion is confused: thought does not direct human life, it informs it; and so the various metaphors of command that lie behind the use in this context of words like 'direct' and 'control' are wildly misleading. A thoughtful comment is not one that was precipitated by cogitation; it is a comment that was meant seriously, uttered responsibly, and so forth. The Cartesian influence on computational psychology is not straightforward, but it is fundamental. Consider, for example, the remark made by Marvin Minsky, one of the leading lights of AI, that the brain is a 'meat machine'. What is interesting about this remark is not the picture of gleeful butchery that it conjures so effectively, but the fact that its author imagines the remark to be a subversive one. Whom does it subvert? It was obviously made *pour épater les bourgeois*; but who are the bourgeois here, and what beliefs are they supposed to cherish? (A Cartesian, of course, would be happy to agree that the brain is a meat machine.) If they are supposed to believe that thought is a property of the brain, but a non-natural property – and it is difficult to see what other view Professor Minsky could be tilting against – then the only hackles that will rise are on the backs of the more mystical champions of ESP and telekinesis. In other words, Professor Minsky simply takes it for granted that thought is a property of the brain, rather than of the living and more or less socialized human being; and that the brain and body are fundamentally distinct, the body a mere prosthesis. Quite unexpectedly, we have discovered a point of view remarkably similar to Descartes': it can be called brain–body dualism, a label that indicates both how it resembles and how it differs from its forebear.

Are thought and calculation, and are the exercise of cognitive skills in general, activities of the brain? (This was question (3) above.) And is this question one that could some day be settled by experiment? Like machines, bodily organs, such as eyes, hearts and brains, have functions, and can benefit or be damaged – the heart, for example, by exercise or nicotine. Like a machine, a heart can benefit or be damaged because the living organism whose life it sustains can flourish or be hurt, and an eye can benefit or be damaged because it enables the creature – a man, for example – whose eye it is to modify his behaviour in the pursuit of his goals. And just as it makes no sense to ask whether a computer is conscious or unconscious, sees or is blind, it makes no sense to ask this about an eye or a brain, unless the use of the psychological predicate is purely metonymical, so that the question is settled by the behaviour of the creature: 'Mine eyes have seen the glory of the coming of the Lord!' is not an assertion whose truth can be confirmed by means of an ophthalmoscope. It is not the eye that sees, or the brain that thinks, any more than it is the mind, as Descartes supposed: it is the living human being whose eye or brain it is.

At the end of her book *Real People*, Kathleen Wilkes asks what, given that computers are '*manifestly* mindless', we can learn from the computational analogy. Her answer is that 'we are like computers in that we are "only" physical systems', and hence the analogy enables us to 'get free of the idea that there must be a "ghost in the machine"'.[15] To be sure, there is no ghost in the machine: I am not a Cartesian soul 'fastened to a dying animal'. But this was established incontrovertibly by the arguments of Kant and Wittgenstein before the invention of computers, and hence without the tangle of confusion to which we are prey if we have recourse to the computational analogy. Moreover it is misleading to express the thought by saying that 'we are "only" physical systems', for human beings are not '"only" physical systems', unless we so stretch the term 'physical system' that it becomes nothing more than a syntactic expedient, a place-holder for any term at all that refers to an 'entity' or a 'something' – these words *are* such place-holders – in the (physical) world. But neither are they physical systems (bodies) plus something else: the distinction between a human being and a physical system[16] is not the stuff of perverse philosophical slogans, or the linchpin of a false theory, but the linguistic precipitate of a form of life which essentially involves the distinctive moral, affective and (for some) religious attitudes we have towards each other. We use the terms 'human being', 'machine', 'physical object', 'purpose', 'function', etc. to demarcate these elemental features of human life; and, like a wedding-ring, a word means what it does in virtue of the use to which it is put.

As so often in philosophy, we end up by reminding ourselves how certain words are used, and we do so because – as I have already said – the source of those problems that philosophical methods are fitted to solve is not our puzzlement about the causes of empirical facts, although it very often seems that way. It is, in fact, a subtle distortion of the pattern of our language that leads us astray, as if ripples on the surface of the water caused us to wonder how the objects under it could have such curious shapes.

All of this may seem too fast. Of course it was fast – not a philosophical argument so much as a whistle-stop tour of some of the arguments, and a few gestures in the direction of others, which suggest that the three questions raised by the computational analogy are not, as they are generally believed to be, empirical questions that will be answered by experiment. An introduction is not supposed to make a case. But one hopes that it will give the reader reason to believe that there is a case to answer.

NOTES

Several colleagues and friends were kind enough to comment on an earlier draft. I am especially grateful to Maria Alvarez, Hanjo Glock, Peter Hacker, Peter Neumann and Stuart Shanker.

1 P. Feyerabend, *Against Method* (London: Verso, 1978), 19.
2 L. Wittgenstein, *Philosophical Investigations* (Oxford: Basil Blackwell, 1953), §18.
3 A. Turing, 'On Computable Numbers, with an Application to the Entscheidungsproblem', *Proceedings of the London Mathematical Society*, XLII (1937), 230–65.
4 K. Gödel, *Collected Papers*, vol. 1 (Oxford: Oxford University Press, 1986), 369.
5 Y. Wilks, quoted in G. Cohen, *The Psychology of Cognition* (London: Academic Press, 1977), 161.
6 G. Cohen, op. cit., 161.
7 In G. P. Baker and P. M. S. Hacker, *Language Sense and Nonsense* (Oxford: Basil Blackwell, 1984), 297.
8 R. L. Gregory, 'In Defence of Artificial Intelligence', in C. Blakemore and S. Greenfield (eds), *Mindwaves* (Oxford: Basil Blackwell, 1987), 242.
9 It might appear tempting to protest against AI enthusiasts that it is no more plausible to suppose that a computer simulating thought is actually thinking than it is reasonable to expect that a computer simulating a tropical storm will get wet. Searle mistakenly allowed himself to be tempted in this way: 'No one supposes that ... a computer simulation of a fire is likely to burn a house down. Why on earth would anyone in his right mind suppose a computer simulation of mental processes actually had mental processes?', *Minds, Brains and Science* (London: BBC, 1984), 37–8. In fact, the analogy is illusory, for as I have argued, 'simulation' means something different in the two cases. See also D. R. Hofstadter and D. C. Dennett (eds), *The Mind's I* (Brighton: Harvester Press, 1981), 73–6.
10 Notice that the third theme of recent psychology, its methodological austerity, conspires here with the first, computationalism. See above, p. 7.
11 L. Wittgenstein, op. cit., §281.

12 K. Wilkes, *Real People* (Oxford: Oxford University Press, 1989), 223.
13 On this issue, see A. Kenny, 'The Argument from Design', in his *Reason and Religion* (Oxford: Basil Blackwell, 1987).
14 M. Midgley, *Beast and Man* (Hassocks: Harvester Press, 1979), 206–7.
15 K. Wilkes, op. cit., 222–3.
16 The distinction is not exhaustive: cats and dogs are neither human beings nor physical systems.

Part I

LANGUAGE AND BEHAVIOUR

1

THE RELATION OF LANGUAGE TO INSTINCTIVE BEHAVIOUR

Norman Malcolm

'Language did not emerge from reasoning'. This remark from *On Certainty* (*OC*, §475) presents an important theme of Wittgenstein's later writing. The idea is most plausible in respect to simple linguistic expressions of fear, pain, surprise, desire. A small child exhibits unlearned, instinctive, behaviour of fear. A dog rushes at it and it recoils with fear, just as a cat would. It would be absurd to attribute to either child or cat the thought, 'This beast may be dangerous, so I had better take avoiding action.'

Wittgenstein's suggestion is that the child is taught or simply picks up from adults, words and sentences that are added to its repertoire of fear-expressive behaviour. In a well-known passage in the *Philosophical Investigations* concerning the transition from non-linguistic to linguistic expressions of pain, Wittgenstein remarks that when a child learns linguistic expressions of pain it learns 'new pain-behaviour' (*PI*, §244). The learned verbal expressions of pain or fear are no more due to thinking or reasoning than are the instinctive pre-verbal behaviours. Wittgenstein calls these first-person utterances, *Äusserungen*, to indicate that they are immediate expressions of pain, fear, surprise, desire and so on, and are not the result of thought.

This conception of certain linguistic expressions as replacements for unlearned reactions was seen by Wittgenstein to extend to some of the sentences that we use to refer to other persons. Not only 'I'm in pain' but also 'He's in pain', can take the place of instinctive behaviour. In *Zettel* Wittgenstein observes that 'it is a primitive reaction to tend, to treat, the part that hurts when someone else is in pain, and not merely when oneself is' (*Z*, §540). Plainly there are instinctive reactions of shock, concern, sympathy, when one sees that another person is injured. We observe something of this sort

27

in lower animals too. In the *Zettel* passage Wittgenstein asks himself what he means by saying that these reactions are 'primitive'; and he answers:

> Surely that this way of behaving is *prelinguistic*: that a language-game is based *on it*, that it is the prototype of a way of thinking and not the result of thinking.
>
> (Z, §541)

Wittgenstein is disagreeing with a 'rationalistic' explanation of this behaviour – for example, the explanation that we have a sympathetic reaction to an injured person 'because by analogy with our own case we believe that he too is experiencing pain' (Z, §542). The actions of comforting or trying to help, that go with the words 'He's in pain', are no more a product of reasoning from analogy than is the similar behaviour in deer or birds. Wittgenstein goes on to say that

> Being sure that someone is in pain, doubting whether he is, and so on, are so many natural, instinctive, kinds of relationship towards other human beings, and our language is merely an auxiliary to, and further extension of, this behaviour. Our language-game is an extension of primitive behaviour. (For our *language-game* is behaviour.) (Instinct.)
>
> (Z, §545)

This same conception is set forth, in more general terms, in *Vermischte Bemerkungen*:

> The origin and the primitive form of the language-game is a reaction; only from this can the more complicated forms grow.
>   Language – I want to say – is a refinement; 'in the beginning was the deed'.[1]

Wittgenstein says here that not only does language replace prelinguistic behaviour, but also that it serves as an extension, refinement or elaboration of that behaviour. What does this mean? An example is the way in which exclamations such as 'It hurts' or 'The pain is here' can, first of all, simply take the place of the instinctive behaviour of caressing, protecting, comforting, the painful part. But the language of sensation provides finer descriptions of sensation than would be possible with purely non-linguistic behaviour. One says, 'It still hurts but not as much as it did yesterday'; or 'There is a slight pain in my hip but not enough to bother me.' These reports could not be conveyed in pre-linguistic behaviour.

As another example consider natural human reactions to heat and cold, such as doffing and donning garments, fanning oneself, huddling near a fire, and so on. The exclamations, 'Hot!', 'Cold!', are learned in connection with such pre-verbal behaviour, and come to be used themselves as responses to heat and cold. But language provides an expansion and refinement far beyond these simple verbal equivalents of pre-verbal behaviour. Predictions, comparisons, warnings, in regard to the heat and cold of objects, which could not be conveyed in wordless behaviour, become possible. The language of the thermometer yields more precise discriminations of heat and cold than could be expressed in non-verbal behaviour. But of course the thermometer would never have been taken to be a measure of heat and cold if there had not been a rough agreement between the contraction and expansion of mercury in a tube and the natural behavioural responses of human beings to heat and cold.

As a more difficult example, let us consider the use of the word 'cause' and of other casual expressions. Philosophers often assume that this causal language originates in observations of constant sequences of events. But this view is too intellectual. It implies that when one event is followed by another we remain in doubt whether the two events are related as cause and effect until we have satisfied ourselves by further observations that an event of the one kind is always in all instances conjoined with an event of another kind: whereupon we call the one, *cause*, the other, *effect*. On this view the thought of a universal rule, and a doubt as to whether the rule is satisfied by the events in question, are present at the very beginning of our employment of causal expressions.

In remarks written in 1937[2] Wittgenstein presents an entirely different conception. Suppose that a child runs into another child, knocking him down. The latter might react by leaping up and hitting or kicking the other one. He would be 'reacting to the cause' of his falling. Wittgenstein says: 'Calling something "the cause" is like pointing and saying: "He's to blame!".'[3] The child would not be doubting or wondering what made him fall. He would not wait to observe what happens in other cases. Nor could he be said to assume that in similar cases the same thing occurs. Wittgenstein remarks:

There is a reaction which can be called 'reacting to the cause'.
– We also speak of 'tracing' the cause; a simple case would be, say, following a string to see who is pulling it. If I then

find him – how do I know that he, his pulling, is the cause of the string's moving? Do I establish this by a series of experiments?[4]

This 'reacting to the cause' can be called 'immediate'. This means, first, that there is no uncertainty, guessing, conjecturing, inferring, concluding. Second, calling it an 'immediate reaction' emphasizes the aspect of action – striking back, chasing away the cat that has hold of the string, pointing in anger at the one who broke the toy. Causal expressions, such as 'He knocked me down', 'The cat is pulling it', 'She broke it', are grafted on to these immediate reactions.

Later on there develops a use of causal expression where doubt, conjecture, testing, experiments, theory, enter in. According to Wittgenstein's conception these are 'second-order features'.[5] Wittgenstein says:

> The primitive form of the language-game is certainty, not uncertainty. For uncertainty could never lead to action.
> The basic form of the game must be one in which we act.[6]

To suppose that wondering whether this caused that, or questioning in one's mind whether the two events are constantly conjoined, comes in advance of, or along with, the first employment of causal words, is putting the cart before the horse. The child who retaliates against the one that crashed into him does not do this because he 'knows' or 'believes' that this caused his fall. He simply does it. It is an instant reaction, like brushing away an insect that is tickling one's skin. One does not make experiments to determine whether the tickling sensation is caused by the insect.

When Wittgenstein says that the primitive form of the language-game with the word 'cause' is 'certainty', he does not mean that the child affirms in his mind the proposition that the other one certainly knocked him down, or that the child has a perception or intuitive awareness of the causal connection between his being crashed into and his falling down. No: Wittgenstein means that the hitting back at the other child is instinctive. This instinctive behaviour is what Wittgenstein calls 'reacting to the cause'. The 'certainty' he is talking about is a certainty in behaviour, not a certainty in propositional thought.

Doesn't the child's reaction at least presuppose that he has the concept of cause and effect? No. In the first place, it is misleading to speak of '*the* concept' of cause and effect, as if there were an essence of causation, a set of necessary and sufficient conditions, a hidden definition of causation that lies behind the differing uses of causal expressions. In the second place, instinctive reactions of this sort would be one source of the learning of causal expressions. Sentences, such as 'He knocked me down', 'He caused me to fall', would be linked to the instant reaction. The understanding of some causal terms would grow out of such reactions, and would not be presupposed by them; just as a child's crying out with pain when injured would be one source of its acquisition of the use of the word 'pain' and would not presuppose that it has 'the concept' of pain.

Wittgenstein's idea is that the child's first learning of causal expressions consists in learning to use them along with, or in place of, unlearned reactions. Being in doubt about the cause of something, learning to investigate by tests and experiments, would be a subsequent addition.

A similar thing occurs in the first learning of names of objects. Wittgenstein remarks that 'Children do not learn that there are books, that there are armchairs, etc. etc., but they learn to fetch books, sit in armchairs, etc.' (*OC*, §476). He imagines someone saying: 'So one must know that the objects exist whose names one teaches a child by ostensive definition'. Wittgenstein replies: 'Why should the language-game rest on knowledge?' (*OC*, §477). And he asks: 'Does a child believe that milk exists? Or does it know that milk exists? Does a cat know that a mouse exists?' (*OC*, §478).

A cat watches a mouse-hole. It would be natural to say that the cat knows, or believes, that a mouse may come out of the hole. But what does this come to? Are we attributing to the cat the propositional thought, 'A mouse may appear'? No. We are only placing this behaviour in the larger pattern of cat-seeking-mouse behaviour. An infant reaches for its milk bottle. Does it 'believe' that what is in the bottle is milk? One could say this. But what would it mean? Just that there is this behaviour of reaching for the bottle from which it has been fed in the past; plus, perhaps, the fact that it will reject the bottle if what it tastes is chalk-water. This is *just doing*. In order to understand it we do not have to suppose that this doing rests on some underlying belief. The belief here is nothing other than this behaviour in these circumstances – not a source of the behaviour. In the case of the infant, words and sentences will gradually emerge from such behaviour. Not so with the cat.

Wittgenstein's conception is sharply at odds with some current views. Noam Chomsky, for example, regards a child's language-learning as a highly intellectual performance. A child is bombarded with what Chomsky calls 'primary linguistic data':

> On the basis of such data, the child constructs a grammar – that is, a theory of the language of which the well-formed sentences of the primary linguistic data constitute a small sample. To learn a language, then, the child must have a method for devising an appropriate grammar, given primary linguistic data. As a precondition for language learning, he must possess, first, a linguistic theory that specifies the form of the grammar of a possible human language, and, second, a strategy for selecting a grammar of the appropriate form that is compatible with the primary linguistic data. . . .
>
> The child approaches the data with the presumption that they are drawn from a language of a certain antecedently well-defined type, his problem being to determine which of the (humanly) possible languages is that of the community in which he is placed. Language learning would be impossible unless this were the case. . . .
>
> To acquire language, a child must devise a hypothesis compatible with present data – he must select from the store of potential grammars a specific one that is appropriate to the data available to him.[7]

On Chomsky's view each normal child is an intellectual marvel right from the start. Before an infant can hold his milk bottle he is already in possession of a theory concerning the general form of every possible human language (as if there were such a thing). When the adults around him utter words this child immediately starts forming and testing hypotheses to determine which of the possible languages is the actual language of the community in which he happens to be placed. Chomsky says: 'Language learning would be impossible unless this were the case'. *Mirabile dictu*!

Suppose a sailor whose native language is French or Russian, is cast ashore on a Pacific island whose inhabitants speak an alien tongue. Since the sailor believes that this island was a Japanese possession for a good many years, he forms the hypothesis that perhaps the language of these people is Japanese. In his travels he has picked up a few words and sentences of Japanese; so he tries out his little bit of Japanese on the inhabitants in order to find out whether they respond with any understanding. It won't be easy, but at least he can make a stab at confirming or disconfirming his hypothesis.

Could the infant do this? Could he address the adults around him with remarks in Japanese, French or Russian? No; he doesn't know any spoken language. So he will have to formulate and test his hypotheses solely in his mind. He will think to himself, 'Was that utterance I just heard a request, or a statement, or a prediction, or was it merely a swear word?' But what evidence could there be that an infant understands these differences?

According to Chomsky, 'The child approaches the data with the presumption that they are drawn from a language of a certain antecedently well-defined type'. So does this infant think to himself, 'I presume that these people speak a subject-predicate language'; or, 'I assume that in this language adjectives agree with nouns in gender and number'?

Suppose there were an especially remarkable child (or, perhaps, an especially backward one) who did *not* 'approach the data' with any assumptions or preconceptions, but despite this handicap did gradually learn the language of his community, just like other children. Chomsky would say, 'It is impossible that there should be such a child'. How does Chomsky know this? Has Chomsky conducted tests with infants who make such assumptions, and infants who don't, and found that only those of the first group do succeed in learning language? Of course not. Chomsky would have no way of determining whether any given infant belongs to one group or to the other. His claim about what a child must do is obviously not based on any tests whatever.

J. A. Fodor correctly draws out an implication of Chomsky's view and fearlessly endorses it. The implication is that a child cannot learn a language unless it already has a language. Fodor holds that both perception and learning require the forming and confirming of hypotheses, and that this in turn requires processes of 'computation'. But computation can only be carried out in a system of representation – that is, in a language. Fodor says: 'Computation presupposes a medium of computation: a representational system'.[8] Fodor argues explicitly that a person cannot learn a language unless he already has a language:

Learning a language (including, of course, a first language) involves learning what the predicates of the language mean. Learning what the predicates of a language mean involves learning a determination of the extension of these predicates. Learning a determination of the extensions of the predicates involves learning that they fall under certain rules (i.e. truth rules). But one cannot learn that P falls under R unless one has a language in which P and R can be represented. So one cannot learn a language unless one has a language.[9]

The unlearned language that one possesses, presumably from birth, is called 'the language of thought'. It is innate, inner and private. It is an 'internal code'. One does learn the predicates of a natural language, such as Spanish or German. But according to Fodor, 'for every predicate in the natural language it must be possible to express a coextensive predicate in the internal code. . . . One can't learn a conceptual system richer than the conceptual system that one starts with.'[10]

These are astonishing contentions. How could one find out whether the innate system of representation that Fodor postulates does actually exist? Certainly not by introspection; for Fodor does not hold that the representations and computations that occur in the innate system are 'consciously accessible'.[11]

A map is a system of representation. One can use a map to make computations, e.g. 'If we continue along the Strand from here it is only four blocks to Trafalgar Square'. It is a matter of observation that newcomers to London tend to lose their way unless they employ maps of the city. One can see whether a person on the street is or isn't consulting a map.

Furthermore, a map can be used incorrectly. This is true of any system of representation. It doesn't follow from the fact that a person arrived at his wanted destination that he used his map correctly. The symbols of a map and its method of projection can be understood or misunderstood. Computations based on the map can be right or wrong. None of this could apply to the innate, inner, private, representational system that, according to Fodor, must exist. Therefore, whether its existence can be verified is not really the issue. Whatever Fodor is talking about, the important point is that it cannot be a representational system.

Fodor thinks it is reasonable to suppose that the 'internal language' has a 'vocabulary'.[12] If there is a vocabulary the items that compose it should have meaning and should be understood. How can either of these things be true of a system that is inner and private? A child grows up in a community of speakers and learns, by imitation and training, the language of the community. This language contains expressions that have a function in some contexts of life and not in others. Another expression is employed in different activities and different circumstances. A normal child gradually masters these differences, not in the sense of being able to describe them, but in the sense of conforming with them in its use of words. When this happens the child is said to 'understand the meaning' of those words. It is only in comparison with the practices of the community of speakers in which the child is reared that the child's utterances are correct or incorrect. The 'internal language' that Fodor postulates could not be subject to such comparison, and therefore the items of its 'vocabulary' could have no employment that was either correct or incorrect – which means that they are not items of a language or of a system of representation.

It is no surprise to learn that, for Fodor, the medium in which the supposed innate language of thought operates is the nervous system. He says: 'The nervous system "speaks" an internal language.'[13] As if neural processes could contain symbols, representations, descriptions. Is a nervous system a member of a community of language-users? Does it apply symbols to objects and situations? Does it sometimes make mistakes and have to be corrected until its practices accord with those of the adult nervous systems of its language-community? Can it be said to understand, or to misunderstand, the items of its 'vocabulary'? The nervous system of a human being is indeed innate. But to say that neural processes constitute a 'language of thought' or a 'representational system', is to use these phrases not merely misleadingly but vacuously.

In contrast, Wittgenstein's conception of the role of instinctive behaviour, does not attribute to the human infant an innate representational system, nor any theories, assumptions or hypotheses – attributions that are initially preposterous and ultimately devoid of content.

Wittgenstein presents a conception that is even more striking than what we have so far considered. Not merely is much of the first language of a child grafted onto instinctive behaviour – but the whole of the developed, complex, employment of language by adult speakers embodies something resembling instinct. To explain this I will refer to some of Wittgenstein's responses to the declarations of

G. E. Moore.

Wittgenstein's last writing, *On Certainty*, is a meditation on Moore's so-called 'defence of common sense'. Moore declares that he knows with certainty that he is a human being, that his body has existed continuously since his birth, that the earth existed for a long time before he was born, that he has often perceived material things, and so on. Moore began his paper, 'Certainty', with the following remarks:

> I am at present, as you can all see, in a room and not in the open air; I am standing up, and not either sitting or lying down; I have clothes on, and am not absolutely naked; I am speaking in a fairly loud voice, and am not either singing or whispering or keeping quite silent; I have in my hand some sheets of paper with writing on them; there are a good many other people in the same room in which I am; and there are windows in that wall and a door in this one.[14]

Moore goes on to assert that it would be ridiculous for him, in his circumstances, to say such a thing as 'I *think* I've got some clothes on', or 'I not only think I have, I know that it is very likely indeed that I have, but I can't be quite sure'. Moore declares that he knows that he has clothes on, and knows all of those other things that he enumerated.[15] In his 'Proof of an External World' he insists that he knew that he was holding up one hand and then the other:

> How absurd it would be to suggest that I did not know it, but only believed it, and that perhaps it was not the case! You might as well suggest that I do not know that I am now standing up and talking – that perhaps after all I'm not, and that it's not quite certain that I am![16]

There seems to be an important insight in Moore's assertions; yet it is not easy to say what it is. Certainly it would have been astonishing if Moore, standing before his audience, had said, 'I think this is a hand, but I could be mistaken', or 'I believe I have clothes on but it isn't absolutely certain'.

If my wife and I were about to go out to dinner, and she called to me from another room, 'Do you have your clothes on?', she would be taken aback if I replied in all seriousness, 'I think so but I may be wrong'. Why is this? Haven't I been wrong about lots of things? So why shouldn't I be cautious here? This uncertainty would be shocking because we do not understand what being mistaken, or discovering that one was mistaken, would be like in such a matter as that. (See OC, §32.)

Of course, there could be circumstances in which uncertainty would be understandable. Suppose I had been knocked unconscious and when I regained consciousness I was tightly bound and blindfolded. If my companion, who was in the same condition, whispered to me, 'Do you have clothes on?' I might whisper back, 'I think so but I may be wrong'. Being in doubt, being mistaken, is intelligible here. If the blindfold were removed I would ascertain whether I have clothes on. But if Moore, lecturing to his audience, were to look at his arms and legs, would he be ascertaining whether he has clothes on? Surely not; any more than in picking a piece of lint from my jacket would I be verifying that I am wearing a jacket. As Wittgenstein remarks: 'Does my telephone call to New York strengthen my conviction that the earth exists?' (OC, §210).

If Moore had declared to his audience that he did *not* have clothes on, was not standing up, did not have two hands, etc., the people there would have regarded him not as mistaken, but as mentally disturbed (OC, §155). Why is this? Apparently because we expect an adult speaker of the language, who is in possession of his faculties, to be able in normal circumstances, to say straight off, without looking for evidence, whether he has clothes on, or whether he is sitting or standing.

This helps to bring out the fact that Moore is wrong in saying that he knows these things. For when a person contends that he is not merely convinced of something but knows it to be so, we expect him to be able to produce evidence in support of this distinction. But Moore was in no position to do this. As Wittgenstein says, if what a person believes 'is of such a kind that the grounds which he can give are no surer than his assertion, then he cannot say that he knows what he believes' (OC, §243).

> My having two hands is, in normal circumstances, as certain as anything that I could produce in evidence for it. That is why I am not in a position to take the sight of my hand as evidence for it.
>
> (OC, §250)

But Wittgenstein's remark that my having two hands is 'as certain' as anything I could bring forward as evidence for it might be misleading. Is it *certain* that I have two hands? Who is supposed to be saying or thinking this; and in what circumstances? One can easily describe a natural context for the sentence, 'It is certain that I have two hands.' Suppose both of my hands were infected and I went to hospital for surgery. As I regained consciousness I heard one nurse ask another, 'Were his hands amputated?' After a moment of panic it seems to me that I can feel my fingers moving inside the bandages. Reassured, I say to myself, 'It is certain that I have both hands.' Whether I am right or wrong this would be a natural use of those words.

The case is exactly the same here as with Moore's assertion, 'I *know* that that's a tree', which he reiterated in philosophical discussion. Wittgenstein said of this:

> 'I know that that's a tree'. Why does it strike me as if I did not understand the sentence?, though it is after all an extremely simple sentence of the most ordinary kind? ... As soon as I think of an everyday use of the sentence instead of a philosophical one, its meaning becomes clear and ordinary.
>
> (*OC*, §347)

Outside of ordinary contexts neither 'I am certain' nor 'It is certain' (that I have two hands) has a clear meaning. Nor can a person who is going about his affairs in ordinary life be said to assume, or take for granted, or presuppose, that he has two hands. Wittgenstein remarks:

> No one ever taught me that my hands don't disappear when I am not paying attention to them. Nor can I be said to presuppose the truth of this proposition in my assertions, etc., (as if they rested on it) whereas it only gets some sense from our other asserting.
>
> (*OC*, §153)

What does Wittgenstein mean by saying that this proposition gets its sense from 'our other asserting'? A clue is to be found in another remark, where he is trying to *find* an underlying sense for Moore's curious insistence that he *knows* that *this* is a hand:

> Doesn't 'I know that that's a hand', in Moore's sense, mean the same or something similar to: I can make statements like 'I have a pain in this hand' or 'this hand is weaker than the other' or 'I once broke this hand', and countless others, in language-games where a doubt as to the existence of this hand does not come in?
>
> (*OC*, §371)

Doubt does not come in! That is where the emphasis should be put. It isn't that in normal life a person is certain, or convinced, or knows, or assumes, or takes for granted, or presupposes, that he has two hands. It is simply that he makes statements about his hands without any doubt as to their existence occurring to him or to others. He use the word 'hand' without a second thought. And it isn't only that he uses this word in *statements* about his hands – he *acts*. A child responds to requests such as 'Hold out your hands', 'Wash your hands', and so on, without considering whether he has hands. This immediate, unthinking, response cannot be said to show that he knows, or is certain, that he has hands. 'Knowledge' and 'certainty' have no application here. Wittgenstein says that the young child 'learns to react in such-and-such a way; and in so reacting it doesn't so far know anything' (*OC*, §538). This learned but unthinking acting also characterizes the use of words by adults, of the word 'hand' and of other names of things. It is 'our *acting* which lies at the bottom of the language-game' (*OC*, §204).

An adult has acquired a confident use of many words. But isn't it an empirical fact that *this* word is used like *this*? (*OC*, §306). And since it is an empirical fact, shouldn't I have empirical grounds for my 'certainty' that the word is used like that? But, as Wittgenstein notes:

> The strange thing here is that when I am quite certain of how the words are used, have no doubt about it, I can still give no *grounds* for my way of acting. If I tried I could give a thousand, but none of them as certain as the very thing they were supposed to be grounds for.
>
> (*OC*, §307)

Absence of doubt manifests itself throughout the normal life of a human being. It appears, first, in advance of any learning: for example, in the spontaneous behaviour of reacting to a cause. This behaviour is 'instinctive' in the primary sense of the word. Second, it appears in the young child when it is taught to respond to orders such as 'Sit in the chair', 'Hold out your hands', and so on, before the child can itself employ words. Third, it appears in the behaviour, due to teaching, of employing the names of objects. At these second and third levels, the confident way of acting and speaking could be called 'instinctive' in a secondary sense.

The absence of doubt, at all three levels, can be called 'instinctive' because it isn't *learned*, and because it isn't the product of thinking.

In the original reacting to something as a cause, there is no thought of whether a similar result will follow upon a similar event. Nor in the sympathetic response to another's injury is there any reflection as to whether this other person has 'the same thing' that I have when I'm in pain. The child who has not yet begun to speak but has reached the stage of responding to orders, such as 'Sit on a chair', could be said to 'know' that this thing is a chair and that the couch, stool or cushion is not a chair. The same could be said of a dog. In neither case does this knowingly imply the overcoming of doubt or the testing of an hypothesis. In both cases the knowledge is nothing other than correct behavioural responses produced by training. The knowledge is not something that underlines and explains the behaviour.

One of the most striking illustrations of what I am calling the 'instinctive' element in the employment of language and in language-like activities, is the way in which people who have been given some instruction in a procedure (such as continuing a mathematical series, or drawing a design, or building a brick wall) will, when told to carry on from there, spontaneously and on their own continue in the *same* way. It would seem that from the original instruction those people could branch out in an indefinitely large number of directions, each one going a different way. It is true that they *could*; but they don't! Almost all of them will go on in a way that the others will agree is the *same* way. This 'agreement in reactions' is impressive. And it cannot be *explained* by saying that they have 'intuitively grasped the rule', or something of the sort. This confident going-on in the same way, without any doubt, cannot be given any rational foundation. This is a reason for calling it 'instinctive'. Without this kind of natural agreement, this instinctive going-on in the same way, there could not be language.

A boy who grows up on a farm is taught that the farm animals need to be fed in the morning, and this becomes one of his daily chores. Now if the animals had ceased to exist for several hours during the night, perhaps they wouldn't be hungry and wouldn't need to be fed. Does the thought of such a possibility occur to the boy? No. Does this mean that he *assumes* that the animals continued to exist throughout the night? On the basis of what could we attribute this assumption to him? On the fact that he does act this way every day, without raising any questions? But why couldn't he act that way *without* an assumption? The case here is the same as in the following example of Wittgenstein's:

Why do I satisfy myself that I have two feet when I want to get up from a chair? There is no why. I simply don't. This is how I act.

(OC, §148)

'There is no why'! There is no explanation. I don't, for example, make an inductive inference from past experience. Wittgenstein says:

The squirrel does not infer by induction that it is going to need stores next winter as well. And no more do we need a law of induction to justify our actions and predictions.

(OC, §287)

As I previously noted, an obsession with 'rationality' is characteristic of much of current philosophical thought. For example, Fodor says:

Perception must involve hypothesis formation and confirmation because the organism must somehow manage to infer the appropriate task-relevant description of the environment *from* its physical description together with whatever background information about the structure of the environment it has available.[17]

If I am sitting in a chair and decide to go for a walk, I need first to get out of the chair. According to Fodor, I must *infer* this 'appropriate task-relevant description'. Why is there a *must* here? Isn't it enough if I simply rise from the chair *without* inferring that this is the appropriate action? Do I need to form a hypothesis about the way to proceed, any more than would a dog?

What is striking is not only that one's first learning of words is an outgrowth of unthinking, instinctive behaviour, but that something of the same kind permeates and surrounds all human acting and all use of language, even at sophisticated levels. The chemist who is conducting an experiment may be in doubt about the outcome of the experiment, but not about the existence of his laboratory. A person who is doing an arithmetical calculation might wonder whether he multiplied correctly, but not whether the figures on the paper changed themselves into other figures (*OC*, §337). This freedom from doubt has not been won by any tests or any reasoning.

Wittgenstein conceives of the absence of doubt that exists at so many points in the daily course of our lives, as not something 'hasty or superficial' but as 'something that lies beyond being justified or unjustified; as it were, as something animal' (*OC*, §§358, 359). It is

41

too fundamental to be either 'unjustified' or 'justified'. It underlies any mastery of words in which a procedure of justification could be framed.

This fundamental thing is *so* fundamental that it is difficult, or perhaps impossible, to describe it in words. One would *like* to characterize it in mental terms – to call it knowledge, or belief, or conviction, or certainty, or acceptance, or confidence, or assumption. But none of these expressions fits: all of them have their appropriate application *within* various language-games, whereas Wittgenstein is trying to call attention to something that underlies all language-games.

But can't one give a characterization at least in *negative* terms of this fundamental thing? Wittgenstein attempts this in many passages. A formulation he frequently resorts to is 'the absence of doubt'. For example, in conversation I say, 'This hand is weaker than the other', or 'I once broke this hand', without (as Wittgenstein puts it) 'a doubt as to the existence of this hand coming in' (*OC*, §371). And he says:

> The fact that I use the word 'hand' and all the other words in my sentence without a second thought, indeed that I should stand before the abyss if I wanted so much as to try doubting their meanings – shows that the absence of doubt belongs to the essence of the language-game.

> (*OC*, §370)

Now it is true that if a previously normal adult began to be in constant doubt about the meanings of ordinary words, not only could he not continue to carry on the everyday employment of language, but also his behaviour would fall into disarray. But is it right to say of me right now that I 'am not in doubt' as to whether this is called a 'hand'? This is a formulation I have resorted to in trying to expound Wittgenstein. But is this the way in which the expressions 'I am not in doubt' or 'He is not in doubt' are used in everyday life? Surely not. One normally says this only in a situation where a doubt has been voiced or felt or anticipated – and for some reason. For example: one person says that he is in doubt as to whether Mr A will come to the meeting since he was absent from the two previous ones. Another person replies: 'I know that he didn't come those other times; but I have no doubt that he will come today because he told me explicitly that he would'. Here a ground for doubt is met by a ground for not doubting. The expression 'I don't have any doubt' is typically used to counter a presented or anticipated reason for doubt. And who, in my present circumstances, has any reason to doubt that this is called a 'hand'?

Wittgenstein says: 'I would like to reserve the expression "I know" for the cases in which it is used in normal linguistic exchange' (*OC*, §260). Of course the same should hold for 'I believe', 'I am certain', 'I agree', 'I assume' and also 'I do not doubt'.

There are indications in *On Certainty* that Wittgenstein is dissatisfied with every attempt to characterize this fact that is so fundamental to language, thought and action. Suppose that a customer tells a greengrocer that he wants ten apples, and the shopkeeper proceeds to count them out. Wittgenstein says:

> If the shopkeeper wanted to investigate each of his apples without any reason, in order to play safe, why doesn't he have to investigate the investigation? And can one speak here of belief (I mean belief as in religious belief, not conjecture)? Here all psychological terms merely lead us away from the main thing.
>
> (*OC*, §459)

In order to have 'absolute certainty' must not the shopkeeper try to determine not only that these things are apples, but also that what he is doing is trying to find out whether they are apples, and in addition that he is really counting them? And if the shopkeeper doesn't do this, is this because he 'believes', or 'knows', or is 'certain', or is 'convinced', or 'assumes', or 'has no doubt', that these are apples and that he is counting them? No. All psychological terms, says Wittgenstein, lead us away from 'the main thing' (*die Hauptsache*).

In later passages Wittgenstein asks himself whether he knows or only believes that his name is L.W., and whether he knows or only believes that the law of induction is true? In regard to the latter he says that it appears to him to be nonsense to say, 'I know that the law of induction is true', and that it would be 'more correct' to say 'I believe in the law of induction' (*OC*, §500). Yet apparently he is dissatisfied with this too, for he goes on to remark:

> Am I not getting closer and closer to saying that in the end logic cannot be described? You must look at the practice of language, then you will see it.
>
> (*OC*, §501)

Logic cannot be described! I take this to mean that it is not appropriate for Wittgenstein to say either that he 'knows', or 'believes', or is 'certain', or is 'convinced', or 'assumes', or 'does not doubt', that his name is L.W., or that this is called a 'hand', or that the law of induction is true. None of these terms is correct.

What does it mean to say: 'You must look at the practice of language, then you will see it'? What do you see? Well, you see *the unhesitating behaviour* with which a person signs his name at the end of a letter or gives his name to a bank clerk; or uses the word 'hand' in statements; or makes inductive inferences; or does calculations; and so on. What you see is this unhesitating way of *acting*. This is the 'logic' of language that cannot be described with psychological words. It is too 'primitive', too 'instinctive', for that. It is *behaviour* that is *like* the squirrel's gathering nuts or the cat's watching a mouse hole. This is why Wittgenstein says it is something *animal* (OC, §359).

Just now I have spoken of this human behaviour as 'unhesitating', and previously as 'confident'. But isn't this a strained use of these words? When I sign my name to a cheque in the normal way, is it correct to say that I do it 'confidently' or 'without hesitation'? It seems not. If, with advancing senility, I sometimes forgot my name, or sometimes write it unconfidently, then an observer could report of me, 'This time he wrote his name confidently, without any hesitation'. Or if I had been given a drug that is supposed to produce amnesia, an observer might report, with surprise, 'Why, he stated his name quite confidently!' But the way in which a normal adult normally comes out with his own name and with the names of familiar objects, cannot be called either 'confident' or 'unconfident', 'hesitating' or 'unhesitating'.

Wittgenstein's remark, 'Am I not getting closer and closer to saying that in the end logic cannot be described? You must look at the practice of language, then you will see it' (OC, §501), may strike one as remarkably similar to an important theme of the *Tractatus*, namely, that there are things that cannot be *said* but *show* themselves. Is this theme of the *Tractatus* re-emerging in Wittgenstein's last writing?[18]

I do not have the space to give this topic the treatment it deserves, but I will make a brief comment. According to the *Tractatus* something can be 'said' only if it is a *contingent* proposition – that is, only if its negation is a logical possibility. If you try to say what is logically necessary your remark is 'nonsense' (*Unsinn*). You are not contrasting one state of affairs with another conceivable state of affairs.

Throughout Wittgenstein's later writings he is describing what he calls 'the grammar' of concepts. His remarks are called 'grammatical' because they are attempts to describe how a certain *expression* in the language is actually used. In a sense, a true grammatical remark is a 'truism' since it merely spells out some feature of our familiar use of an expression. But in philosophy we get confused about the language we speak, and so a truistic grammatical remark, when brought to bear upon a particular confusion, can sometimes be illuminating.

A true grammatical remark expresses a *logically necessary truth*. Take the sentence, 'If you *know* that *p*, then *p* is *true*'. It isn't that the verb 'to know' *had* to be used that way. But it *is* normally so used that if one person says 'Jones knew that *p*', and another person concludes, 'So *p* was true!', the latter is making a logically valid inference.

Would Wittgenstein, in his later period, have thought that whenever a philosopher says, 'If you know that *p*, then *p* is true', he is uttering 'nonsense'? I think not. It would be a matter of how the philosopher is *taking* this sentence. If what he wants to say is that there is a certain 'mental state' called 'knowing', which is such that if a person knows that *p*, then the fact that *p* is contained in or guaranteed by that 'mental state', then Wittgenstein would say, 'Nonsense!' (see *Z*, §408; *OC*, §356). But if the philosopher only meant that this is how the verb 'to know' *is used*, Wittgenstein would not say 'Nonsense!'; nor would he hold that this philosopher was trying to say something that could not be 'said'. No longer does he hold the view that any remark that expresses something non-contingent is 'nonsensical' and must finally be 'thrown away' (*Tractatus*, 6.54).

On Certainty is full of grammatical remarks. An example is this: 'The child learns by believing the adult. Doubt comes *after* belief' (*OC*, §160). Wittgenstein is trying to express, in this remark, something that is necessarily true about the concept of doubting – namely, that a person's behaviour and utterances can be rightly described as 'doubting', only if they occur against a background of things that the person *accepts*.

The difficulty confronting Wittgenstein in *On Certainty* is not that what he is trying to state is a logical or conceptual necessity. It is instead a problem concerning *the words* in terms of which the necessary truth can be stated. Is, for example, the word 'accepts', that I used just now, the right word? Can it be said that the small child 'accepts' that what he is told to sit on is a 'chair'? Isn't this too sophisticated a term to apply to him at this stage? Nor can one say that he 'agrees' that it is a chair, nor that he 'believes' this, nor even that he 'does not doubt' it. As previously noted, if a child has not yet begun to speak, but has learned to respond with discrimination to the orders, 'Sit on a chair' and 'Sit on a stool', we are ready to say that the child 'knows' that a chair is a chair and that a stool is not a chair. We are ready to say the same of a dog. The word 'knows' merely refers here to that learned discriminative behaviour, not to some mental state that *explains* the differential response.

We have the inclination to suppose that all mastery of language, as well as all meaningful behaviour, is based on and emerges from mental states or attitudes that should be expressible in psychological terms. But what we find is that all of the psychological terms either redescribe, or else presuppose, *ways of acting*. It is these ways of acting that provide the foundation for the psychological concepts. They are 'the main thing' (*die Hauptsache*), which *shows* itself when one reflects on the practice of language, but which itself is not supported by any mental process or structure.[19]

NOTES

The following editions of works by Wittgenstein are cited in the text:

OC   *On Certainty*, ed. G. E. M. Anscombe and G. H. von Wright, trans. D. Paul and G. E. M. Anscombe (Oxford: Basil Blackwell, 1969).

PI   *Philosophical Investigations* (Oxford: Basil Blackwell, 1953).
      Tractatus Logico-philosophicus, trans. D. F. Pears and B. F. McGuinness (London: Routledge & Kegan Paul, 1961).

Z   *Zettel*, ed. G. E. M. Anscombe and G. H. von Wright, trans. G. E. M. Anscombe (Oxford: Basil Blackwell, 1967).

1   L. Wittgenstein, *Vermischte Bemerkungen*, ed. G.H. von Wright and Heikki Nyman, 2nd edn (Frankfurt: Suhrkamp, 1978), 65; published under the title *Culture and Value*, with English translation by Peter Winch (Oxford: Basil Blackwell, 1980), 31.

2   L. Wittgenstein, 'Cause and Effect: Intuitive Awareness', *Philosophia* 6/3–4 (1976), 391–425; selected and edited by Rush Rhees, English translation by Peter Winch. (I am deeply indebted to Rush Rhees for leading a faculty seminar at King's College in 1979–80 on the topic of Wittgenstein's writings on causation, and also to my other colleagues at King's College who participated in the discussions.)

3   Ibid., 410.

4   Ibid., 416.

5   Ibid., 420.

6   Ibid., 421.

7   N. Chomsky, *Aspects of the Theory of Syntax* (Cambridge, Mass.: MIT Press, 1965), 25, 27, 36.
8   J. A. Fodor, *The Language of Thought* (Hassocks: Harvester Press, 1975), 27.
9   Ibid., 63–4.
10 Ibid., 85, 97.
11 Ibid., 49.
12 Ibid., 123.
13 Ibid., 122.
14 G.E. Moore, *Philosophical Papers* (London: Allen & Unwin, 1959), 227.
15 Ibid., 228.
16 Ibid., 146–7.
17 Fodor, op. cit., 50.
18 Thomas Morawetz, in his *Wittgenstein and Knowledge* (Hassocks: Harvester Press, 1980), 51, says that in *OC*, §501, 'There are echoes of Wittgenstein's *Tractatus*'.
19 This chapter was presented as the *J. R. Jones Memorial Lecture*, University College of Swansea, May 1981. (I am grateful both to Bruce Goldberg and Rush Rhees for their criticisms of an earlier draft of this essay.)

2

MECHANISM AND MEANING

Bruce Goldberg

In recent years numerous philosophers and psychologists have contended that human beings are robots, or automata, or computing machines. Connected with this view is the further idea that to explain human behaviour, or some aspect of it, is in effect to write a 'program' for a machine capable of simulating that behaviour. Such a program will be a characterization of the internal processes responsible for the behavior of the 'device', human being or machine. As Jerry Fodor puts it:

> understanding the operations of a computer capable of simulating a given form of behavior is tantamount to understanding the behavior itself.[1]

The present paper offers a criticism of this view, with primary emphasis on the form in which it is defended by Fodor. He has, I believe, explored the philosophical foundations of mechanism in greater detail than many writers who share his general outlook. The paper consists of two parts. In the first I discuss Fodor's view concerning what can be learned about human beings from a machine which is able to simulate the speaking of a language. I argue that, given Fodor's idea of a machine simulation, the conclusion he draws about meaning and internal states is unjustified. In the second part of the paper I examine the theory of meaning Fodor defends, and on which his mechanistic conception of human beings rests. I try to show that the theory is untenable, and that it is so for reasons similar to those Fodor offers against a related view of meaning.

I

The idea of 'computer simulation' or 'machine simulation' has, notoriously, been used in a wide variety of ways, and Fodor undertakes to clarify it. He offers the following criterion for simulation:

> I propose to say that a machine successfully simulates the behavior of an organism when trained judges are unable to discriminate the behavior of the machine from the behavior of the organism in relevant test situations.[2]

Employing this criterion, Fodor criticizes Turing's test for determining when a machine can be said to simulate intelligent, or 'cognitive', human behaviour. Turing proposed

> that a machine simulation of human cognitive behavior should be considered to be successful if competent judges cannot distinguish between the machine and a person on the basis of their answers to questions of the judges' devising.[3]

This is unacceptable, Fodor says, since we can imagine a machine which, though it is able to answer questions put to it, cannot behave in anything like the way human beings do. That is,

> Turing's test, strictly interpreted, does not provide a sufficient condition for successful simulation of human cognitive behavior [since] it could be passed by machines that are incapable of indefinitely many performances that lie well within the capacities of normal humans; performances that may well be argued to constitute types of intelligent behavior. Thus, the ability of a machine to pass Turing's test would not, by any means, entail that it could also obey such simple commands as 'Mind the baby while I go shopping.' This is in part because the ability of a machine to win at Turing's game would not ensure that the machine is able to integrate the results of its putative mentations with its ongoing behavior in anything like the normal human fashion.[4]

The trouble with Turing's proposal, in other words, is that it does not require that the machine be able to act in a way consistent with its utterances. And if we imagine a radical enough disparity between what a machine says and what it does then it is clear that we can imagine a 'question-answering machine' which would not be said to be capable of intelligent behaviour. Thus Turing's criterion does not, though it should, rule out a machine which, though it can answer questions about how to boil water, 'routinely puts the kettle in the icebox when told to brew the tea'. Of such a machine, Fodor holds, it could not be said 'that it can think, that it is rational, or that its behavior is intelligent'. That is, Turing's test does not require that the machine be able to integrate its alleged thought 'with its ongoing behavior in anything like the normal human fashion',[5] and that *is* a condition for the simulation of intelligent human behaviour.

Fodor thus concludes that Turing's question-answering machine is a very limited device, and that it is

> in fact, precisely what it seems to be: a question-answering machine, a device that simulates one of the indefinitely many behavioral capacities which jointly constitute the rationality of a normal person – the ability to provide reasonable answers to questions that are put to him in his native language. It is a very long step from doing this to satisfying sufficient conditions upon the simulation of intelligent human behavior *tout court*, and it is perhaps not a step in any very clearly defined direction.[6]

At this point in his discussion Fodor (rightly, I think) requires a great deal of a machine for it to be said to be capable of simulating intelligent human behaviour. For example, it should be able to carry out a command like 'Mind the baby while I go shopping.' Fodor calls this a 'simple' command, but given what might be involved in minding a baby, it is clear that the machine Fodor has in mind is a very sophisticated sort of device. It must be capable of a wide variety of behaviours. Presumably it can do such things as preparing formula, changing diapers, getting a doctor, talking to a Jehovah's Witness who comes to the door, and so on. Fodor doesn't provide a detailed list of the abilities such a machine would have to have, but it is certainly very large. In any event, the point I wish to emphasize in connection with Fodor's idea of simulation is that when he speaks here of the machine simulation of intelligent human behaviour he has in mind a machine capable of behaving like a human being.

But when he comes to discussing a machine which is said to simulate the speaking of a language – an activity that is itself, presumably, a form of intelligent or 'cognitive' behaviour – Fodor demands much less of the machine than one might have expected.

A machine simulates the speaking of a language, Fodor says, simply, when it can produce or 'enumerate' all the sentences of the language.[7] Concerning such a machine – let us call it M1 – Fodor comes to the central conclusion of his argument for mechanism, namely, that certain inferences may be made about M1's internal processes and that these inferences hold for human beings as well. Since M1 can produce all the sentences of English, it can produce ambiguous sentences, identical strings of sound with different meanings. And since this is so, Fodor argues, M1 must contain different internal states the output of which is the same 'phonemic sequence'. Consider, for example, the sentence 'John likes old men and women.' This can be understood as 'John likes (old) (men and women)' or as 'John likes (old men) (and) (women).' If M1 can produce both these sentences, Fodor says, it must contain within it two different causal states or causal sequences both of which result in the production of 'John likes old men and women.'

This is a far-reaching conclusion. From it, Fodor believes, we can learn something about the causal processes taking place in human brains when we speak. Since we, like M1, can produce ambiguous sentences there must be different brain states or different neural sequences responsible for causing the same set of sounds. Fodor states the argument concerning M1 as follows:

> Consider a device that purports to be . . . equivalent to some speaker in that it claims to be capable of enumerating precisely the set of sentences that the speaker will accept as grammatical. In order for the putative . . . equivalence to hold, it must be the case that the behavioral repertoire of the machine includes a sequence that corresponds to 'John likes old men and women.' The present question, however, is whether it must include *two* such sequences, one corresponding to the bracketing (old men) (and) (women) and one corresponding to the bracketing (old) (men and women).[8]

The answer to the question, Fodor believes, is yes. M1 must contain two different internal sequences each terminating in the phonemic sequence 'John likes old men and women.' The machine, and so human beings, must be capable of going through these two different internal causal sequences. Each sequence must be contained in its program.

I want to point out that this conclusion about meaning and

internal states is arrived at by considering a machine which, though it is supposed that it can produce the ambiguous sentence in question – indeed it is supposed that it can produce, or 'enumerate', every sentence of the language – need not satisfy the conditions for successful simulation Fodor proposed earlier. Nothing, it should be noted, is said about the ability of M1 to integrate its 'utterances' with the rest of its behaviour in a way like that of a human being, or about its ability to deceive trained judges in relevant test situations.

What if it cannot? That is, suppose that M1 behaves like the earlier question-answering machine. Imagine that its sentence production does not tie up with the rest of its behaviour in anything like the normal human way. Suppose, for example, that it says, from time to time, 'I'd like to brew the tea', but completely ignores the offered kettle. When told that the baby is sleeping it routinely says, 'Here I stand. I can do no other.' And so on. If M1 were to behave in this way, it would seem, whether or not it can 'enumerate' every sentence of the language, what it is doing is not speaking a language. Paraphrasing Fodor's earlier criticism of Turing's question-answering machine, the sentence-producing machine Fodor describes is precisely what it seems to be, a sentence-producing machine, a device that simulates one of the indefinitely many capacities which jointly constitute the linguistic ability of a normal person. As Keith Gunderson writes, in a related context:

> if the case where the machine X-es is really the same and not just vaguely analogous to the case where the man X-es, then we should be safe in making further assumptions about the machine's general capabilities and performances . . . In the case of certain computer outputs – a poem for example – we have hitherto understood the result in question to be such that its production required certain general skills or capacities on the part of human beings. And human beings who possessed such general skills or capacities could be safely assumed to be able to do a number of other things too. Hence if the machine truly writes poems – which would be the only sort of case where we would be justified in assuming that it was able to understand a language, reason, and reflect – then we would also be able to assume that the machine is also capable of a wide range of other activities, in which verbal, thinking, reasoning, and reflecting creatures are capable of participating.[9]

It would seem then that – since M1 does not simulate the speaking (or understanding) of a language – whatever might be true about the relationship between M1's sentences and its internal states, one could not expect much light to be shed on what is involved in the speaking and understanding of language by human beings.

But I think that the error in Fodor's treatment is a more serious one than merely that of selecting an inadequate model of simulation to illustrate his claim about meaning. For I want to suggest that the claim – where there are different meaning there must be different internal states – is not in fact based on considerations about machine simulation. It rests, rather, entirely on the philosophical theory of meaning Fodor adopts. According to this theory the meaning of a sentence *is* an internal state of the person or machine producing it. From this, of course, it will follow that if there are different meanings there must be different internal states. But this theory of meaning is untenable. It is so, I believe, for the same reason Fodor gives in rejecting a related view of meaning.

II

Fodor holds that the meaning of a sentence is an internal state of its 'producer'. He calls this internal state the 'message'. It is a mental structure which accompanies the physical sentence or 'wave form', as Fodor calls it.[10] On Fodor's view, when someone speaks, and means something by what he says, there is a 'message' in his mind. This message is then 'transformed' by mechanical operations taking place inside the speaker. The result of the transformation is the 'wave form'. This process is then reversed in the hearer. He 'retrieves' the mental structure with which the speaker began.

But the idea that meaning something by a sentence involves transforming a message into a wave form, or 'assigning a message to a wave form',[11] is untenable. It is so, I want to say, because the notion of a message is a confused one. The problems with it are exactly those Fodor himself raises against a theory of human thought proposed by the psychologist Jerome Bruner.

According to Bruner, there is a stage of human development, during childhood, when thinking is done by, or in, images – when thoughts *are* images.[12] Fodor holds that Bruner's theory is not a scientific hypothesis at all, even a false one, but is rather, strictly speaking, incoherent. It makes no sense to say that thoughts are images. The argument Fodor employs against Bruner, which he describes as 'entirely convincing', is derived from Wittgenstein:

A picture of John with a bulging tummy corresponds to John's being fat. But it corresponds equally to John's being pregnant since, if that is the way that John *does* look when he is fat, it is also, I suppose, the way that he *would* look if he were pregnant. So, if the fact that John is fat is a reason to call a picture of John with a bulging tummy true, then the fact that John isn't pregnant is as good a reason to call a picture of John with a bulging tummy false. (A picture which corresponds to a man walking up a hill forward corresponds equally, and in the same way, to a man sliding down the hill backward; Wittgenstein, *Philosophical Investigations*, §139.) For every reason that we might have for calling a picture true, there will be a corresponding reason for calling it false. That is, there is no reason for calling it either. Pictures aren't the kind of things that can have truth-values.[13]

An image can't be a thought since any given mental image will be capable of a great variety of interpretations. The very same image can mean this or that, and be true or false, depending on the way it is taken.[14] Bruner has failed to focus on this fact. He supposes that the mental image refers by 'resemblance'. This view founders, however, since the same image can be said to resemble many different things. Fodor concludes that

> there isn't much sense to be made of the notion that ... entertaining an image is identical to thinking *that* such and such is the case.[15]

But, on Fodor's view, entertaining a 'message' *is* identical to thinking that such and such is the case. In holding this, it seems to me, Fodor has failed to appreciate the scope of the argument employed against Bruner. For the conclusion of that argument is not that an image can't be a thought, but that no mental structure, or better, no structure at all, can play the role Bruner attributes to images. It is this role that is misconceived, not the particular candidate Bruner has selected to play the role.

An image, it is clear, can be taken or interpreted in a variety of ways. Fodor says, for example:

> Suppose that what one visualizes in imaging a tiger might be anything from a full-scale tiger portrait (in the case of the ideticist) to a sort of transient stick figure (in the case of

poor imagers like me). What makes my stick figure an image of a tiger is not that it looks much like one (my drawings of tigers don't look much like tigers either) but rather that it's *my* image, so I'm the one who gets to say what it's an image of. My images (and my drawings) connect with my intentions in a certain way; I *take* them as tiger-pictures for purposes of whatever task I happen to have in hand.[16]

This is the reason Bruner is mistaken in supposing that images refer by 'resemblance'. In order for an image to do this, one might say, the image itself would have to determine what it resembles, and this it doesn't do. That is, in order for an image to have the property Bruner treats it as having the image itself would have to determine the way it is to be taken. But an image clearly does not determine the way it is to be taken since, as we have seen, the same image can be taken in a number of different ways. For this reason, if I understand him, Fodor concludes that 'there isn't much sense' in the supposition that images are thoughts.

But this same point applies to messages as well. After all, aren't my messages *my* messages? Why don't I have the same freedom with regard to my messages that I have with regard to my images? In fact, in supposing that entertaining a message is having a thought Fodor is supposing that messages, unlike images, do determine their own interpretation. His idea of a message, that is, is that of a mental structure that can be interpreted in only one way. Images are ambiguous but messages, Fodor says, must be 'ambiguity-free'.[17]

It is, however, this idea, of a mental structure that can be interpreted in only one way, which is incoherent. This can be seen perhaps more clearly by noticing that Fodor has given no meaning to the terms he uses to describe the role messages are supposed to play. He says that a message 'displays' the information communicated by sentences.[18] What does the word 'display' mean here?

The question arises because Fodor says of images also, as he does of messages, that they display information.[19] But, as we have seen, the way in which messages display cannot be the way images display. For images don't display anything until they are taken a certain way. Messages, however, are thought of as displaying what they do *intrinsically*. They must be thought of, Fodor says, as displaying the meaning of a sentence

explicitly, in a way that the sentence itself fails to do.[20]

But why should messages differ in this respect from images? Messages, like images, are mental structures. How is it that they are immune from even the possibility of ambiguity? Indeed, what does it even mean to say that they are? For it seems clear that any structure, mental or physical, could be used, or taken, or interpreted in a variety of ways. There is no such thing as an object that admits of only one possible use, an object which is intrinsically unambiguous. Fodor's entire view of language and mind would appear to rest on a notion which is unintelligible, in the same way that Bruner's notion that images are thoughts is unintelligible.

The confusion in this view of meaning can be seen further in Fodor's account of the constituents of messages. A message is said to be composed of elementary, not-further-analysable units.[21] The meaning of a sentence, Fodor holds, is a structured arrangement of atomic concepts,[22] but it hardly needs saying that the notion of an atomic concept has never been satisfactorily clarified. Moreover, it needs to be asked at this point: how could a view justifiably be considered to be scientific, not to say correct, which has at its foundation such a notorious philosophical dead end as that of an elementary meaning particle?[23]

In support of the claim that mechanism represents a viable approach to understanding the nature of language, Fodor cites the work of Noam Chomsky. Chomsky's theory of 'transformational grammar', he believes, is a scientific, mechanistic account of language which is being fruitfully developed. In the light of what has been said, however, it can be seen that Chomsky's theory does not provide an illustration of the viability of mechanism. For the objections to Fodor's view apply equally well to Chomsky. Indeed, Chomsky advances the very same set of theses we have been considering. A language, Chomsky says, is a combination of 'sound and meaning'. It has 'an inner and an outer aspect'. The outer aspect, the sound (Fodor's 'wave form'), he calls the 'physical signal' or 'phonetic form'.[24] The inner aspect, the mental structure which is the meaning of the sentence, he calls the 'deep structure':

> It is the deep structure underlying the actual utterance, a structure that is purely mental, that conveys the semantic content of the sentence.[25]

The deep structure is produced 'when the sentence is uttered'. It is 'a mental accompaniment to the utterance'.[26]

Chomsky is no clearer about the nature and function of this alleged structure than was Fodor. Thus, he says, in different places, that it is the meaning, that it represents the meaning, that it expresses the meaning, that it specifies the meaning, that it determines the meaning, that it expresses the intrinsic meaning of the sentence, and, somewhat more expansively, that it 'incorporates all information relevant to a single interpretation of a particular sentence'.[27]

What Chomsky actually should have said, from his own point of view, is not that this structure expresses the intrinsic meaning of the sentence, but that it intrinsically expresses the meaning of the sentence. It cannot express the intrinsic meaning of the sentence because, on Chomsky's view, sentences do not have intrinsic meaning. Sentences acquire meaning because they are associated with, by being 'transformations' of, internal structures. It is the internal structure which has intrinsic meaning. Chomsky is right in denying intrinsic meaning to sentences, but he is wrong in affirming it of some other object. There is no such object. The idea of a structure with 'intrinsic meaning', a structure which displays meaning 'explicitly', is literally senseless.

Moreover, Chomsky, like Fodor, is altogether unclear about the constituents of this supposed object. His own detailed work has gone into developing another part of the theory. The nature of the internal structure, he says, is 'being left unspecified pending further insights into semantic theory'. Chomsky says enough on this topic, though, to show the direction of his thinking, and the central idea is one we have already encountered. The deep structure is composed of 'basic content elements', 'minimal "meaning-bearing" elements'. A theory erected on such a foundation, it would seem, rests on air.[28]

Apart from the incoherence of its central concepts, one can see that the view Fodor defends fails to represent correctly many facts about language. Thus, Fodor holds that in order for someone to understand a sentence his internal language mechanism must construct the message by means of a series of operations. Among these operations is the 'decomposing' of the sentence into its parts, the words, which are then replaced by the atomic meaning elements. This view of the supposed processes required for understanding reflects the idea that the meaning of a sentence, the message, is a 'compositional function' of the meanings of its words, which are in turn compositional functions of atomic concepts. But, apart from the incoherence of the notions of an atomic concept and a message, when someone says something the meaning of his remark is not simply a 'function' of the meanings of the words, any more than the humour in a remark is a function of the humour in the words, or the friendliness of a remark is a function of the friendliness of the words. Meaning, humour, friendliness – all these are functions of many things, the words, the way they are said, what they are said in response to, the relationship of the people involved. They are functions of the way what is said is 'integrated', as Fodor puts it, into a flow of 'ongoing behavior'.[29]

Fodor's claim about messages and understanding seems to get support from considering overly simple, and misleading, examples. If one restricts one's attention to such sentences as 'John likes old men and women' or 'A wise man is honest' it is easy to come to the conclusion that understanding a sentence requires a 'construction' or 'computation' of its meaning, employing the antecedently available meanings of the words. And then one is naturally inclined to suppose that there must be an internal 'dictionary' in which such meanings are stored, and 'retrieval mechanisms' to make them available.[30] Consider, however, the following sentence:

(a) He didn't want to spend another year being Dr No.

It is quite easy to think of many possible interpretations of this remark, many situations in which it might be used. The range narrows greatly, though, when it is heard following the sentence: 'Sullivan decided to resign from the Censorship Board.' Even if the notions of an atomic concept and an internal dictionary were intelligible, what plausible 'entry' might there be for 'Dr No' from which the mechanism could 'construct the message'? Yet many people who speak English would have no trouble at all with the remark in that context.

The extent to which meaning results from or depends on the embedding of language into the flow of human activity is perhaps more clearly seen in the following example. A general led a coup attempt that failed and he fled the country. The government, which had been shaky, gradually strengthened its position and, as a consequence, moderated its hostility toward the opposition. The general, through sympathizers, also made gestures of reconciliation and a somewhat friendlier climate emerged in the country. The government's original intention was to have the general shot if they caught him but now, eleven months later, at a press conference, the People's Prosecutor is asked: 'What is your position with regard to General Barrios?' He replies:

(*b*) I think that in the interest of tranquillity this case ought to be de-dramatized.

In this situation it is clear what is being said. The general got the message. He knew that he was not going to be executed. Indeed, he knew many other things, e.g., that he wouldn't be tortured or imprisoned – that he was going to be treated leniently. When he returned home, he was questioned for a few hours and released, assured of 'complete and total freedom on the condition that he refrain from any further political activity'.

But if one imagines (*b*) being said in a quite different situation its meaning changes radically. Suppose it to be said during a discussion between the Prosecutor and one of his assistants. Suppose that it follows the assistant's observation: 'It is clear that he must be caught and killed. Now, do we have a trial or is this one for the back room?' Obviously what (*b*) means and how it will be understood in a particular case depends crucially on the context in which it is spoken. But in developing his view of language Fodor appears to have ignored what he most emphasized at the outset, namely, the importance of seeing how what human beings say is integrated into the flow of their actions.

At this point a reply along the following lines might be made: 'Certainly the context in which a remark is made is relevant to the way it will be interpreted by a hearer. Understanding a sentence involves many psychological processes, of different kinds, and a complete theory of linguistic communication would include them all. Thus, in explaining why a hearer in a particular situation interprets a sentence as he does, a complete psychological theory would undoubtedly refer to such features of the situation as what the hearer's relevant beliefs are, what he is doing, what attitudes he has toward the speaker, and so on. The account of sentence understanding being offered is intended only as part of such a more comprehensive theory. Its focus is on one central aspect of the processes leading to understanding, namely, the hearer's transformation of the wave forms. And its goal is to characterize this "purely linguistic" factor in communication, to discover the internal operations involved in carrying out these transformations.' That is to say,

> the internalized system of rules [governing the transfor-
> mations] is only one of the many factors that determine

59

how an utterance will be ... understood in a particular situation. The linguist who is trying to ... construct a correct grammar is studying one fundamental factor that is involved in performance, but not the only one. ... There is no reason why one should not also study the interaction of several factors involved in complex mental acts and underlying actual performance, but such a study is not likely to proceed very far unless the separate factors are themselves fairly well understood.[31]

However, the only reason for thinking that there is such a factor involved in someone's understanding what is said to him – internal operations yielding messages – is that on this view of language to understand a sentence *is* to have a message in one's mind. Of course, were understanding identical with having a message (or a deep structure or a picture) in one's mind, there would be compelling reasons for assuming the existence of a program or grammar which governs the mental processes involved in the construction of messages. It would be natural to suppose further that there are processes in the brain causally responsible for those in the mind, that there is a 'neural substructure' of the mental mechanism awaiting scientific discovery. But, if the argument of the present chapter is correct, this analysis of the notion of understanding is unacceptable, for the same reason that the analysis of the notion of meaning is unacceptable, namely, that the idea of a message, upon which both analyses rely, is itself an unintelligible idea.[32]

What is correct in Fodor's account, I think, is its emphasis on the treatment of meaning as a relational property of sentences. That meaning must be so treated follows from the fact that there are ambiguous sentences, that the same 'phonemic sequence' can be taken or understood in different ways. Sentences, clearly, are not themselves intrinsically unambiguous. The error in Fodor's account, however, comes in his treatment of 'disambiguation', in the supposition that for a sentence to be disambiguated, for it to have one meaning rather than another, it must be associated with a structure which is itself intrinsically unambiguous: that is, his mistake lies in supposing that the relation to be sought is that of the sentence to an object.

There is an alternative. It would be to see sentences as becoming disambiguated, as acquiring the meaning they have, because of, among other things, the relation in which they stand to the flow of action around them: that is, to see disambiguation as positional. A particular remark in a given situation will be taken a certain way. But this does not require that a structure be attached to it. The case is no different, I want to suggest, from the acquisition of such a thing as humour by a sentence. In a particular situation some sentence *s* will be found funny, while in other situations *s* will not be found funny. In this case, no more than in the case of meaning, is there a need for supposing that different structures attach to the sentence in the different contexts.

The idea of positional disambiguation can be illustrated by means of the example Fodor referred to earlier. Figure 1 is ambiguous:

Figure 1

one might see it as a man walking up or sliding down a hill. But if the picture appears in a particular sequence (Figure 2) it will not be seen in the second of these ways:

Figure 2

In this sequence it is a man walking up a hill. I don't mean, of course, that the picture can only be seen in that way. The attempt to find a picture that can only be seen in one way is, as has already been noted, a doomed one. But if this is so then the most one could get is a picture that will be seen in one way rather than another. And that is what we have in the above example. The picture is disambiguated because it occupies the position it does.

The moral is this: the notion of sentence meaning cannot be rendered intelligible unless sentences are seen, essentially, against the background of and embedded into the flow of characteristic patterns of human behaviour. To say this is really to say nothing more than that if the life surrounding a remark were quite different from what it is, if the behavioural flow were not what it is, then the remark would not have the meaning it does.

This result has already been anticipated in Fodor's discussion of machine simulation. It was seen there that if a machine (or a person) did not behave in the right way, the normal human way, then it would not be speaking a language. In this sense, if there is something logically presupposed by language and meaning, it is not the existence of internal displaying structures but rather the existence and character of human life itself. For it is only given the normal flow of behaviour that a sentence can have the kind of position required for it to mean something.

It may seem that a Contextual Theory of Meaning is here being contrasted with and offered in place of an Internal Structure Theory of Meaning. But that is not so. For, I want to suggest, not only is the Internal Structure Theory misconceived, but the very idea of a theory of meaning, in the sense in which Fodor tries to provide one, is itself misconceived. What is Fodor's theory supposed to do? His theory is intended to offer a general account of how a sentence acquires the meaning it has. It does so by association with a structure. And connected with this, as we have seen, is the idea that there is such a thing as a 'complete specification', a 'final analysis', of the meaning of a sentence. As against this I want to say that there is no justification for treating meaning as a property of an altogether different kind from other properties of sentences. The remarks people make to each other are meaningful. But they are also powerful, fanciful, witty, cautious, friendly, ironic. With respect to each of these properties it is possible to explain to someone why a remark has it. Such an explanation may be given in the form of words or gestures or pictures or some combination of these. However – and this is the essential point – there is no 'preferred form' that the explanation must take. In the first place, the kind of explanation given will depend on the kind of question being asked, on who is asking it, on what he already knows, and so on. Explanations, it has been observed, are 'interest-relative'.[33] In the second place, there is no preferred form because the idea of such a preferred form or complete specification is an unintelligible one. In this sense, there is no more a Theory of Sentence Meaning than there is a Theory of Sentence Power.

In his attempt to understand linguistic meaning Fodor, along with many other writers, seeks something at the moment of utterance, something which exists at a point-instant. This is the intrinsically unambiguous structure. If one had a 'cut-out' of the mind at the moment it appears one could read off the meaning of the sentence associated with it. And one could do so, not only without knowing what the circumstances of utterance are, but even without knowing what the sentence itself is. One could say: whatever sentence is associated with this structure means such and such. But this 'static' conception of meaning fails to preserve the insight that the functioning of language, that the very idea of a language, cannot be understood unless what people say to each other is viewed as part of the continuing flow of human action and reaction. That is to say that one must look, not at a point-instant, but rather along the horizontal.

It can be seen, in Fodor's defence of mechanism, how a number of widely held views about language come together:

1 Sentences acquire meaning by association with internal structures.
2 Linguistic communication is an encoding–decoding process in which these internal structures are transformed (encoded) into sounds which are then retransformed (decoded) into internal structures.
3 This encoding–decoding is carried out by mechanisms in the brain.

Fodor's treatment also reveals how these views are grounded ultimately in the concept of an intrinsically unambiguous meaning structure, a structure which represents 'in so luminous a way that no room is left for differing interpretations'.[34] If the argument of this chapter is correct, these ideas are, strictly speaking, unintelligible. I believe that this is part of what it means to say that conceiving of human beings as mechanisms is a mistake.[35]

NOTES

1 J. Fodor, *Psychological Explanation* (New York: Random House, 1968), 121.

2 Ibid., 123.
3 Ibid., 124–5. See also A. Turing, 'Computing Machinery and Intelligence', *Mind* 59 (1950), 433–60.
4 Fodor, *Psychological Explanation*, 125.
5 Ibid., 125–7.
6 Ibid., 126. For a somewhat more extended version of this critique of Turing, from which Fodor's version is derived, see K. Gunderson, *Mentality and Machines* (Garden City, New York: Doubleday & Co., 1971), ch. 2.
7 Fodor, *Psychological Explanation*, 138.
8 Ibid., 138 (emphasis in text).
9 Gunderson, op. cit., 48, 50–1.
10 J. Fodor, *The Language of Thought* (New York: Thomas Y. Crowell, 1975), 111, 151. Since Fodor advocates a form of the Psycho-Physical Identity Theory he believes that this internal structure is, in fact, in the brain (*Psychological Explanation*, 107 ff).
11 Fodor, *The Language of Thought*, 151.
12 J. Bruner, 'On Cognitive Growth', in J. S. Bruner, R. R. Oliver and P. M. Greenfield (eds), *Studies in Cognitive Growth* (New York: John Wiley & Sons, 1966).
13 Fodor, *The Language of Thought*, 181 (emphasis in text). The reference to Wittgenstein is to *Philosophical Investigations* (Oxford: Basil Blackwell, 1969).
14 Fodor, *The Language of Thought*, 191.
15 Ibid., 181 (emphasis in text).
16 Ibid., 191 (emphasis in text).
17 Ibid., 121.
18 Ibid., 151.
19 Ibid., 191.
20 Ibid., 114.
21 Ibid., 123.
22 J. A. Fodor (with J. J. Katz), 'The Structure of a Semantic Theory', in J. A. Fodor and J. J. Katz (eds), *The Structure of Language* (Englewood Cliffs, New Jersey: Prentice-Hall, 1964), 496.
23 Indeed, it is precisely this view of language – requiring intrinsically unambiguous structures composed of simple, unanalysable units – against which the argument of Wittgenstein referred to by Fodor is directed. This point is discussed in detail by Norman Malcolm in *Memory and Mind* (Ithaca: Cornell University Press, 1977), 152 ff. Wittgenstein's insight that the *Tractatus* rests on the incoherent notion of a structure that '*shows* its sense' (*Tractatus Logico-Philosophicus* (London: Routledge & Kegan Paul, 1961), 4.022), Malcolm says, is the key to his subsequent abandonment of its view of language and mind: 'In the *Tractatus* he had conceived that in order for thought and language to be possible there must be something (a picture, a proposition, a thought) that depicts a state of affairs in the world in so luminous a way that no room is left for differing interpretations. It would be something that, as it were, contained its interpretation, its application, *in itself*. In *The Blue Book*, the *Grammatik*, and the

Investigations, Wittgenstein is saying that it is an illusion to think that there might be such a thing' (op. cit., 157, emphasis in the text).

24   The quotations are from N. Chomsky, *Language and Mind* (New York: Harcourt Brace Jovanovich, 1972), 17; N. Chomsky, *Cartesian Linguistics* (New York: Harper & Row, 1966), 32; *Language and Mind*, 29; *Cartesian Linguistics*, 52.

25   *Cartesian Linguistics*, 35.

26   *Language and Mind*, 17; *Cartesian Linguistics*, 34.

27   *Cartesian Linguistics*, 38; *Language and Mind*, 25, 104, 106, 136; N. Chomsky, *Aspects of the Theory of Syntax* (Cambridge, Mass.: MIT Press, 1970), 16. Sometimes Chomsky uses the term 'deep structure' to refer to an intermediate product of the supposed transformational process. When this is so, the final produce is referred to as the 'semantically interpreted deep structure' (*Aspects of the Theory of Syntax*, 29). At other times, as in the quoted passage, 'deep structure' is the term for the final product itself. This perhaps partially accounts for some of the differences in role attributed to the deep structure.

28   The quotations are from N. Chomsky, *Topics in the Theory of Generative Grammar* (The Hague: Mouton, 1969), 13, 58; *Language and Mind*, 138. It is worth noting that while Fodor says that his view of mind is based on Chomsky's approach to language (*Psychological Explanation*, ix) Chomsky says that his approach to language rests on Fodor's view of meaning (*Aspects of the Theory of Syntax*, 161–2).

29   *Psychological Explanation*, 125. At times Fodor expresses dissatisfaction with the decompositional account of understanding. He says at one point that the processes required for understanding may not involve decomposition into simple units but may be carried out instead by means of 'stereotypes, exemplars, images, or what have you' (*The Language of Thought*, 153). In view of Fodor's critique of the image theory, this suggestion is a surprising one. And indeed he says, concerning it: 'The issues here are terribly difficult. . . . If your concept of a dog is, in large part, a representation of a stereotypic dog, how do you go about determining what *falls under* the concept?' (ibid., emphasis in the text). But, given this idea of what a concept is, it is not possible to determine what falls under the concept. As Fodor has shown, what a representation, exemplar, or image is of, depends on how it is taken, how it is used 'for purposes of whatever task I happen to have in hand' (ibid., 191). That is, if 'I'm the one who gets to say what it's an image of' (ibid.) I cannot learn from it what falls under it, since it does not have a 'range' until I give it one. And since this is so, Fodor's alternative suggestion concerning the supposed processes of understanding does not represent an improvement.

30   The quotations are from Chomsky, *Language and Mind*, 168; Fodor, *The Language of Thought*, 117; Fodor (with Katz), 'The Structure of a Semantic Theory', 494; Fodor, *The Language of Thought*, 115.

31   Chomsky, *Language and Mind*, 27.

32   The parallel *Tractatus* view of understanding is described by Malcolm as follows: 'To understand the meaning of a physical sentence is to come into the possession of something (*not* the sentence) the

meaning of which *shows* itself – something the meaning of which is transparent, self-revealing, unambiguous. It is something that not only does not require interpretation but *cannot* be interpreted. It is where interpretation ends' (op. cit., 140, emphasis in the text). The notion of such a self-revealing, unambiguous structure, Malcolm shows, leads to the further idea that its constituents must be 'simple' elements (ibid., 149). I have examined some other aspects of this concept of a 'meaning terminus' in 'The Correspondence Hypothesis', *Philosophical Review* 77 (1968), 438–54.

33 H. Putnam, *Meaning and the Moral Sciences* (London: Routledge & Kegan Paul, 1978), 41. Putnam also contends, as we have here, though for somewhat different reasons, that '"meanings" just ain't in the *head*!' ('The Meaning of "Meaning"', in *Mind, Language, and Reality* (Cambridge: Cambridge University Press, 1975), 227, emphasis in the text).

34 Malcolm, op. cit., 157.

35 I would like to express my gratitude to Stephen Braude for his many valuable comments and suggestions.

3

THE ENDURING RELEVANCE OF WITTGENSTEIN'S REMARKS ON INTENTIONS

Stuart Shanker

Purpose consists in the determination of an action by its agreement with the agent's expectation.

R. B. Perry, 'Purpose as Tendency and Adaptation'

When you get the picture of 'being determined' out of your mind, then you get rid of the puzzle.

L. Wittgenstein, 'Lectures on Sense Data'[1]

THE CONTINUITY IN MECHANIST THOUGHT

It is an inescapable fact of contemporary philosophy that Wittgensteinians have been typecast as the field's reactionaries, consigned to that role by their stubborn refusal to share in the excitement of theory-construction. Indeed, the situation worsens daily, for these are (paradigm-) revolutionary times that we live in, or so we are constantly being told. It is quite true, as this book has been designed to illustrate, that cognitive science has revived interest in a host of perennial philosophical problems; but whether computationalism or connectionism represent the bold new initiatives that their advocates have assumed is another matter. Where the cognitivist contends that Wittgensteinians have taken their lead from a figure who, however gifted, was responding to behaviourist and *Gestalt* outlooks that have long since been superseded, Wittgensteinians have sought to trace the constancy in mechanist presuppositions and perplexities. Far more is involved here than defending Wittgenstein's enduring relevance for the philosophy of psychology, however; the real issue at stake is the significance of Wittgenstein's conviction that 'people will keep stumbling over the same puzzling difficulties and find[ing] themselves staring at something which no explanation seems capable of clearing up' because 'our language has remained the same and keeps seducing us into asking the same questions'.[2] Thus, if there has been a marked emphasis in Wittgensteinian writings on the nature of the framework sustaining cognitive science, it is because of the manifest continuity in mechanist thought, exhibited as much by the problems which remain of central concern as the theories and methodologies that are designed to resolve them.

No better example of the paramount role which the framework plays in the evolution – and frustration – of mechanist thought can be found than in the persisting preoccupation with the nature of purposive behaviour. Intentions are more than just an embarrassment (or perhaps, an acid test) for mechanist theories; for cerebral models must come to naught unless there is 'some way to map the cognitive representation into the appropriate *pattern* of activity', and it is intentions which constitute this crucial intermediary that is 'needed to bridge the gap from knowledge to action'.[3] Already this century we have witnessed the demise of two major movements, both of which foundered over their inability to overcome the mechanist presuppositions of their predecessors: will cognitive science go the same way as behaviourism and cybernetics?[4] To be sure, cognitive scientists will insist on the revolutionary character of their novel paradigm, but it must be remembered that much the same thing was said of cybernetics when it was introduced. Admittedly, Rosenbleuth, Wiener and Bigelow's stated intention to rehabilitate purposive explanation in a mechanist context (by defining purposive behaviour as that which is 'controlled by negative feedback' in the 'attainment of a goal') signified a profound departure from behaviourist attitudes; but we must not overlook the fact that the founders of cybernetics saw themselves as working within a behaviourist framework,[5] and similarly, that the fathers of cognitive science saw themselves as working within a cybernetic framework. Thus, just as Rosenbleuth, Wiener and Bigelow insisted that their goal was to give 'a uniform behavioristic analysis [which] is applicable to both machines and living organisms, regardless of the complexity of the behavior',[6] so too Miller, Galanter and Pribram reported that their 'fundamental concern ... was to discover whether the cybernetic ideas have any relevance for psychology'.[7]

What was primarily novel about 'Behavior, Purpose and Teleology' was the manner in which the authors sought to render teleological explanation scientifically respectable by treating the feedback mechanisms in homeostatic systems as both purposive and subject to the laws of causality. But far from just rewriting the logical form of teleological explanation in order to bring out what they saw as its fundamental contrast with the antecedent-consequent form of causal laws, there are several points which stand out in the original cybernetic analysis of 'purpose'. To begin with, there are the central claims that purposive behaviour is defined in terms of the goal-directed movements of a system interacting with its environment, where the goal is said to be a part of the environment with which the system interacts. Hence the existence of a goal is a necessary condition for the attribution of purposive behaviour. This in itself was sufficient to stimulate a heated philosophical debate over the nature of purposes, but before considering the highlights of the latter it should also be borne in mind that goals on the cybernetic model are the 'final condition' towards which a system is directed (in space or time). Furthermore, the system is controlled by internal and external factors, in which case it cannot be said to exercise a choice. All of which represents, as Richard Taylor effectively brought out, a radical change in the meaning of 'purposive' or 'goal-directed' behaviour as traditionally understood.[8] For in purposive behaviour the relevant goal can be far removed or even non-existent without undermining the purposiveness of that behaviour; indeed it even makes sense to speak of purposive behaviour occurring 'for its own sake' (as e.g. in singing).

More importantly, the internal relations which bind the concept of purpose to consciousness, cognition, belief and volition are rendered external. For the upshot of Rosenbleuth, Wiener and Bigelow's argument is that there is no logical obstacle to describing cybernetic systems as purposive even though they can exercise no choice, and cannot be said to be trying to attain their goal, or even to be aware that such is their goal (as e.g. in the case of guided missiles). There is, of course, nothing to stop one from introducing a technical notion of 'cybernetic purpose', by which will be understood the state of equilibrium that the feedback mechanisms of a homeostatic system are designed or have evolved to maintain. But, as with the case of radical behaviourist theories, if the logico-grammatical distinction between purposive behaviour and causal sequences is undermined, the result is not a 'new understanding' of but, rather, the abandonment of the notion of (intentional) action and the creation of yet another misleading homonym. Which is another way of raising the central question whether, while they recognized the significance of this issue, Rosenbleuth, Wiener and Bigelow actually succeeded in reconciling causality with teleological explanations? And the first things to notice here are the striking continuities which cybernetics bears to its mechanist forebears. For example, Rosenbleuth and Wiener insisted that

> if the term purpose is to have any significance in science, it must be recognizable from the nature of the act, not from the study of or from any speculation on the structure and nature of the acting object. . . . [Hence] if the notion of purpose is applicable to living organisms, it is also applicable to non-living entities when they show the same observable traits of behavior.[9]

As a corollary to this they articulated the standard behaviourist thesis that multiple observations are needed to verify the existence of purposive behaviour.[10] Most importantly, the theory is committed to a picture of a *continuum of purposive behaviour*, now said to be governed by the 'orders of prediction' enjoyed by the system in question.[11] Thus the reflex acts and tropisms studied by the founders of behaviourism can indeed be seen to be purposive (albeit of a lower order), complex actions are treated as nested hierarchies of bodily movements, and consciousness can be neither co-extensive with sensation nor a necessary condition of action (since the argument does not distinguish between mechanical and biological systems) but, rather, must be epiphenomenal.[12]

There are a number of important objections that have been raised against the conceptual distortions induced by the cybernetic analysis of 'purposive behaviour' by cognitivists as well as Wittgensteinians; from the standpoint of the former, however, the root of these problems lies not in its causal orientation, but rather, in the absence of 'a mechanistic analogy of specifically psychological processes, a cybernetic parallel of the mind–body distinction'.[13] This lacuna is to be filled by the computationalist distinction between an embodied schema and its neurophysiological components. These internal representations are models of both goal and alternative procedures for pursuing it which 'mediate between stimulus and response in determining the behavior of the organism as a whole'.[14] Such an action-plan is 'an internal representation of possible action that functions as a model guiding intentional behaviour'.[15] It is this which accounts for the purposiveness of a system's movements, not the misguided supposition that there must be a goal which is a part of the environment with which the system interacts. On the assumption of a fundamental analogy between the hierarchical problem-solving structures introduced by Newell and Simon (in *LT* and *GPS*) and the 'procedural routines within a computer program', the crux of the post-computational version of the mechanist thesis thus lies in the premiss that 'Insofar as a machine's performance is guided by its internal, perhaps idiosyncratic model of the environment, the overall performance is describable in intensional terms.'[16] Once the mechanics of human (and animal) purposive action have been grasped it will be seen that philosophical objections which dwell on the logical grammar of ordinary mechanical versus intentional concepts are simply vacuous appeals to semantic inertia; not because intentional concepts are eliminable, but, rather, because there is room for both (given the different levels on which the same behaviour can be described).

While post-computational mechanists are committed to the logical possibility of empirical reducibility, therefore, they need not regard this as anything more than a distant prospect. Hence the much-celebrated shift from bottom-up to top-down approaches – i.e. to the computer simulation of the internal representations and processes that guide purposive behaviour, rather than the neural mechanisms in which these schemata are embodied. For 'We can only postulate such models on behavioral grounds, and hypothesize that they correspond to actual neurophysiological mechanisms.'[17] The cognitivist is thus engaged in the task of mapping function-theoretic automata onto behavioural outputs that are now seen to be mediated by internal representations acting on inputs, where the 'explanatory power of a machine model of behavior depends on the extent to which the details of the underlying information-processing are functionally equivalent to the psychological processes actually underlying behavior'.[18] This argument raises a number of profound issues on the nature and interpretation of models and automata (as formalistically conceived), consideration of which must be deferred for another occasion.[19] Our immediate concern is with the post-computationalist's endeavour to provide the non-causal mechanist account of purposive behaviour which eluded Rosenblueth, Wiener and Bigelow by postulating a species of 'action-plans', neurally embodied, that are 'closely analogous to the sets of instructions comprising procedural routines within a computer program' – that is, internal representations both of 'the goal or putative end-state of an intention' and a possible plan of action for bringing about that state.[20]

Although this argument is committed to the (remote) possibility of discovering the neural mechanisms of these internal models – and thus of the discovery of causally sufficient conditions for purposive behaviour – all of the emphasis is on the manner in which these models *guide* an agent's behaviour.[21] Not surprisingly, this theory has led to a growing bond between cognitivists and those ethologists who, following in Pavlov's footsteps, have added servo-mechanisms to the list of 'elemental units' driving the behaviour of insects and animals. It remains to be seen whether a cybernetic framework offers a promising approach to such studies; that is, whether the classic S–R paradigm (or some enhanced post-computational version) does not distort the nature and organization of the systems involved.[22] Our interest here is not with this (putatively) technical matter, however, but rather with the conceptual problems involved in the mechanist assumption that cognitive science can discover the building-blocks of *all* behaviour, be it tropistic, reflexive, or purposive. That is, our concern is with the persisting influence of the continuum picture – with the crucial premiss that (all) actions are complex sequences of 'planned' movements which 'are controlled by an organism's internal representation of its universe'.[23]

This theme is very much the basis for the functionalist thesis that purposive behaviour is directed by an organism's internal condition – its 'state of receptivity'. (For example, a cat will react differently to a touch on its cheek depending on whether or not it is stalking prey.[24]) We must be careful, however, not to confuse an agent's intentions when performing some action with the physical state that he, she or it is in when thus engaged. Or at least we must be clear that this argument presupposes that intentions are mental states which can alter an organism's reactions to external stimuli, and thus, that there is no categorial difference between bodily states and (e.g.) the manner in which the desire for promotion will shape one's reaction to such an event.[25] Furthermore, at a still more fundamental level the argument presupposes that without some such mechanism we will be unable to 'map the cognitive representation into the appropriate *pattern* of activity'.[26] But as we shall see in the following sections, where cognitive scientists – like all mechanists – disregard the philosophical problems involved in these assumptions (as a result of their unswerving faith that any such obstacles will be removed by empirical means), Wittgenstein was to struggle with them throughout his later writings on the philosophy of psychology.

THE HARMONY BETWEEN INTENTIONS AND ACTIONS

It is commonplace for cyberneticians and cognitivists alike to speak of purposive behaviour as those actions which are *guided* by an agent's intentions;[27] and how else could we explain this phenomenon if not in causal terms? To disclaim – on the grounds of neurophysiological ignorance – any knowledge of the relevant structures is not so much an evasion of duty as a confirmation of the mechanical picture which dominates here. Likewise, to fall back on the prospective form of teleological explanation does not in itself suffice to remove causality from the system; for the claim that

> behaviour is a function of what it serves to bring about, rather than some other unrelated factor, is a fact (if it is one) about the form of the antecedent; it is not a claim to dispense with an antecedent altogether or the invocation of an unobservable one.[28]

But purposive behaviour must not be confused with mere statistical regularity; the alternative (mapped out by automata theory) is to take this function-theoretic terminology as more than metaphorical, in which case the relation between intentions and goals should be seen as quasi-normative (in the sense 'disclosed' by Turing) rather than causal. Certainly this is an approach which harmonizes closely with what has become standard practice in the philosophy of language, and would it not be possible to say that an intention guides an agent in much the same way as does a rule? Indeed, do we not have here the perfect opportunity for the post-computational argument; for what could be more inviting than to argue that purposive behaviour is that in which an organism's actions are guided by the internal representations which are physically embodied in its central nervous system? At any rate, there would seem to be a conceptual gap here which can only be filled by an account that confronts the causality built into the 'folk theory' of intentional discourse and attempts to reconcile this with the 'non-contingent' relation between purpose and behaviour.[29]

This immediately calls into play the battery of arguments which Wittgenstein launched against Turing's attempt to treat computation as a causal sequence by reducing rule-following to its 'non-cognitive components'.[30] Without our going over that material again here, it is important to note that Wittgenstein first explored the themes he was to raise in response to Turing's thesis in the context of a discussion of the relation between 'ideas' (under which broad category are included intentions, purposes, desires, expectations, wishes etc., as well as concepts and rules) and their corresponding actions or applications. Our problem is that we regard an idea as 'like a mechanism whose workings we do not know': 'we expect every idea to have tentacles or affinities, so that it predetermines what will satisfy it'. But 'The agreement we want is not experiential at all. It is not a question of experience whether a thing will agree with our general idea, as it is with a mechanism about which we cannot predict with certainty'.[31] Just as in the case of rule-following, where what is needed is to explain the nature of the certainty which governs the applications of a rule, so too the first step towards understanding the relation between intentions and actions is to see that 'The connexion which is not supposed to be a causal, experiential one, but much stricter and harder, so rigid even, that the one thing somehow already *is* the other, is always a connexion in grammar'.[32] The manner in which this applies to intentional concepts is 'completely expressed in the fact that the state of affairs satisfying the expectation of p is represented by the proposition p'.[33] It is not the information (or rather lack of it) conveyed here that is important, however, but simply, that this is tautological – that it is impossible to specify the meaning of intentional terms independently of the states of affairs with which they are in accord.

When Wittgenstein first broached this topic after his return to Cambridge he insisted that 'the essential difference' between his own and Russell, Ogden and Richards' conception of the harmony between intentions (expectations, desires, purposes) and the behaviour which satisfies them lay in the fact that this is 'an internal relation, whereas in their view this is an external relation'.[34] In so far as this is precisely the move embraced by cybernetics, his objection to Russell's theory of desire is no less pertinent to the present discussion:

> I believe Russell's theory amounts to the following: if I give someone an order and I am happy with what he then does, then he has carried out my order. (If I wanted to eat an apple, and someone punched me in the stomach, taking away my appetite, then it was this punch that I originally wanted.)[35]

If this was indeed Russell's intention then, in his haste to absorb behaviourism, he had clearly failed to think through the logical absurdities entailed by such a thesis.[36] If we only learned as a matter of experience what complied with an order or satisfied our desires, then whatever event occurred would have to be deemed the meaning of that command or the nature of that desire, regardless of our expectations (assuming there is any basis for retaining such a notion). Moreover, it would no longer be tautological to say that the command or desire p is satisfied by p. But it is only because of this grammatical foundation that it makes sense to speak of disobeying an order, failing to act on one's intentions, satisfying one's desires or attaining one's goals – and knowing when one has done so.[37] Unlike causes, intentions determine those actions which fulfil them just as much when they are not as when they are carried out; for 'it is in language that an expectation and its fulfilment make contact'.[38] Thus, the whole question of how intentional concepts determine those actions with which they are in accord is but one instance of the family of problems grouped under 'the harmony of language with reality'.[39]

One possible problem with Wittgenstein's argument is that this mention of 'internal relations' might encourage one to suppose that what we are dealing with are just like external relations, except that the two entities or events involved are bound to one another necessarily.[40] To forestall this confusion Wittgenstein explained in *Lectures on the Foundations of Mathematics* that an

> internal relation is never a relation between two objects, but you might call it a relation between two concepts. And a sentence asserting an internal relation between two objects, such as a mathematical sentence, is not describing objects but constructing concepts.[41]

Similarly, the relation between purposes and the actions which satisfy them is forged by a rule of grammar laying down the connection between two concepts (i.e. 'X's purpose in doing Φ' means the same thing as 'the purpose that is satisfied by Φing'), not two events (one mental and the other behavioural). And it is for this – logical – reason that, to paraphrase what Wittgenstein says elsewhere in *Remarks on the Foundations of Mathematics*: 'If I have once expressed an intention I am bound in what I do further. But of course that only means that I am bound in my *judgement* about what is in accord with the intention and what not'.[42] In other words, we must distinguish between two senses of 'determines': the *causal* – in which something brings about a future event – and the *grammatical* – in which rules are laid down for the use of words.

Without this conceptual distinction we find it philosophically puzzling that it is possible (although not necessary) to frame an intention before acting upon it, or to predict someone's future behaviour on the basis of their expressed intentions. We are troubled by the fact that

> even if my wish does not determine what is going to be the case, still it does so to speak determine the theme of a fact, whether the fact fulfils the wish or not.' We are – as it were – surprised, not at anyone's knowing the future, but at his being able to prophesy at all (right or wrong).[43]

Moreover, as Wittgenstein himself stressed:

> in many cases someone else cannot predict my actions, whereas I foresee them in my intentions . . . [and thus] my prediction (in my expression of intention) has not the same foundation as his prediction of what I shall do, and the conclusions to be drawn from these predictions are quite different.[44]

Prima facie this seems to confirm the Cartesian picture of the subject's privileged access to his own 'mental states' and indirect knowledge of other people's intentions. In all these cases our knowledge rests, however, not on an inductive hypothesis, but rather, on the basic fact of logical grammar that intentions are *internally related* to the actions which satisfy them:

> 'The proposition determines in advance what will make it true.'
> Certainly, the proposition 'p' determines that p must be the case in order to make it true; and that means:
>   (the proposition p) = (the proposition that the fact p makes true).
> And the statement that the wish for it to be the case that p is satisfied by the event p, merely enunciates a rule for signs:
>   (the wish for it to be the case that p) = (the wish that is satisfied by the event p).[45]

Great care must be taken to clarify the normative sense in which these rules of grammar are to be construed; for

> Those propositions which seem to be analogous to experiential propositions about mechanisms, for example, that such-and-such an action or use will 'agree with' or 'follow from' an

idea, are not really analogous, since they are *rules*. And this is why they have the appearance of certainty which the analogous propositions about mechanisms do not have.[46]

The internal relation between a purpose and the action which fulfils it is no more temporal than is that between the rule '+2' and the series '102, 104, 106 . . .'. For the meeting-point between intentions and actions is in language, not the future:

> The *a priori* statements about agreement of something with an idea are misleadingly put in the form that the thing *will* agree with the idea, as though it were a question of time. But time does not enter in. One might as well say that 2 plus 2 made 4 yesterday or would a thousand years hence.[47]

Thus the certainty we possess as to the action an agent must perform in order to satisfy his intentions excludes the possibility of doubt precisely because it excludes the 'time axis' which is a source of the underlying tension in the mechanist framework.

It may not be at all clear, however, what bearing this conclusion has on the nature of purposive explanation; for given that the relation between intentions and actions is internal, it is far from obvious why this should preclude the possibility of treating it as temporal as well. After all, if an agent decides at t to Φ at t_1, and then does so, there is clearly a temporal relation between his initial decision and subsequent behaviour. To this Wittgenstein responds that we must distinguish between the rule of grammar involved and its applications – i.e. the temporal relation which subsists between the time (if there is one) at which an agent formed an intention (learned a rule) and the time at which he acted (applied the rule) versus the logico-grammatical relation which renders that action the satisfaction of that intention (application of that rule). As in the case of rule-following, the latter governs our accounts of the former – i.e., of what counts as acting in accord with an intention; whereas on the causal picture we are led to postulate the exact opposite as the case, by treating that action as the result of being guided by that intention. That is, we are led to confuse the logical consequences that the bearing of an agent's reasons (motives, wishes etc.) have on the description of his behaviour with the physical consequences of his engaging in that behaviour. But while one's reasons for Φing may be to bring about x, it is the action which has this effect, not one's reasons or intentions. Moreover, an agent's forming the intention to Φ no more brought about his Φing than his learning the rules of chess brought about his playing a game. Nor could his reasons for forming the intention (learning the rules) be said to bring about his actions; for his reasons either justify or explain the nature of his behaviour, they do not bring about his forming (or acting upon) that intention. Indeed, even the suggestion that an agent Φd at t_1 because he had so decided at t is potentially misleading, in so far as the typical sorts of appropriate explanation for why he Φd at t_1 are those that present the agent's reasons for Φing (and perhaps, some such rider as that he had not changed his mind since t, that he possessed the ability to Φ, that the circumstances allowed him to Φ, etc.).[48]

The drift of this argument is to bring us to see just how misleading it is to speak of purposive as 'something more' than causal behaviour,[49] or of action as a 'species of behaviour'.[50] On such a picture, action is seen as consisting in the mental state of directing or guiding a set of bodily movements towards a given end. It is as if the same set of movements exercised without the influence of this mental pilot would yield automaton-like behaviour.[51] And, of course, there is an element of truth in this; for without the evidence of an agent's purpose in Φing we may indeed be constrained to describe his behaviour as 'mechanical' (e.g. when someone is in a trance). But how do we establish the presence or absence of such intentions? There are any number of cases where this can be achieved on the basis of direct observation. For example, we can see straight off that the players on a pitch are engaged in a purposeful activity; conversely, we can see that a dervish whirling himself into a frenzy is not. There is no room here for error or doubt: even if the two teams were only trying to convince the spectators that they were playing a game they would still be behaving purposefully, while it is absurd to suppose that a dervish frothing at the mouth with upturned eyeballs and mutilating himself is only simulating frenzy. Then there are a wide range of cases where it is apparent that an agent is behaving purposefully but not at all clear what that purpose is: this might be resolved by further observation, or perhaps only by questioning the agent, but in any event we are dealing here with actions that are hinted at but not confirmed (or even belied) by the immediately observed behaviour. There are also cases where an agent appears to be behaving randomly but, as subsequent testimony reveals, was in fact acting purposefully (e.g. the latest dance craze) or the converse (e.g. the latest dance craze). Finally, there are cases where an agent might exhibit patterned movements without engaging in an action (e.g. somnambulism) or might not display any movements at all yet is none the less performing an action (e.g. feigning sleep).

In none of these cases do we observe or infer the attendance of a mental state; rather, we judge whether the behaviour involved warrants the attribution of an intentional concept. For it is the nature of the latter which fixes the demands we make upon the former, not the reverse: i.e., it is the complexity of the concept which determines whether it makes sense to say of a given species of behaviour that it constitutes Φing (*infra*). But 'In philosophy we are always in danger of giving a mythology of the symbolism, or of psychology: instead of simply saying what everyone knows and must admit.'[52] The mythology that Wittgenstein had in mind here is that there must be some hidden mechanism (whether mental or material) to account for overt purposive behaviour.[53] By explaining behaviour in terms of intentions we are neither reducing the latter to the former nor *inferring* the presence of an intervening mechanism; for as the above examples demonstrate, appropriate behaviour *justifies*, it does not entail the attribution of intentions. That one can display purposive behaviour without entertaining a purpose, or conversely, conceal one's intentions, merely attests to the fact that such criterial evidence is defeasible: not that in assigning intentions we are framing hypotheses or forming inductive generalizations on the basis of introspected experiences. If intentions were hidden mechanisms then first- and third-person statements would be '*hypothetical* in the sense that further experience can confirm or disprove the causal nexus'.[54] In which case, even if we accepted the sincerity of someone's avowed intention we could never be certain of its truth. But we can be as certain of what an agent intends as that twice 2 is 4 even though these two kinds of certainty belong to different language-games; for what they have in common, as this example illustrates, is the exclusion of doubt.[55]

Moreover, if the relation of intentions to actions were contingent it would indeed make sense to speak (without qualification) of having intentions without knowing it, of inferring, learning, suspecting, or even making mistakes as to what one intends.[56] But '"I know what I want, wish, believe, feel, . . ." (and so on through all the psychological verbs) is either philosophers' nonsense, or at any rate *not* a judgment *a priori*.'[57] That is, apart from such cases as when an agent is undecided (and in that sense uncertain) as to which course of action to pursue, or when prodding someone to confess or confront their real motives for an action, it is nonsensical to ask whether one is certain as to what one intends.[58] For what else could one respond to such a question other than 'The intention that I should Φ is the intention that really *I* should really Φ.' If a further explanation of this assurance is wanted I would go on to say 'and by "I" I mean myself, and by "Φ" I mean doing this . . .'; 'But these are just grammatical explanations, explanations which *create* language. It is *in language* that it's all done'.[59] Wittgenstein's point is not that intentions can only be attributed to creatures that possess the ability to speak a language, however,[60] but rather, that the 'mechanism' set into play by the application of intentional concepts is linguistic, not physiological or functional.[61]

This use of the term 'mechanism' must not be confused with the 'misleading analogy' that a 'causal nexus seems to be established by a mechanism connecting two parts of a machine' which leads us to view (e.g.) 'willing as an immediate non-causal bringing-about'.[62] Rather, it underlines the reason why the 'mechanism' set into play by an agent's deciding to Φ is *conceptual*: viz., this establishes the 'meaning' of his behaviour.[63] In the case of third-person statements we create certain expectations as to how an agent will subsequently behave or will respond to questioning (a point which is particularly relevant to those situations in which there is nothing overt to distinguish between movement and action). In the case of first-person reports the speaker himself arouses certain expectations which, should they fail to materialize, *may* indicate the presence of countervailing factors, or might just as well signify that the agent changed his mind, but in any event license the demand for some explanation as to why the agent failed to Φ (without entailing that there must be an answer!). This is still not enough to dispose of the mechanist challenge, however, for it is always possible to respond that 'changing one's mind' is itself the result of a 'countervailing factor' (i.e. that it manifests a conflict of action-plans). Indeed, the cognitivist may even harbour hopes of resolving those cases which are currently deemed inexplicable by traditional psychology (e.g. where the agent himself cannot explain why he failed to Φ, or perhaps, why he did). Certainly, as far as all of the above objections are concerned, he will respond that these definitely belong to the category of embarrassments, but they are in no way *a priori* obstacles to the successful explanation of how intentions 'somehow influence and guide [an] agent's actions'.[64]

'AN INTENTION IS EMBEDDED IN ITS SITUATION'

As was remarked at the close of the preceding section, the fact that the post-computational analysis of intentions opens up a whole gamut of linguistic complications does not faze the cognitivist in the least; for these can easily be dismissed as the consequences of a paradigm-conflict and not the symptoms of hidden conceptual truths. Indeed, the cognitivist remains confident that, however convincing the foregoing argument may be on the logical relation between intentions and actions, it does nothing to address the central issue at stake here, viz.,

> What are intentions? What, for instance, is the intention to buy a loaf of bread? Theoretical psychologists offer differing answers to these questions, for they disagree about the nature and importance of intentions. Not all allow that intention is a useful systematic concept, and even those who do so define it in significantly different ways. My central thesis is that any specific instance of intention is a highly structured phenomenon arising within a highly structured system, and that the nature of intention as a psychological reality cannot be understood unless this fact is taken into account.[65]

But then, this way of presenting the matter presupposes that the use of intentional concepts mirrors that of causal and the task of psychology is to identify the motive difference between the two. To be sure, we are constantly invited to make such an assumption by intentional language. The very fact that we speak of having or describing an intention, of learning what someone's intentions are or of doubting whether someone has the intentions they expressed, all point us in this direction. Wittgenstein repeatedly warns, however, that our basic mistake in the philosophy of psychology (as in the philosophy of mathematics) is to assume that all propositions are used descriptively,[66] or that all names are to be construed referentially.[67] This is not to be confused, however, with Davidson's claim that descriptions of intention are syncategorematic;[68] for where Davidson regards this as signifying that the use of 'intention' is to generate new descriptions of actions in terms of their reasons (terminating in something like 'His desire to π and his belief that Φing would lead to π caused him to Φ'), Wittgenstein's intention here as in the discussion of rule-following was to bring us to forsake the causal point of view *in toto*.

At first it seems that any help which Wittgenstein was disposed to lend on the actual use of intentional concepts was largely confined to the negative. Thus he bluntly warns that 'Intent, intention, is neither an emotion, a mood, nor yet a sensation or image. It is not a state of consciousness. It does not have genuine duration.'[69] If this appears to take us little further in response to the question of what intentions are if not mental states, it is because we are meant to see that the question itself is the source of our problem:

> Our mistake is to look for an explanation where we ought to look at what happens as a 'proto-phenomenon'. That is, where we ought to have said: *this language-game is played*. The question is not one of explaining a language-game by means of our experiences, but of noting a language-game.[70]

All of the various passages scattered throughout Wittgenstein's writings on the philosophy of psychology in which he seeks to flesh out the dogmatic claim made in §178 of *Remarks on the Philosophy of Psychology* (quoted at the start of this paragraph) are intended to undermine the picture that is the origin of our confusion here, and thereby bring us to discern the nature of the language-game that is played with intentional concepts. For the latter cannot be grasped while we are in the grip of the former – i.e. while we are still operating within the original framework of the mechanist/vitalist debate. Whether one subscribes to vital entelechies, neural nets, S–R or conditioning contingencies, feedback loops, function-theoretic tables, or action-plans, the fact is that in all these cases one has assumed that reasons, wishes, purposes, intentions, plans, decisions, etc. all somehow *bring about* their outcomes. And if one accepts the premiss that the family of intentional concepts must somehow 'guide' the behaviour which satisfies them, they must exist and execute this 'influence'[71] somewhere. It is thus in order to escape the consequences of this (ultimately Cartesian) framework that Wittgenstein counsels us to 'Look on the language-game as the primary thing'.[72]

By this Wittgenstein clearly meant to highlight the subtle effects involved in the use of intentional concepts (e.g. that 'I intend to Φ' can be used to express defiance or determination, to instil confidence etc.). But there is still a deeper point to be gleaned from the claim that 'An intention is embedded in its situation, in human customs and institutions.'[73] Once again we find an echo of the fundamental theme presented at §281 of *Philosophical Investigations* which, in the present context, can be paraphrased to read: 'Only of a living human being and what resembles (behaves like) a human being can one say: it has intentions; it acts for a reason; acts for no reason; knows what it is doing; discovers what it is doing; wants to Φ; refrains from Φing'. Whereas Wittgenstein's concern in §281 is to clarify the manner in which human beings serve as the paradigm subjects for the use of psychological concepts, what is at issue in this chapter is the (interrelated) manner in which human behaviour serves as the paradigm for the family of concepts subsumed under *action*.[74] Just as it is the complexity of the behaviour manifested by an organism which determines whether or not there are sufficient grounds for the attribution of a perceptual faculty, so too to grasp an agent's intention is to grasp the nature of his action, where to do the latter just is to take in the situation (customs and conventions). That is, it is to see the action *as an action* – to explain behaviour in a manner which takes it out of the realm of causality by embedding its description in the grammatical nexus of intentional concepts (a point which Wittgenstein illustrates with the example that 'Only in a quite particular musical context is there such a thing as three-part counterpoint').[75]

The application of intentional, like that of normative concepts, is thus determined by the complexity of the behaviour manifested by an agent (e.g. that it satisfies such judgments as 'He Φ'd intentionally', 'He intended to Φ', 'His reason/purpose/motive for Φing was . . .' etc.). Immediately following the well-known passage in *Remarks on the Foundations of Mathematics* in which Wittgenstein explored the criteria which would license us in saying that two chimpanzees were following rules, he continued: 'But suppose that already the first time the one chimpanzee had *purposed* to repeat this procedure? Only in a particular technique of acting, speaking, thinking, can someone purpose something. (This "can" is the grammatical "can.")'[76] That is, to say of an agent that he intends to Φ he must exhibit that species of behaviour rendered appropriate by the institution of Φing. Moreover, the point which Wittgenstein stressed in the preceding passage is equally relevant here; for what is going on in the chimpanzees' mind has no more bearing on the question of whether they are acting intentionally than on whether they are following a rule.[77] Rather, it is on the basis of what an agent says or does that we judge whether he intends to Φ. To say of someone that he has expressed or demonstrated the intention to Φ is both to treat Φing as an action and to assume that (circumstances allowing) he can be counted upon to Φ; *not* because intentions are such failsafe mechanisms, but rather, because this 'expresses our inability to depart from *this* concept. (Or ought I to say "refusal"?)'[78]

The only kind of 'guidance' involved here, therefore, is logical: viz. we speak of the purposes whereby an agent guides his behaviour when he cites those purposes as his reasons for Φing (e.g. when justifying his actions), or when there are grounds for attributing such a purpose when explaining the nature of someone's actions. This point rests on the familiar themes that the concept of action is internally related to that of agent,[79] and that by describing an agent's reasons for an action we are (logically) excluding the possibility that his behaviour was caused. As even the defenders of causal theories of action will quite readily acknowledge, this is characterized by the attribution of reasons and the logico-grammatical prohibition which this involves of the range of epistemological notions outlined above that only obtain in causal contexts. On the classic Davidsonian argument, however, redescribing an action by giving its reason may explain it in one sense but does not suffice to answer the question of how reasons explain actions; e.g. redescribing an agent's raising his arm as an act of signalling does not explain how an intention to signal brought it about that he raised his arm.[80] But this is the very question which is rendered senseless by having described his behaviour in intentional terms – i.e. by having seen (and asserted) that he 'raised his arm'. Thus, we do not redescribe his 'action of raising his arm' as the act of signalling; unless his behaviour satisfied the criterial demands of some intentional concept (e.g. to signal) there would be no grounds for describing his arm movements as an action in the first place. Hence we are not redescribing, we are describing or substantiating our description of that behaviour as an action by supplying an agent's reasons – i.e. reasons 'explain actions', not in the causal sense that they bring about behaviour, but in the constitutive sense that they establish that a species of behaviour is legitimately described as an action.

Herein lies another key insight into the logical nature of the internal relation between intentions and actions. Mechanists have sought to capitalize on the facts that someone's intention to Φ does not entail that in the absence of countervailing factors that agent will Φ, or that someone's having Φ'd does not entail that they intended to Φ or were aware of any reasons for Φing. But while both claims are clearly true, mechanist attempts to draw a reductionist conclusion from them tend to focus unduly on a single intentional concept, and more importantly, ignore the complexity of intentional concepts. For whereas 'X's arm is rising' invites a causal explanation, 'X raised his arm' does indeed entail some form of intentional explanation. The familiar claim that the question why some event occurred permits either a causal or an intentional response should thus be treated with caution. To be sure, there are a number of verbs which can be used to denote either an action or a causal sequence (e.g. 'Why did X cry out?'); but in many cases the very question that we ask removes the possibility of a causal response (e.g. 'Why did X prevaricate?').[81] And this in itself is indicative, not of the fact that such concepts are theory-laden, but rather, of the manner in which intentional concepts 'fix the meaning' of behaviour – of the crucial difference between the questions 'Why did X raise his arm?' and 'Why did X's arm rise?'.[82] To answer the former in causal terms or the latter in terms of the agent's intentions may indeed be intelligible, but only in so far as it serves (tacitly) to reformulate the question.

This theme that an agent's behaviour cannot be separated from its situation does not appeal to the (overly restrictive) claim that the concept of human behaviour is confined to that of action (although there is clearly a bias in this direction). Overlooking the varying uses of 'behaviour' employed by biologists, physiologists, sociologists etc., there are indeed instances in which we speak of a human being's 'mechanical behaviour' – viz., precisely those in which the application of intentional concepts (and those of moral responsibility) is suspended. But that in no way licenses the assumption that the same behaviour can be described in either intentional or causal terms. The danger here is that of treating behaviour as a category-neutral, pre-linguistic phenomenon (viz., a 'colourless set of movements') which as such can be described in either causal or intentional terms – i.e. of conceding that causal descriptions may be excluded from purposive explanation but insisting that this does not preclude a distinct causal explanation of the same behaviour. The problem with this argument is that it fails to consider what exactly would be involved in the causal description of manifestly purposive behaviour. Consider, for example, Gasking and Jackson's memoir of 'Wittgenstein as a teacher':

> At times [he] would break off, saying, 'Just a minute, let me think!' and would sit for minutes on end, crouched forward on the edge of a chair, staring down at his upturned palm. Or

he would exclaim with vehement sincerity: 'This is as difficult as *hell*!'[83]

What would it mean to give a causal account of *this* behaviour? (A related question which mechanists should consider is: do we infer from his behaviour that Wittgenstein was indeed thinking during these pauses; what would we say to someone who persistently expressed some doubt as to whether Wittgenstein really was thinking?)

Obviously, one must not confuse the 'behaviour' of his nervous system while lecturing with 'Wittgenstein's behaviour'; such a misplaced neurophysiological report would in no sense be describing the 'same thing' as Gasking and Jackson, although it would clearly be describing something. But we could not even begin to understand a misguided mechanist who insisted that what he was describing just was Wittgenstein's behaviour; in Wittgenstein's words, one may well have believed that he suffered while lecturing, but could one 'also *believe* that he wasn't an automation? It would go against the grain to use the word in both connexions. (Or is it like this: I believe that he is suffering, but am certain that he is not an automaton? Nonsense!)'[84] To be sure, the question of 'Why Wittgenstein behaved in this way' admits of different kinds of answer; for example, that he was struggling to clarify his thoughts, that the act of closing his eyes and blocking out sound caused certain neuro-transmitters to fire more rapidly, that the lack of attention which he had received as a child made him turn in on himself to find his own answers to the problems that troubled him. But what such examples illustrate is not the manner in which the same behaviour can be explained in either intentional or causal terms; rather, it is the pertinence of Wittgenstein's general warning that 'the meaning of a question is given by its method of answering it'.[85]

It is thus in the restricted sense that 'we judge an action according to its background within human life'[86] that the use of intentional and mechanical concepts exclude one another – a logico-grammatical barrier which cannot be circumvented by exploiting the ambiguity of 'behaviour'. That is, the identity of the behaviour is itself fixed by the context in which it is embedded – a point which bears as much on the subtleties involved in the discrimination of behaviour as on the 'reasons versus causes' debate, as Wittgenstein brings out with his distinction between

Pain-behaviour and the behaviour of sorrow. – These can only be described along with their external occasions. (If a child's mother leaves it alone it may cry because it is sad; if it falls down, from pain.) Behaviour and kind of occasion belong together.[87]

But just as it is a mistake to generalize the concept of 'reasons',[88] so too we must not suppose that these contexts are static. If it gradually emerged that Köhler's chimpanzees were trying to use a stick as a tool, or like Thorndike's cats, that the possibility of so using a stick had accidentally occurred to them, it would no longer make sense to describe their behaviour in (micro or molar) S–R terms; conversely, the more we read of the speaker's thoughts and behaviour in *The Outsider*, the less willing are we to treat him as a fully rational agent.[89] But as the latter so abundantly makes clear, this should be regarded as a source of the richness of life and its literature, not the bane of philosophers and psychologists. For the fact that one may act intentionally for no reason at all, or even for someone else's reasons, does not entail that the concept of action can be severed from the entire family of intentional concepts.[90] But then, this very premiss has been built into the mechanist framework as one of its defining features.

In his remarks on the philosophy of mathematics Wittgenstein warned that

> The philosopher easily gets into the position of a ham-fisted director, who, instead of doing his own work and merely supervising his employees to see they do their work well, takes over their jobs until one day he finds himself over-burdened with other people's work while his employees watch and criticize him. He is particularly inclined to saddle himself with the work of the mathematician.[91]

The same counsel no doubt applies to the philosopher of psychology, but here one finds oneself sorely tempted to pursue just such a course.[92] For at the heart of the subject are a number of concepts which are not just ambiguous, but whose shades of meaning lie in the very realms which are opposed. Most serious of all are the consequences of either overlooking or of deliberately renouncing any such ambiguity. Thus the question 'What do reflex and intentional actions have in common *qua* species of behaviour?' cannot but lead us to transgress this logico-grammatical boundary.[93] Nor is this nothing more than an etymological coincidence; for the driving force behind the mechanist concept of 'reflex actions' stemmed from just such an assumption. Thus to acquiesce in this linguistic custom is to concede *ab initio* the legitimacy of a misguided mechanist theory! Despite these dangers built into the framework, however, Wittgenstein's admonition still has considerable weight. For the point of the warning is not to thwart the exposure of misleading constructions, but rather, to encourage us to interpret rather than theorize, which, of course, should forestall the fruitless search for the *Merkmale* of a family-resemblance concept. And the futility of such an endeavour has indeed been demonstrated by those who have sought to provide rigid definitions of 'intention' and 'action'. No matter how comprehensive the latest offering, some exception has always been found to elude the net of necessary and sufficient conditions – as much a consequence of shifting contexts as the unending supply of counter-examples.

To dispute the claim that such a conclusion would deal a devastating blow to the juvenile science of psychology is merely to question the paradigm of 'science' whereby one approaches psychology,[94] and thus the manner in which mechanists have sought to impose an inappropriate framework on intentional behaviour. By denying the significance of purposive terms the founders of behaviourism in effect renounced the possibility of closing what they regarded as the metaphysical hiatus between intentions and actions. Recognizing the importance of purposive concepts, the cyberneticians sought to fill this gap, thereby endeavouring to dispel mystery with theory. Artificial Intelligence scientists have continued the latter enterprise, refining the processes involved through the medium of recursive programs and replacing the notions of an 'idea of a goal' and 'procedures for obtaining it' with neurally embodied 'internal representations' whereby the agent's behaviour is controlled. Thus, the embodied souls of classical epistemology have been displaced by the embodied rules and representations of modern thought. As a prolegomenon to consideration of the provenance of the latter concepts, one of the questions that the present chapter has touched on is not so much how as *why* so many pre-computational mechanists anticipated the latter cognitivist themes.[95] The answer that has been explored is that, running right through the history of mechanist thought is this premiss that there is a gulf between purposes and actions which in some way must be bridged. Here, as elsewhere, Wittgenstein's response to this mystery was to 'dissolve' it; to demonstrate that, 'Like everything metaphysical the harmony between thought and reality is to be found in the grammar of the language.'[96] And therein lies the essence of the enduring relevance of his remarks on intentions.

NOTES

As I hope they will appreciate, I am deeply indebted to Jack Canfield, Peter Hacker, Ed Reed and Sören Stenlund for the searching questions which they raised in response to an earlier draft of this paper.

1 R.B. Perry, 'Purpose as Tendency and Adaptation', *Philosophical Review* 26 (1917); L. Wittgenstein, 'The Language of Sense Data and Private Experience' (Notes taken by Rush Rhees of Wittgenstein's Lectures, 1936), *Philosophical Investigations* 7 (1984).

2 L. Wittgenstein, *Culture and Value*, ed. G.H. von Wright and Heikki Nyman, trans. Peter Winch (Oxford: Basil Blackwell, 1980), 15.

3 George A. Miller, Eugene Galanter and Karl H. Pribram, *Plans and the Structure of Behavior* (New York: Holt, Rinehart & Winston, 1960), 13, 10.

4 Perhaps 'demise' is too strong a term, since both fields continue to attract considerable support; it might thus be better to speak of 'paradigm displacement'.

5 Cf. Stephen E. Palmer and Ruth Kimchi, 'The Information Processing Approach to Cognition', in Terry J. Knapp and Lynn C. Robertson (eds), *Approaches to Cognition* (Hillsdale, New Jersey: Lawrence Erlbaum Associates, Publishers, 1986), 60 ff, and F.H. George, *Cognition* (London: Methuen & Co., 1960), 32: 'It must be emphasized very strongly that cybernetics as a scientific discipline is essentially consistent with behaviourism, and is indeed a direct offshoot from it. Behaviourists, in essence, are people who have always treated organisms as if they were machines.'

6 Arturo Rosenbleuth, Norbert Wiener and Julian Bigelow, 'Behavior, Purpose and Teleology', *Philosophy of Science* 10 (1943), 24, 22.

7 Miller, Galanter and Pribram, op. cit., 3.

8 See Richard Taylor, 'Comments on a Mechanistic Conception of Purposefulness' (1950) and 'Purposeful and Non-Purposeful Behavior: A Rejoinder' (1950), in Walter Buckley (ed.), *Modern Systems Research for the Behavioral Scientist* (Chicago: Aldine Publishing Company, 1968).

9 Arturo Rosenbleuth and Norbert Wiener, 'Purposeful and Non-purposeful Behavior' (1950), in Buckley, op. cit., 235.

10 Ibid., 236.

11 E.g. 'it is possible that one of the features of the discontinuity of behavior observable when comparing humans with other high mammals may lie in that the other mammals are limited to predictive behavior of low order, whereas man may be capable potentially of quite high orders of prediction' (Rosenbleuth, Wiener and Bigelow, op. cit., 223).

12 Ibid., 235; cf. K.M. Sayre, *Consciousness: A Philosophic Study of Minds*

and Machines (New York: Random House, 1969).

13 Margaret A. Boden, *Purposive Explanation in Psychology* (Cambridge, Mass: Harvard University Press, 1972), 107.

14 Margaret A. Boden, 'Intentionality and Physical Systems' (1970), in Margaret A. Boden, *Minds and Mechanisms* (Ithaca: Cornell University Press, 1981), 58.

15 Margaret A. Boden, 'The Structure of Intentions' (1973), in *Minds and Mechanisms*, 134.

16 See Allen Newell and Herbert A. Simon, 'The Logic Theory Machine: A Complex Information Processing System', *Transactions on Information Theory* (Institute of Radio Engineers, 1957); Allen Newell and Herbert A. Simon, 'GPS, A Program that simulates Human Thought', in Edward A. Feigenbaum and Julian Feldman (eds), *Computers and Thought* (New York: McGraw-Hill, 1963); Margaret A. Boden, *Purposive Explanation in Psychology*, 128. It should be noted that this argument marks a shift in focus from the subject of machine intelligence to that of cognitive modeling. For the very fact that these internal representations can be mechanically simulated, thereby enabling us to describe cybernetic systems in purposive terms, might also 'provide a key to understanding the way in which the corresponding [human or animal] behavior is actually produced' (ibid., 142).

17 Boden, 'Intentionality and Physical Systems', 60.

18 Boden, *Purposive Explanation in Psychology*, 144.

19 See S.G. Shanker, 'The Dawning of Machine Intelligence', *Philosophica* 42 (1989).

20 Boden, 'The Structure of Intentions', 134; cf. Miller, Galanter and Pribram, op. cit., 378.

21 See Boden, *Purposive Explanation in Psychology*, 155.

22 See Edward S. Reed, 'An Outline of a Theory of Action Systems', *Journal of Motor Behavior* 14 (1982).

23 Miller, Galanter and Pribram, op. cit., 12.

24 See C.R. Gallistel, 'Precis of Gallistel's *The Organisation of Action: A New Synthesis*', *The Behavioral and Brain Sciences* 4 (1981), 616.

25 See Fred Dretske, *Explaining Behavior* (Cambridge, Mass.: the MIT Press, 1988), 110.

26 Miller, Galanter and Pribram, op. cit., 13.

27 E.g. in her article on 'Purpose' Margaret Boden explains at the outset that 'We commonly explain what people (and perhaps animals) do by assuming they have some purpose in doing it, some idea in mind which guides their activity towards their goal in an intelligently flexible fashion' (in Richard Gregory (ed.), *The Oxford Companion to the Mind*, (Oxford: Oxford University Press, 1987), 664).

28 Charles Taylor, 'The Explanation of Purposive Behaviour', in Robert Borger and Frank Cioffi (eds), *Explanation in the Behavioural Sciences* (Cambridge: Cambridge University Press, 1970), 55.

29 See S. G. Shanker, 'Wittgenstein versus Turing on the Nature of Church's Thesis', *Notre Dame Journal of Formal Logic* 28 (1987); K. M. Sayre, *Cybernetics and the Philosophy of Mind* (Atlantic Highlands: New Jersey, Humanities Press, 1976).

30 See S. G. Shanker, *Wittgenstein and the Turning-Point in the Philosophy of Mathematics* (London: Croom Helm, 1987).

31 L. Wittgenstein, *Wittgenstein's Lectures: Cambridge 1932–1935*, ed. Alice Ambrose (Oxford: Basil Blackwell, 1979), 80, 84–5.

32 L. Wittgenstein, *Remarks on the Foundations of Mathematics*, ed. G. H. von Wright, R. Rhees and G. E. M. Anscombe, trans. G. E. M. Anscombe, 3rd edn (Oxford: Basil Blackwell, 1978), I §128.

33 L. Wittgenstein, *Philosophical Remarks*, ed. Rush Rhees, trans. R. Hargreaves and R. White (Oxford: Basil Blackwell, 1975), 66.

34 Ibid., 63.

35 Ibid., 64 cf. Friedrich Waismann, *Principles of Linguistic Philosophy* (London: Macmillan, 1965), 116–7.

36 Cf. Bertrand Russell, *The Analysis of Mind* (London: George Allen & Unwin, 1971), 32.

37 Malcolm makes a related point in his debate with Armstrong. Armstrong holds that intentions can be described under two distinct guises: on the level of ordinary language they bear a logical connection to those actions with which they are in accord, whereas on a reductionist level (where they are identical with brain-states) they are contingently related to the behaviour they bring about. But, as Malcolm explains, this would entail that it is logically possible that the intention to Φ might be satisfied (under different causal laws) by πing. Where Malcolm treats this as a *reductio*, however, Armstrong 'cannot see any serious difficulty here'. He concedes that 'there seems to be a difficulty in the particular case which Malcolm proposes' (D. M. Armstrong and Norman Malcolm, *Consciousness and Causality* (Oxford: Basil Blackwell, 1984), 148), but this he thinks is due to the interlocking network of intentional concepts involved and not to any inherent weakness in the argument. In reply to this Malcolm can only fall back on reiterating the logical character of the relation between intentions and actions, to which Armstrong quite naturally responds that he and Malcolm seem to be 'taking yet a further turn around the [mulberry] bush' (ibid., 209). He then spells out his reasons for believing that there is no logical reason why the intention to Φ might not have been the intention to π. But, as Malcolm had sought to clarify (197–8), the problem is not that the intention to Φ might have been a different intention but rather, the logical absurdity involved in the suggestion that the intention to π might have been satisfied by the act of πing.

38 L. Wittgenstein, *Philosophical Investigations*, §445; cf. Wittgenstein, *Philosophical Remarks*, 69, and L. Wittgenstein, *Philosophical Grammar*, ed. Rush Rhees, trans. Anthony Kenny (Oxford: Basil Blackwell, 1974), 134, 161–2.

39 L. Wittgenstein, *Philosophical Grammar*, 162.

40 As Wittgenstein himself had originally thought (cf. L. Wittgenstein, *Tractatus Logico-Philosophicus*, trans. D. F. Pears and B. F. McGuinness (London: Routledge & Kegan Paul, 1961), 4.123).

41 L. Wittgenstein, *Lectures on the Foundations of Mathematics: Cambridge, 1939*, ed. Cora Diamond (Hassocks: The Harvester Press,

1976), 73.

42 L. Wittgenstein, *Remarks on the Foundations of Mathematics*, VI §27.

43 L. Wittgenstein, *Philosophical Investigations*, trans. G. E. M. Anscombe 3rd edn (Oxford: Basil Blackwell, 1973), §461.

44 Ibid., 224.

45 L. Wittgenstein, *Philosophical Grammar*, 161–2.

46 L. Wittgenstein, *Wittgenstein's Lectures: Cambridge 1932–1935*, 87.

47 Ibid.

48 It is thus important to note that, in contrast to the above remarks on the internal relation between intentional concepts and the actions with which they are in accord, that it is *not* tautologous to say 'He Φd at t_1 because he had so decided at t'. In fact, this might be false, and if it were indeed true, would generally be deemed a highly unsatisfactory (if not rude) response to the question 'Why did he Φ?'

49 Charles Taylor, *Explanation of Behaviour* (London: Routledge & Kegan Paul, 1964), 55.

50 Dretske, op. cit., 6.

51 For, as theorists of action have long emphasized, the identical movements might in one context be purely reflexive while in another constitute an action (e.g. contrast blinking with winking).

52 L. Wittgenstein, *Philosophical Remarks*, §24.

53 Cognitive science is, of course, committed to just such a *tertium quid* between thought and action; what Wittgenstein was querying was not the nature of this 'mechanism', but the assumption that *anything* could be interposed here (cf. Friedrich Waismann, *Ludwig Wittgenstein and the Vienna Circle*, ed. Brian McGuinness, (trans.) Joachim Schulte and Brian McGuinness (Oxford: Basil Blackwell, 1979), 154 ff). Lest it be thought that this represents a covert attempt to attribute remarkable prescience to Wittgenstein it should be emphasized that his target here was his own abortive attempt, in the early 1930s, to apply the picture theory to intentional concepts. What does bear noting are the significant parallels between cognitivism and Wittgenstein's proposal to treat intentions as logical pictures (representations) of future actions.

54 Waismann, *Principles of Linguistic Philosophy*, 120.

55 Thus Wittgenstein asks: '"But, if you are *certain*, isn't it that you are shutting your eyes in face of doubt?" – They are shut' (Wittgenstein, *Philosophical Investigations*, 224.)

56 Cf. ibid., §246.

57 Ibid, 221.

58 Ibid, §247; cf. L. Wittgenstein, *Last Writings*, ed. G. H. von Wright and Heikki Nyman, trans. C. G. Luckhardt and M. A. E. Aue (Oxford: Basil Blackwell, 1982), §§881–2.

59 L. Wittgenstein, *Philosophical Grammar*, 143.

60 Cf. Wittgenstein, *Philosophical Investigations*, §647.

61 See John F. M. Hunter, *Intending* (Halifax: Philosophy in Canada, 1978), 17.

62 L. Wittgenstein, *Philosophical Investigations*, §613.

63 See Waismann, *Principles of Linguistic Philosophy*, 111 ff.

64 Boden, 'The Structure of Intentions', 134.

65   Ibid., 133.
66   L. Wittgenstein, *Philosophical Investigations*, §317.
67   Ibid., §244.
68   Donald Davidson, 'Actions, Reasons, and Causes' (1963), in *Essays on Actions and Events* (Oxford: Clarendon Press, 1980), 8.
69   L. Wittgenstein, *Remarks on the Philosophy of Psychology*, 2 vols, ed. G. H. von Wright and Heikki Nyman, trans. C. G. Luckhardt and M. A. E. Aue (Oxford: Basil Blackwell, 1980), II §§178.
70   L. Wittgenstein, *Philosophical Investigations*, §654, 655.
71   In the full etymological sense of the term.
72   Ibid., §656.
73   Ibid., §337.
74   Cf. Dretske: 'It may be that one finds the conditioned behavior of simple creatures, such as rats and pigeons, too simple, too rigid, and too nonadaptive to qualify as goal-directed or purposeful, and hence too simple to be explained in terms of *reasons* (what the animal believes and desires). Although in *some* sense the rat is pressing the bar *in order to get food*, this isn't the kind of deliberate, intentional, intelligent behavior that we humans exhibit in our quest to satisfy our desires and realize our purposes' (op. cit., 119–20). But the explanation for this hesitation is no more a result of the putative distinction between implicit and explicit beliefs than a 'simple dislike of rats'. As this passage intimates, the problem here is that the further we move from the human paradigm of intentional concepts, the less willing are we to describe insect and animal behaviour as goal-directed or purposeful. The very attempt to distinguish between 'implicit' and 'explicit' beliefs attests to this strain; significantly, if we move still further away from the paradigm (e.g. to tropisms) the temptation to postulate such 'conative states' disappears. Cf. George M. Wilson, *The Intentionality of Human Action* (Amsterdam: North-Holland, 1980).
75   L. Wittgenstein, *Last Writings*, §948.
76   L. Wittgenstein, *Remarks on the Foundations of Mathematics*, VI §43.
77   See S. G. Shanker, 'Wittgenstein versus Turing on the Nature of Church's Thesis', cf. Wittgenstein, *Philosophical Grammar*, 143.
78   L. Wittgenstein, *Remarks on the Foundations of Mathematics*, IV §30. Herein lies one of the more subtle ways in which the concept of intention departs from that of rule. For it is puzzling but not nonsensical to suggest that X sincerely intended to Φ, possessed both the opportunity and the ability, and yet failed to Φ, or to offer any explanation or justification for his behaviour. Malcolm illustrates this with the example of someone regularly announcing their intention to go on a diet (and just as regularly failing to keep their word). But the relation between intention and execution can only take so much strain before we are forced to deny the agent's sincerity (Armstrong and Malcolm, *Consciousness and Causality*, 88).
79   As the etymology of the latter – viz. something which acts to bring about changes in itself or its environment – bears out.
80   Davidson, 'Actions, Reasons, and Causes', 10.
81   Cf. Davidson, 'Agency', in *Essays on Actions and Events*, 45.

82   Cf. Wittgenstein, *Philosophical Investigations* §§612 ff: One problem with this tired example is that it obscures the subtle nuances which figure in the description of behaviour. Compare 'Why did the dancer raise her leg?', 'Why did the dog raise its leg?', 'Why did the centipede raise its leg?', 'Why did the table raise its leg?' Contrast these with 'Why did the dancer's leg rise?', 'Why did the dog's leg rise?', 'Why did the centipede's leg rise?', 'Why did the table's leg rise?'

83   In K. T. Fann, *Ludwig Wittgenstein: The Man and His Philosophy* (New Jersey: Humanities Press, 1967), 52.

84   L. Wittgenstein, *Philosophical Investigations*, §178.

85   L. Wittgenstein, *Philosophical Grammar*, 387; see Shanker, *Wittgenstein and the Turning-Point in the Philosophy of Mathematics*, ch. III.

86   L. Wittgenstein, *Remarks on the Philosophy of Psychology*, §624.

87   L. Wittgenstein, *Zettel*, ed. G. E. M. Anscombe and G. H. von Wright, trans. G. E. M. Anscombe (Oxford: Basil Blackwell, 1967), §492.

88   I am indebted to Jack Canfield's unpublished 'Reasons' for this point.

89   See Shanker, 'The Dawning of (Machine) Intelligence'; cf. A. I. Melden, *Free Action* (London: Routledge & Kegan Paul, 1961), 192–3, and Waismann, *Principles of Linguistic Philosophy*, 111–12.

90   Sayre maintains that someone under hypnosis who shakes hands with a trained animal illustrates the fact that the concept of action is not internally related to that of conscious intention and that external causes can bring about an agent's actions (*Consciousness: A Philosophic Study of Minds and Machines*, 30–1). But we should compare the case of an agent controlling someone or something's movements with controlling someone's actions (e.g. an anaesthetist who administers succinylcholine with a hypnotist who mesmerizes someone to go limp.) Unless *some* intentional concept applies (e.g. he was trying to relax or had an uncontrollable urge to shake hands with the lion) there would be no grounds for introducing action-terms to describe his behaviour. Furthermore, the fact that an agent may have had a reason for an action does not entail that he was aware of that reason. (He may even have acted for a completely different reason; see Roy Lawrence, *Motive and Intention* (Evanston: Northwestern University Press, 1972), 18 ff.)

91   L. Wittgenstein, *Philosophical Grammar*, 369.

92   Cf. G. H. von Wright, *Explanation and Understanding* (Ithaca: Cornell University Press, 1971) 193.

93   Cf. Dretske, op. cit., 7.

94   For an extremely important introduction to the direction in which the theory of action can and should be taken, see Jeff Coulter's *Mind in Action* (Oxford: Polity Press, 1989).

95   e.g. Tolman, Hull (in the early work 'Knowledge and Purpose as Habit Mechanisms', *Psychological Review* 37 (1930)) and, according to Bruner, McDougall (Jerome Bruner, 'Preface to the Beacon Press Edition', in William McDougall, *Body and Mind* (Boston: Beacon Press, 1961)).

96   L. Wittgenstein, *Philosophical Grammar*, 162.

4

CONVERSATIONS
WITH APES

Reflections on the scientific study
of language

John Dupré

Contemporary attempts to teach a form of language to great apes date from the work of Beatrice and Allen Gardner.[1] While a number of earlier attempts were made to teach spoken languages to domestically raised chimpanzees,[2] these were uniformly unsuccessful. The insight pursued by the Gardners was that the failures might be due as much to the apes' lack of suitable vocal mechanisms as to their lack of linguistic aptitude.[3] They therefore attempted instead to teach their charges – notably the chimpanzee Washoe, undoubtedly the best-known of the talking apes – American Sign Language, or Ameslan. The Gardners claimed considerable success for this project, Washoe acquiring a vocabulary of well over a hundred signs[4] and significant conversational skills. Since then a number of other chimpanzees have been instructed in sign language[5] as well as a pair of gorillas[6] and an orangutan.[7] A rather different strategy has been pursued by David Premack,[8] Duane Rumbaugh[9] and Sue Savage-Rumbaugh,[10] who attempted to teach chimpanzees wholly artificial symbolic systems. In the first case this involved learning to place variously coloured and shaped metal pieces in sequence on a magnetic board, and in the latter two, pressing keys on a specially designed computer keyboard. The difference between the sign language and other approaches will be discussed further below.

Numerous interesting questions are raised by this research. I shall divide the present discussion into three broad categories. First, I shall briefly consider what it is these various apes have really learned to do. Second, in the main part of the chapter, I shall consider a variety of objections that have been posed to claims that such apes have acquired genuinely linguistic abilities. These objections reveal how the research under consideration raises important methodological questions about the scientific study of language. And finally I shall consider some of the varied goals and interests underlying this research programme and its criticisms.

WHAT DO APES LEARN?

The assertion that apes have, to some limited degree, mastered a language has engendered enormous controversy. One major issue has concerned whether apes ever acquire any kind of syntactic capacity.[11] Given the widely held Chomskyan idea that the indefinitely productive powers of language, grounded in syntax, are of its essence, this has often been interpreted as showing that pongid utterances[12] are not really linguistic at all. On the other hand, it seems widely conceded within the debate that the question: what is required for syntactic competence, is an extremely obscure one, and I shall here side-step it.

What is fairly clear is that apes can be taught to use quite substantial repertoires of symbols (the gorilla, Koko, apparently the star in this area, is said to have a vocabulary of around 150–600 words, depending on the strictness of the criteria employed).[13] Slightly more contentiously, it may be said that apes can perform certain speech-acts. These two claims are sufficiently illustrated by the kind of performance of which these apes are most widely agreed to be capable, that of demanding. Requesting various foods and drinks, tickles and other preferred amusements figure largely in the reported utterances of language-trained apes. Given that these requests are effected by the use of essentially arbitrary symbols (signs, selection of keys marked with geometric symbols, etc.), it seems clear that these apes can use symbols. Against this it is sometimes argued that all that has happened is that the apes have been conditioned, in a crudely Skinnerian way, to bring about certain desired results. On this view an ape said to be signing 'Give me banana' is doing essentially the same as a rat trained to press a red lever to obtain a food pellet.

One might perhaps retort that the rat has indeed been taught that red means 'pellets', and thus has acquired a minimal semantic competence. Generally the intended force of the criticism is that the ape, and a fortiori the rat, does not know that its sign, say 'X', means banana. And certainly one is not inclined to attribute this knowledge to the rat, presumably because it seems more parsimonious to attribute to the rat merely the causal belief that pressing the lever produces food. The critic wants to say the same of the ape, that signing 'give me banana' is essentially similar to shaking the tree to make the bananas fall off. Presumably rebuttal of this criticism should not be taken to require showing that apes have explicitly semantic beliefs, e.g. the belief that 'X' means bananas. Mastery of this kind of semantic ascent would surely exclude most small children and many adults from our linguistic communities; sentences such as '"banana" means bananas' are pretty sophisticated bits of philosophical gadgetry. A much more reasonable demand would be that to qualify as using 'X' as a symbol one should be able to do more with it than merely make requests (though compare the notorious language games in Wittgenstein's *Philosophical Investigations*, §§1–7).

It would appear that this latter demand has been quite thoroughly addressed in recent ape-language research. The fact that an ape's ability to use a symbol in a particular way does not entail its possession of all the capacities we might naturally associate with knowing the meaning of a common noun is nicely demonstrated by some of the experiments of Savage-Rumbaugh.[14] For example, apes can be taught to produce utterances appropriate for requesting different available kinds of food, while giving no indication that they can respond appropriately as addressees of the same utterances, e.g. in selecting the named object from a group of objects. (A similar separation between linguistic production and reception has also been noted in the linguistic development of children.) On the other hand, this is equally clearly not the typical case for trained apes. In the experiments referred to above, once the animals acquired the capacity of responding to, as well as producing, particular kinds of utterance, they had no trouble in generalizing this facility to newly acquired signs. Much more striking illustrations of the flexible use of signs can be drawn from the reports of Patterson's work. She reports cases of descriptions by her gorillas of events present and past, and the production of jokes, threats and insults. Koko is reported as using signs while playing with her dolls (though apparently she is embarrassed to be discovered doing this), and even as discussing death:

MAUREEN (an instructor): Where (do) gorillas go when (they) die?
KOKO: Comfortable hole bye.
MAUREEN: When (do) gorillas die?

KOKO: Trouble old.
(Words in parentheses do not actually appear as signs in the original Ameslan.)[15]

Without constituting brilliant dialogue or philosophy, such reported interchanges surely suggest more than conditioned reflexes. However, their significance has been seriously questioned. I shall now look in more detail at the kinds of attacks that have been launched against the conclusions that these apes reveal any genuine linguistic capacity.

CRITICISMS OF APE-LANGUAGE RESEARCH

It will be helpful in considering the criticisms of research on the linguistic capacities of apes to distinguish sharply between the sign-language projects of the Gardners, Fouts, Terrace, and Patterson, and the artificial languages of Premack, Rumbaugh and Savage-Rumbaugh. Somewhat crudely, one may see the former as motivated by the goal of maximizing the level of communication with the subjects, as against the latter, in which greatest importance was attached to the possibility of acquiring clean, unambiguous and well-controlled data. Thus in the first category, taking as exemplary the work of Patterson, one is struck by the establishment of rapport between subject and researcher over a long period of time. Patterson emphasizes, for example, ways in which the communicative intent of her subjects can be revealed, at least to the experienced observer, in ways that transcend the 'literal' interpretation of strings of signs; novel and unexpected productions are given particular emphasis. At the other extreme, in Premack's experiments the possible behaviour of the subjects is tightly constrained by the experimenter. The ape is typically given access to only a very limited number of signs, thus facilitating quantitatively tractable predictions and analysis of the ape's response to particular promptings. This sharp dichotomy is something of a caricature: on the one hand, the artificial-language researchers discuss the affective connections established with their charges, and Savage-Rumbaugh, for instance, attaches considerable importance to unanticipated and spontaneous productions (the chimpanzees in her experiments appear to have had continuous access to a larger range of signs than those in Premack's, though not the full repertoire available to Koko or Washoe); on the other hand, Patterson, the Gardners and other sign-language experimenters devote serious effort to fairly rigidly controlled tests of their apes' vocabulary. However, I think the contrast fairly indicates the emphasis of the different experiments, and also serves to differentiate the main lines of criticism of these experiments.

Two prominent critics of ape-language research, Jean Umiker-Sebeok and Thomas Sebeok, usefully distinguish three major lines of such criticism.[16] These are (1) inaccurate observations and/or recording of ape behaviour; (2) the over-interpretation of ape behaviour; and (3) the unintended modification of an animal's behaviour towards desired results. I shall look next at each of these kinds of criticism.

Complaints about inaccurate observation and reporting are directed most especially against the research using sign language. David Premack,[17] for example, cites a study by M. S. Seidenberg and L. A. Petitto[18] (collaborators of Terrace), suggesting that comparisons between tapes of Washoe's performance and the published reports of the Gardners often fail significantly to agree. For example where Washoe is reported as replying to a question with the signs for 'you me', the actual response as seen on the videotape was 'you me you out me'. Premack remarks that 'the Gardners appear to have assumed . . . something like "if we can extract from the ape's garbled message what the ape is trying to say, so can the ape"'. But while this assumption may certainly sound very 'unscientific', further reflection may lead one to wonder. After all, if what the ape is producing really is a kind of language, then we should surely not be surprised that the listener will typically be required to contribute a measure of interpretation to the communicative interaction. Literal transcriptions of conversations even between linguistically competent human adults typically look very different from grammatically correct written language; yet this does not lead us to doubt that successful and intentional communication is taking place. Even with the significantly more aberrant utterances of human children, we are prepared to believe that parents often understand what is being said.

Two particular circumstances reinforce the reasonableness of charity in these cases. First, it is often remarked that apes, especially chimpanzees, are typically operating at a high level of activity and even excitement. The repetitive linguistic style which often *is* literally transcribed seems highly consistent with this trait.[19] More significantly, the particular characteristics of a signed language such as Ameslan seem to necessitate greater subtleties of speaker interpretation even than normal English conversation.[20] Native users of sign, it appears, use a number of cues such as location of the sign in the space around the body, direction of glance, or facial expression to convey various syntactic and other aspects of an utterance that cannot economically be conveyed with independent symbolic units. Thus the translation from sign to a spoken language is intrinsically more complex even than that between spoken languages. So the claims that those who have worked with particular signing apes for long periods of time can acquire considerable and subtle capacities to interpret what they are saying cannot simply be dismissed on the basis of naïvely literal interpretation.

The preceding points begin to illustrate the difficulties with the second general line of criticism, that the behaviour of apes is often wishfully over-interpreted in the light of the experimenter's expectations. They do not, of course, show that any such interpretations of ape utterances in sign language are in fact well grounded. Indeed, it would be beyond my competence to make any general judgment on this question. What I do want to emphasize at this point is that there appear to be fundamental conflicts between intrinsic features of this kind of research and commonly held ideals of scientific enquiry. Most obviously, it is widely supposed that data requiring interpretation, even debatable interpretation, by the researcher are scientifically unacceptable. Of course, since the decline of classical positivism – indeed largely responsible for that decline – there has been a widespread realization that to some extent all data are interpreted in the light of some theoretical background. Observations and descriptions of electrons, tectonic plates or pecking orders cannot exist independently of the theoretical contexts in which these terms are given significance. Nevertheless, various factors commonly maintain the trappings of objectivity despite this realization. First, the theoretical background may, at a particular historical moment, be uncontroversial. Thus, for example, contemporary anti-realism in philosophy of science notwithstanding, the observation of an electron passing through a cloud chamber is often considered paradigmatically objective. Second, it is considered very important that scientific data be replicable. Without in any way mitigating the role of interpretation in the description of data, this does provide a strong kind of intersubjectivity. Any researcher, it is supposed, can confirm that a certain kind of experiment does indeed have a certain kind of outcome.

It is clear that neither of these bases for claims of objectivity can readily be applied to ape-language research. What the controversial interpretations of ape signings require is the theoretical background assumption that the apes, when signing, are attempting to communicate something. But far from being uncontroversial, this is precisely what the critics are inclined to deny. Yet clearly it would be impossible to investigate the possibility that apes are saying something without at least the working hypothesis that this is what they are trying to do. Replicability is an issue that I shall discuss further below. But it is worth pointing out here that it has a quite paradoxical relation to this kind of study. Roughly, the more impressive a bit of linguistic behaviour is, the less likely it is to be replicable. The exact contrast which underlies scepticism about ape language is that between language as a creative and spontaneous form of behaviour, and stereotyped performances which may be taken as no more than causal and semantically innocent manipulation of the environment. By definition the latter, but not the former, would be susceptible of predictable and reliable replication.

In addition to these apparently impassable barriers to certain conceptions of acceptably objective data generation, there is a feature of this research that may well seem more positively, and objectionably, subjective. Ideals of scientific objectivity typically include a central role for the detached and dispassionate observer. Yet it is clear, and generally admitted, that someone who has devoted a substantial portion of his or her life to working with a highly intelligent and appealing creature will be anything but detached and dispassionate.[21] An obvious feature of this affective connection between researcher and subject is that the researcher will typically be anxious for the success of their subjects in language acquisition -- very likely as anxious as typical human parents that their children be educationally successful. But an emotional commitment to a particular outcome of an experiment is complete anathema to conceptions of scientific objectivity. (Whether scientists are typically wholly disinterested in the results of their experiments is hardly beyond question. Given the structure of rewards in the scientific professions, this would constitute almost incredible high-mindedness. But that is another topic.)

But as with the other aspects of objectivity one may suspect that these apparent drawbacks are inevitable in this research. It is after all possible that the ape, like the human child, will learn only if someone with whom it feels an affective connection shows some sign of caring that it does so. Much of human learning might well be inaccessible to a thoroughly disinterested and 'objective' study. In addition, to return to an earlier point, it might well be that the possibilities for comprehension of the linguistic efforts of an ape may be vastly greater for someone intimately familiar with its interests and its idiosyncracies than for the dispassionate and disinterested scientific observer.[22]

The general tenor of the preceding discussion may be summarized as follows. It is highly plausible that what these criticisms of ape-language research really illustrate are very basic conflicts between ideals of scientific research and certain kinds of language study. Everyday language is, after all, typically learnt in a highly emotive context, and affective aspects of communication, even between competent speakers, can hardly be divorced totally from the aseptic-ally semantic. Moreover, language without interpretation is plainly an incoherent conception; and this may be so in a sense that precludes the study of controversial candidates for language in ways that meet scientific conceptions of freedom from interpretation. Perhaps we might have more idea of the linguistic capacity of apes if the research had been carried out by literary critics.

Research using artificial languages has been motivated, to a considerable extent, by the attempt to avoid these divergences between the methodology of the Ameslan research and assumed norms of scientific enquiry. Sequences of coloured shapes or computer keystrokes provide, by contrast, thoroughly 'clean' and unambiguous data. Another virtue of the approach is apparent from the preceding discussion. I noted above that a prerequisite for interpretation of the more interesting and suggestive utterances of apes was the working hypothesis that the apes were trying to communicate. This suggests an obvious circularity, though not necessarily a vicious one, in the process of interpretation. It is an attractive goal to ground this hypothesis in some more rigorously analytic demonstration that apes can, indeed, use symbols with communicative intent. *Prima facie*, just such support can indeed be gained from the artificial-languages research.

Probably the most analytically detailed study of ape symbol acquisition is the work of Sue Savage-Rumbaugh.[23] The most distinctive feature of this research is the attempt to break down and test independently a range of different possible ways in which an ape may be using symbols. A noteworthy result of this work is the observation that apes often cannot, without specific training, generalize from one kind of symbol use to others, which leads Savage-Rumbaugh to be sceptical whether all the apes studied in the experiments under consideration have acquired this full range of skills. However, her work does appear to show that apes can learn to use and understand symbols, refer to objects that are not present, make spontaneous comments and announce their intended actions. In one particularly interesting series of experiments, an ape was required to request from another tools (keys, straws, magnets, etc.) which it required to gain access to food, demonstrating its ability to use language to facilitate co-operative enterprises. And apes have even been able to teach symbols to one another. (Patterson and Linden amusingly recount an attempt by Michael, a later gorilla addition to her experiments, to instruct one of his trainers in the use of a sign.[24] Fouts reports attempts by Washoe to teach sign to an adopted infant chimpanzee.[25]) Finally, it appears that some apes acquire a significant understanding of spoken English. Patterson and Linden also claim this ability for Koko, though Savage-Rumbaugh, on the basis of negative results with her principal subjects (the chimpanzees Sherman and Austin), views this claim with scepticism. However Savage-Rumbaugh does report more recent work with the pygmy chimpanzee (*Pan paniscus*) Kanzi, showing that this ape has acquired an understanding of a number of spoken words.[26] (This rather remarkable animal apparently acquired significant linguistic ability, including this partial comprehension of spoken English, with no deliberate training. Savage-Rumbaugh speculates that this rare and little-studied species may have substantially greater linguistic aptitude than the common chimpanzee (*Pan troglodytes*). Patterson's occasional suggestions that the gorilla is more talented than the common chimpanzee cannot be dismissed out of hand. And orangutans, despite their more languid temperaments, are reported to do better than either chimpanzees or gorillas on various cognitive tests.[27] Species partisanship is an amusing occasional subtext to this topic.)

Savage-Rumbaugh's research is richly adorned with all the trappings of respectable scientific research: controls of various kinds, 'double-blind' experiments, careful statistical analyses of data and unambiguous recording of data by computers. The evidence seems impressively marshalled that apes can, if properly instructed, communicate, and do so with full intention.

However, these scientific virtues have not sufficed to silence the critics. This brings me to the third, and perhaps most pervasive, kind of criticism of ape-language studies, the problem of inadvertent cueing, or manipulation of the animal to produce the desired result. This is sometimes referred to as the 'Clever Hans effect' after the notorious performing horse that convinced many that it was capable of doing arithmetic. Hans, when given an arithmetical problem, would tap his hoof a number of times corresponding to the solution of the problem. Investigation eventually revealed that Hans responded to extremely subtle cues from his interrogators that he had tapped long enough, and thus learned to stop at the correct point. More generally, it is known that animal trainers can develop extremely subtle ways of influencing and controlling the behaviour of their charges. Although great efforts have been made by ape-language researchers to eliminate these possibilities, it seems very difficult to devise experiments that eliminate every possible channel of communication other than that intended by the researchers. In almost all such experiments a researcher is present with the ape. Indeed, this is hardly avoidable. Umiker-Sebeok and Sebeok, noting that apes do not normally sit quietly through their tests, remark:

> Experimenters must spend a good deal of time interacting with the animal just to get it under sufficient control to enable them to administer the test, hardly what one would call ideal experimental conditions. If cueing is feasible even when a subject is sitting still and attentive, it is even more so under the chaotic circumstances created by an ape's natural response to such man-made rules.[28]

Though it may be deplorable that apes show so little dedication to the advancement of science, reluctance to sit quietly through batteries of psychological tests is hardly indicative of a lack of intelligence.

Researchers often attempt to eliminate the possibility of cueing by using so-called double-blind strategies, in which the observer of the ape's performance is distinct from the experimenter who poses the problem, and thus does not know the correct response. This strategy can produce problems of its own, most notably that the elaborate and artificial procedures involved are likely to discourage the ape's co-operation. Patterson reports that Koko frequently did refuse to co-operate in such tests and would, for example, on occasion give the same answer to every question. This provides a striking instance of the problem of the dependence of interpretation on antecedent belief. To Patterson, perfectly convinced that Koko is capable of performing the task (identifying familiar objects), it is obvious that Koko is expressing her resentment of a boring activity. Umiker-Sebeok and Sebeok, on the other hand, for whom Koko's competence is extremely questionable, wonder sceptically whether these sessions were included as sets of false responses in the analysis of the experiment.

Even when the apes do co-operate, the sceptic is likely to be unconvinced. The more complex the experimental situation becomes, it almost seems, the more possible channels for unintended communication are opened up. It is not hard, for example, to imagine cues the supposedly blind observer may use to guess what the ape 'means' (perhaps its non-linguistic behaviour). And indeed, as Umiker-Sebeok and Sebeok emphasize, the experimenters, outside observers, blind observers, naïve observers etc. do not necessarily exhaust the *dramatis personae*. In the interests of producing hard and objective data (or press copy) there is usually a camera or a videorecorder being operated; no doubt the operator will often understand the experiment well enough to know what response is expected, and to provide a possible source of cues to the animal.

Central to the proliferation of these doubts is an important methodological issue. This is the commitment to explanatory parsimony.[29] Occam's razor is alleged to cut away at the claims of the ape researchers in two directions. First, following on the preceding discussion, if there is some channel through which a human observer or participant might have led the ape to the correct answer to a question or an appropriate utterance, then it is assumed more parsimonious to conclude that this happened than that the ape has exhibited the ability to produce its utterance or response unaided. Second, Occam's razor is commonly employed against the more creative and innovative uses of language by apes, which, it is suggested, may more parsimoniously be attributed to error or luck. A widely cited example is the production by Washoe of the signs 'water bird' when first confronted with a swan. Critics note that Washoe was presented, on this occasion, with both water and a bird, so it is gratuitous to suppose that her utterance involved the imaginative synthesis of referring to the swan as a water-bird. Rather differently, Patterson reports that Koko, in a particularly obstinate mood, was refusing to produce the sign for drink (thumb against the mouth with fist clenched), which she had previously made thousands of times. Eventually, grinning, she made the sign, but to her ear rather than her mouth. Patterson interpreted this as an exercise in humour.[30] Predictably, critics[31] see this as more plausibly interpreted as a mistake.[32]

It is hard to adjudicate particular disputes. But one point should be stressed. Parsimony is hardly an objective, theory-independent concept. *Why* is it more parsimonious to assume some complex and covert channel of communication in a double-blind experiment than to suppose that the ape knows what it is doing? If you believe that the ape is in fact capable of the performance in question, the latter explanation is surely more parsimonious. Again, in the Koko anecdote, to Patterson, confident that Koko could sign 'drink' if she wanted, the interpretation as a joke is quite natural. The sceptic, disinclined to credit the linguistic aptitude of the ape, will tend to view any alternative explanation as more plausible. Either way, what interpretation is natural, or 'parsimonious', depends heavily on antecedent belief. It will, of course, be objected that the charitable assumption is question-begging, since that is what it is the object of the experiment to reveal. But this is irrelevant to the prior probabilities that one may attach to the apes having, or lacking, the sort of capacity being investigated.

I should perhaps say that there is more of interest in the Clever Hans phenomenon than my discussion may have suggested. The general point is that, independent of controversial questions about linguistic apes, there is a great deal of communication possible between humans and animals. Sebeok remarks that '[t]wo way zoosemiotic communication is thus not the issue, but such communication by *verbal* means between man and animalkind is another matter.'[33] Sebeok's objections to the ape-language research are grounded in his view that 'the Clever Hans effect informs, in fact insidiously infects, all dyadic interactions whatever, whether interpersonal, or between man and animal, and by no means excepting the interactions of living organisms with a computer'.[34] (One wonders only why this should be 'insidious'; what linguistic essence should ideally be distilled from this non-linguistic noise?) He also stresses that the range of non-verbal means of such communication is yet poorly understood. But while it is possible that many ape-language researchers may be naïve about these means of communication, it is difficult to see why their existence should cast doubt on the kinds of artificially established channels of communication they assert. Indeed, one would think the opposite. Thus I do not see how the Clever Hans effect, for all its intrinsic interest, need push us towards a sceptical interpretation of purported ape utterances.

One final point about the Clever Hans objections is particularly important. As with Clever Hans himself, the kind of performance for which cueing is most plausible is that in which decisively correct or incorrect answers are available. Thus, perhaps ironically, it is the experiments which offer clean, unambiguous data that seem most vulnerable to this line of attack. By contrast, when the ape produces an utterance that is novel and unexpected, this kind of criticism seems wholly inapplicable. (Thus in these cases the critic moves to the very different ground of suggesting chance or error.) Patterson's report of Koko chatting with her dolls, but rapidly ceasing on discovering that she was observed, is hardly to be understood as unconscious cueing by the experimenter. This will, on the other hand, be dismissed as 'anecdotal', the most damning term in the lexicon of scientific norms, applied to reports which most signally fail to meet desiderata of adequate controls and replicability (see, for example, the dialogue cited in n. 32). The irony is that it is precisely the predictable, replicable responses that *do* meet these desiderata that are vulnerable to the suspicion of cueing. It would seem, then, that ape-language research is impaled squarely on the horns of a methodological dilemma. On the one hand, the more controlled and predictable the behaviour of the animal is made, the harder it becomes to fend off the accusation of manipulation, conscious or otherwise. On the other hand, the more freedom the animal is given, and the more spontaneous and uncontrolled its utterances, the further the reports of its behaviour will sink into the scientific netherworld of the 'anecdotal'. A more optimistic interpretation is possible, however, that these kinds of research are mutually supporting of the conclusion that the ape is, indeed, intentionally and often successfully engaging in modest feats of linguistic communication. To the extent that methodological constraints threaten to preclude *a priori* the possibility of establishing this result, we should perhaps rather question the methodology.

I believe that there are, indeed, important grounds for deep suspicion of the appropriateness to this kind of research of various of the methodological norms that have been mentioned in the preceding discussion. Tying together ideas of objectivity, replicable versus anecdotal results, and the undesirability of affective or 'interpretative' relations between the experimenter and the subject, is a conception of the appropriate role of the scientific investigator nicely expressed by H. Hediger, another prominent critic of ape-language research. Hediger writes: 'The ideal condition for all such experiments would be complete isolation of the experimental animal from the leader of the experiment.'[35] But if, as is surely not unreasonable, the goal of the 'leader of the experiment' is to communicate with the experimental animal, this seems a serious restriction. If one supposes further that linguistic communication is inextricably involved with a range of expression beyond mere stringing together of signs – as, I assume, do Umiker-Sebeok and Sebeok, though such expression will no doubt fall within the proscribed category of 'cueing' – the demand is, in addition to being impossible, misguided in its motivation. This difficulty can, as I have suggested, be seen in relation to a very general picture of the role of the scientist. The ideals of scientific enquiry I have been discussing constantly presuppose the picture of an active (though impartial) observer set against a passive object of study. But in fact, most obviously though not only in the case of sign-language research, what is being investigated in ape-language studies is *interaction* between two intelligent subjects. Perhaps it will be thought that the very question at issue is whether the ape *is* an intelligent subject, or rather a passive object, responding mechanically if complexly to its stream of inputs. I shall say something bearing on this issue in the conclusion. It is my impression, though, that researchers involved in the ape-language experiments would not, with good reason, take this question very seriously.

THE GOALS OF APE-LANGUAGE RESEARCHERS AND THEIR CRITICS

As interesting as the methodological prejudices revealed in the debate over ape-language research is the range of objectives detectable both in the practitioners of this research and their critics. Some of these motives and concerns, laudable or otherwise, are tangential to my present interests. Laudably enough, for example, Savage-Rumbaugh's work is directed towards improved methods for teaching language to mentally impaired children. This kind of goal is quite frequently an explicit component of ape-language research. Perhaps less laudably, one can detect some fairly overt disciplinary in-fighting. Umiker-Sebeok and Sebeok, for example, discussing some research on dolphins in a context which leaves little doubt that they intend the same to apply to ape research, remark that by contrast with these unpromising efforts, computers will 'within the next decade' be able to talk in, if not listen to, English. They continue: 'for computers to achieve the implied level of sophistication, vast but justifiable funding will be required; money spent on chimerical experimentation with speechless creatures of the deep to be hominified is, however, tantamount to squandering scarce resources'.[36] As they immediately point out, apes, too, are expensive to maintain; economic competition in the multi-billion dollar world of contemporary science is, perhaps unsurprisingly, often not far beneath the surface of scientific controversy.

My present interest, however, is rather with the questions about the natures of apes and humans which dominate the official rationales for this research. The subsequent discussion can naturally be divided between the questions, What can this research tell us about apes? and, What can it tell us about humans?

I am inclined to some scepticism about how productive a method of learning about apes the research under consideration is likely to prove. As Umiker-Sebeok and Sebeok remark in the quote above, the process to which thes apes are being subjected is one of domestication or even 'hominification'. It is not quite correct to refer to these animals as 'domestic' apes, since domestication is best seen as the co-evolution over a substantial period of time of a symbiotic relationship between humans and another species; merely 'socialized' animals are a rather different matter.[37] But neither domestic nor socialized animals are a reliable model for learning about the natures of their free-living relatives without careful attention to the effects of these processes on their behaviour. Domestic cats and dogs may, by now, be a sufficiently interesting quasi-natural kind to deserve study in their own right, and their relation to undomesticated relatives can be systematically explored; none of this can plausibly be said for so rare and exotic an artefact as the language-trained ape. In the case of apes we would surely do better to consider the observations of primatologists such as Jane van Lawick-Goodall or Dian Fossey, who have devoted years of their lives to the study of these creatures in their natural habitats. It is true that despite this extensive observation, the means by which apes in the wild communicate remain shrouded in obscurity. There is little doubt that there is much here to be learned. A quite elaborate system of calls used by vervet monkeys, assumed to be much simpler animals than the great apes, to identify differentially various kinds of predators has been described in some detail,[38] and is only one of a wide range of animal communication

...s that are at least partly understood. One further point that well illustrates the communicative capacities of untrained primates is the following. An important criterion of intentional communication, as has often been noted,[39] is the possibility of communicating deceptively. Duane Quiatt[40] has usefully surveyed an impressive range of evidence that apes, and even monkeys, are quite up to this feat. It would be remarkable, then, if social animals as intelligent as chimpanzees or gorillas did not employ some quite sophisticated means of communication. But apart from providing minor encouragement to the search for these means, there is no reason to expect the linguistic achievements of highly socialized apes to throw much light on this question. The fact that the odd chimpanzee has been propelled into space will hardly help us understand how chimpanzees manage to swing through the trees.

Much deeper philosophical interests, however, are frequently, if not universally, connected with interpretations, positive or negative, of ape-language experiments. Frequently the name of Descartes is invoked to connect these experiments with long-standing and continuing debates about the internal lives of animals. One pervasive theme is that the research will illuminate the supposed problem of the internal lives of animals, or their lack of any. Of most obvious pertinence to the present topic is the Cartesian thesis that language is the only reliable indicator of genuine mental process. Also relevant is the corollary, that behaviour in general has only contingent relations to the underlying mental processes that it might be held to reflect. While for reasons that have little to do with my assessment of ape-language experiments I believe neither thesis, the continued good health of both is evident in much of the debate over these experiments.

Terrace[41] contrasts the view of Descartes, that animals are 'mechanical beasts' with Darwin's opinion that animals engage in 'forms of thinking . . . homologous to human thought'. He then remarks that '[u]ntil recently, there has been little concrete basis for choosing between the contradictory positions of Darwin and Descartes.' He continues by locating the studies of ape language acquisition in an incipient body of work in cognitive psychology that is beginning to cast the balance of evidence in favour of the Darwinian approach. While Terrace is explicitly including the ape-language studies within a wider range of work in cognitive psychology, language-training might seem to have particular relevance. If the question is whether animals have any thoughts at all, then perhaps the best way of finding out is to provide them with an opportunity of expressing them.

Although most researchers on the cognitive capacities of animals are, like Terrace, explicitly opposed to the Cartesian conception of animals as 'mechanical beasts', it is striking that they typically concede most of the remainder of the Cartesian perspective. Even those most ardent in defence of the cognitive achievements and capacities of non-humans frequently accept the Cartesian assumption that animal thought and even consciousness, since conceptually independent of behaviour, are in principle impossible to demonstrate.[42] In ape-language research the same tendency is readily discoverable. Savage-Rumbaugh motivates her research into the variety of uses to which apes may put symbols by questioning the assumption of previous researchers that 'when an ape "correctly" uses a symbol, it had some referent clearly in mind', and thus was using the symbol to name an object.[43] And while she is surely correct to argue that naming may be a complex activity, she appears not to question this Cartesian characterization of what would constitute referential use of a word. And this, surely, leaves it wholly obscure how any variety of referential uses would address the supposed issue, what the ape has 'clearly in mind'.

The untenability of these Cartesian presuppositions cannot be adequately addressed here.[44] What they require is philosophical exorcism rather than empirical research, as should perhaps be clear from the frequency with which scientists in their grip admit that, strictly speaking, no evidence could establish any of the desired conclusions about the minds of animals. For the present, I shall focus on the relation of ape-language research to some related contemporary philosophical views. I hope that this will at the same time throw some light on the inadequacy of the Cartesian perspective.

More recent philosophical views about the connection between thought and language may also seem to give particular significance to ape-language research. By contrast to Descartes' view that language is a reliable symptom of something quite distinct from it – thought – Donald Davidson has claimed that language is a necessary condition of thought.[45] Although, again, the arguments for and against this position cannot be thoroughly examined here,[46] ape-language research does provide a curious perspective on this claim. For if Davidson's position were correct, then what would be at issue in the ape-language controversy would be not merely whether apes could be taught to talk, but whether they could be taught to think.

The idea that the apes trained by the Gardners and others differed from their wild or untrained conspecifics in that they alone possessed the rudiments of thought is so much less plausible than the idea that they have simply been taught a rudimentary form of human language as to cast doubt on the suggestion that these two contingencies might be essentially equivalent. One reason for this is that the communicative abilities of language-trained apes seem so clearly continuous with those of animals outside the educational elite. This connects with a point emphasized earlier, that even human linguistic communication is not totally different in kind from the range of non-verbal communication that provides a crucial part of its context.

At first sight a more modest proposal is that of Peter Carruthers,[47] that the thought of animals, since they lack language, must not be conscious. I say 'at first sight' more modest, because this suggestion is in fact part of a revival of the preposterous Cartesian thesis that non-human animals are not conscious at all. The considerations adduced in the previous paragraph against using language to defend such an apartheid[48] view of human versus animal communication seem equally relevant here. Consideration of Carruthers's rationale for this neo-Cartesian (or perhaps better, neuro-Cartesian) doctrine must await another place. His discussion does, however, raise one further important issue. Questions about animal consciousness, far from constituting merely an abstruse philosophical debate, are directly relevant to an ethical issue that has recently, and appropriately, come to the forefront of philosophical debate. Specifically, a number of thinkers have recently questioned the ethical legitimacy of the *prima facie* horrendous treatment of animals in factory farming and scientific research (not to mention 'recreations' such as hunting). Carruthers, on the basis of the thesis just mentioned, claims that these practices are not only permissible but, in so far as they conduce to human welfare, obligatory.[49] While, as I hope I have made clear, I do not think the moral repugnance of this conclusion depends in any way on the success (or failure) of animal-language projects, they do, perhaps, provide useful rhetorical ammunition. Unless one adopts the absurd view that it is permissible (or obligatory) to torture any animal except an educated ape, a defender of Carruthers's position will have to defend the apartheid view of human communication, with ape language falling on the animal side of this divide. I hope I have at least indicated some obstacles to this strategy.

Finally, then, there is the question whether this research has anything to tell us about ourselves. For the most part, this question is simply the obverse of the preceding one. That is to say, much of the official motivation for the research concerns the question whether humans are, or are not, radically discontinuous from the remainder of the animal kingdom. And the major remaining bastion for defenders of this discontinuity is the view of language as something categorially distinct from any lesser system of communication. Again, I think that this position is to be refuted not by seeing whether apes can learn our language, but rather by, first, investigation of the complex and interesting lives of animals in their natural environments and, second, philosophical dismantling of the naïve views of language it presupposes.

The most influential view of language that is commonly appealed to in defence of the radical-discontinuity thesis is that of Noam Chomsky,[50] which sees language as a uniquely human cognitive organ. But even should this (somehow) turn out to be true, it seems irrelevant to the issue under discussion. For presumably the issue concerns the kinds of things humans can do, not the organs that they may use to do them. I take it that the only serious candidates for capacities with which a language organ might uniquely endow humans are communication and thought. But there are many kinds of non-linguistic behaviour that facilitate communication, and many non-linguistic manifestations of thought.[51] To argue that the existence of a special organ of language shows that only humans can think or communicate would be comparable to arguing that only fish, being uniquely equipped with a swim-bladder, can swim.

So finally, for all its undoubted charm, I do not think the research on the linguistic aptitude of apes will tell us much about either ourselves or apes that we could not learn at least as well in many other ways. It does, however, provide the occasion for a wealth of interesting observations on the reactions and assumptions of those who engage in, or attack, this area of study. And perhaps even charm is not a totally negligible scientific virtue.

NOTES

1 I am grateful to Regenia Gagnier and Debra Satz for pointing out a number of obscurities in an earlier draft.
2 For a brief summary, see Ann Premack, *Why Chimps Can Read* (New York: Harper & Row, 1976), ch. 2.
3 'Two-Way Communication with an Infant Chimpanzee', in A. M. Schrier and F. Stollnitz (eds), *Behavior of Non-Human Primates*,

vol. IV (New York: Academic Press, 1971), 117–83.

4 The actual number may be much higher, perhaps several hundred. Criteria of various degrees of stringency are applied to decide whether the animal has genuinely mastered particular signs.

5 See Roger Fouts, 'Acquisition and Testing in Four Young Chimpanzees', *Science* 180 (1973), 978–80; Herbert Terrace, *Nim* (New York: Columbia University Press, 1987).

6 Francine Patterson and Eugene Linden, *The Education of Koko* (New York: Holt, Rinehart & Winston, 1981).

7 H. Lyn Miles, 'Apes and Language: The Search for Communicative Competence', in J. de Luce and H. T. Wilder (eds), *Language in Primates* (New York: Springer, 1983).

8 'Teaching Language to an Ape', *Scientific American* 227 (1972), 92–9.

9 *Language Learning by a Chimpanzee: The Lana Project* (New York: Academic Press, 1977).

10 *Ape Language* (New York: Columbia University Press, 1986).

11 Notable among those questioning the syntactic capacities of apes has been one of the leading researchers in the area, Herbert Terrace (op. cit.).

12 I use the term 'utterance' throughout to refer to the alleged linguistic productions of apes. Obviously apes do not, strictly, 'utter', but this usage has become standard.

13 Patterson and Linden, op. cit., 84.

14 Op. cit.

15 Patterson and Linden, op. cit., 191.

16 'Questioning Apes', in T. A. Sebeok and J. Umiker-Sebeok, *Speaking of Apes* (New York: Plenum, 1980), 9.

17 *Gavagai* (Cambridge, Mass.: Bradford Books/MIT Press, 1986), 32.

18 'Signing Behavior in Apes: A Critical Review', *Cognition* 1 (1979), 177–215.

19 Striking confirmation of this construal is provided by the work of Miles (op. cit.) on the orangutan, a much more languid and phlegmatic beast. Her subject, Chantek, rarely made immediate repetitions. In a very similar vein, it is sometimes suggested that chimpanzees cannot really converse, partly on the grounds that they so frequently interrupt their human interlocutors. Chantek, apparently, had no more tendency to interrupt his trainer than vice versa.

20 See, e.g., Jane H. Hill, 'Apes and Language', in Sebeok and Umiker-Sebeok (op. cit.), 336; Terrace, op. cit., 237–8. Terrace provides a useful general description of sign language, ibid., 235–54.

21 See Umiker-Sebeok and Sebeok, op. cit., 5–8.

22 Miles (op. cit., 57) and others have suggested that the failure to recognize the importance of establishing rapport with his subject, Nim, may account for some of Terrace's negative results.

23 Op. cit.

24 Op. cit., 170.

25 'Chimpanzee Language and Elephant Tails: A Theoretical Synthesis', in de Luce and Wilder, op. cit., 1–3.

26 Op. cit., 382–97.

27 Miles, op. cit., 47.
28 Op. cit., 44n.
29 Umiker-Sebeok and Sebeok, op. cit., 14–21.
30 Patterson and Linden, op. cit., 77.
31 e.g. Umiker-Sebeok and Sebeok, op. cit., 16.
32 On the topic of pongid recalcitrance, Patterson observes (op. cit., 6) that 'Koko has often been driven to her most creative uses of language through her obstinate refusal to submit to dull routine.' In illustration, she cites the following dialogue. Cathy, a trainer, had signed to Koko, 'What's this?', pointing to a picture of Koko.
    'Gorilla, signed Koko.
    Who gorilla?, signed Cathy . . .
    Bird, responded Koko.
    You bird?, asked Cathy . . .
    You, countered Koko, who by this age was frequently using the word *bird* as an insult.
    Not me, you bird, retorted Cathy.
    Me gorilla, Koko answered.
    Who bird?, asked Cathy.
    You nut, replied Koko, resorting to another of her favorite insults. (Koko switches *bird* and *nut* from descriptive to pejorative terms by changing the position in which the sign is made from the front to the side of her face.)
    After a little more name-calling Koko gave up the battle, signed *Darn me good*, and walked away signing *Bad.*'
    It is easy to see how this little anecdote will be seen as failing a range of desiderata of scientific method. My general point, however, is that this is insufficient to show that it is impermissible to take such reports at face value.
33 'Looking in the Destination for What Should Have Been Sought in the Source', in Sebeok and Umiker-Sebeok, op. cit., 426.
34 Ibid., 409.
35 'Do You Speak Yerkish? The Newest Colloquial Language With Chimpanzees', in Sebeok and Umiker-Sebeok, op. cit., 446.
36 Op. cit., 27.
37 For a detailed discussion, see Thomas J. Daniels and Marc Bekoff, 'Domestication, Exploitation, and Rights', in M. Bekoff and D. Jamieson (eds), *Explanation and Interpretation in the Study of Animal Behavior: Comparative Perspectives* (Boulder, Colorado: Westview Press, 1990). I am grateful to Marc Bekoff for drawing my attention to this distinction.
38 See Robert M. Seyfarth, 'What the Vocalizations of Monkeys Mean to Humans and What They Mean to the Monkeys Themselves', in Rom Harré and Vernon Reynolds (eds), *The Meaning of Primate Symbols* (Oxford: Oxford University Press, 1984); and Dorothy L. Cheney, 'Category Formation in Vervet Monkeys', in Harré and Reynolds, op. cit.
39 See, e.g., Wittgenstein, *Philosophical Investigations* (Oxford: Basil Blackwell, 1953), §§249–50.

40 'Devious Intentions of Monkeys and Apes', in Harré and Reynolds, op. cit., 9–40.

41 In Savage-Rumbaugh, op. cit., ix.

42 See, e.g. Donald R. Griffin, *Animal Thinking* (Cambridge, Mass.: Harvard University Press, 1984); Marian Stamp Dawkins, 'From an Animal's Point of View: Consumer Demand Theory and Animal Welfare', *Behavioral and Brain Sciences* 13 (1990), 1–9.

43 Op. cit., 10.

44 The *loci classici* are Wittgenstein's *Philosophical Investigations*; and Gilbert Ryle, *The Concept of Mind* (London: Hutchinson, 1949). The latter shows quite decisively how, even for the case of humans, a vast range of behaviour beyond the linguistic can sufficiently ground the attribution of intelligence and thought. I have tried to apply some of these insights specifically to questions about non-human mental states in 'The Mental Lives of Non-Human Animals', in Bekoff and Jamieson, op. cit.

45 See 'Thought and Talk', in S. Gutenplan (ed.), *Mind and Language* (Oxford: Oxford University Press, 1975); and 'Rational Animals', *Dialectica* 36 (1982), 318–27 (reprinted in *Actions and Events: Perspectives on the Philosophy of Donald Davidson*, ed. E. LePore and B.T. McLaughlin (Oxford: Basil Blackwell, 1985)).

46 Davidson's conclusions about animals are criticized by Richard Jeffrey, 'Animal Interpretation,' in LePore and McLaughlin, op. cit.; and in my 'Mental Lives of Non-Human Animals', op. cit.

47 'Brute Experience', *Journal of Philosophy* 86 (1989), 258–69.

48 I borrow this term from an insightful paper on the meanings of animal signals by Roy Harris ('Must Monkeys Mean?' in Harré and Reynolds, op. cit., 116–37).

49 Op. cit., 268.

50 e.g. *Language and Mind* (New York: Harcourt, Brace & World, 1968).

51 See, again, Ryle, op. cit., *passim*.

Part II

PERCEPTION AND REPRESENTATION

5

SEEING, REPRESENTING AND DESCRIBING

An examination of David Marr's computational theory of vision

Peter Hacker

A NEW DISCIPLINE HAS BEEN CREATED . . .

When David Marr's posthumous book *Vision* was published in 1980 it appeared to many scientists, psychologists and neurophysiologists alike, that at last a key to understanding the nature of vision had been found. What Marr and his collaborators at MIT had discovered, it seemed, was 'a theory of perception that integrated work in neurophysiology, psychology, and artificial intelligence and that gives us some of the most profound insights into the nature and functioning of the brain we have had yet'.[1] Indeed, it was claimed, 'a new discipline has been created that brings together much of philosophy, psychology, artificial intelligence, and neurophysiology, and that opens up the exciting possibility of uncovering some of the mysteries of the brain'.[2] These are high claims; indeed, too high. I shall argue in this paper that what Marr describes constitutes, as might be expected from a specialist in artificial intelligence, the outline of a novel approach to the problems of the theory of 'machine-vision', i.e. the theory underlying the design of machines that can identify what lies before them as a consequence of light falling upon a sensor. But Marr's theory is neither an explanation nor even a description of animal or human vision. This is not because the putative neurophysiological 'realization' of Marr's abstract theory remains highly problematic even at the level of the neurological activity of the prestriate cortex or striate cortex, let alone beyond. It is rather because the application of the computer ('machine-vision') analogy to the brain of a creature which can see rests on an array of conceptual confusions. It is the

119

purpose of this paper to lay bare *some* of these incoherences.

Marr 'adopted a point of view that regards visual perception as a problem in information processing. The problem begins with a large grey-level intensity array, which suffices to approximate an image such as the world might cast upon the retinas of the eyes'.[3] This image is conceived to be the informational input for the visual informational processing system.

The output, Marr argues, is the construction of efficient and useful symbolic descriptions of objects in view. Vision, therefore, 'is the *process* of discovering from images what is present in the world and where it is'.[4] It is the process of transforming the information implicit in an image into an explicit description of what is seen. The central problem for the computational theorist therefore is the choice of a series of *representations* which can make explicit the information. As in any information-processing problem, Marr explains, there are four different levels of analysis. First, at the lowest level, lies the description of the basic component and circuit analysis: how do transistors (or neurons) or diodes (or synapses) work? Second, how do the particular mechanisms, e.g. adders, multipliers, memories, which are assemblies made from the basic components, operate? Third, what are the computational schemata or algorithms? And finally, at the highest or most abstract level, what is the theory of the computation? The latter, Marr contends, is both the most important and the most neglected. It is the most important in as much as the nature of the computations underlying perception – the algorithms that transform one representation into another – depend more upon computational problems that have to be solved than upon the particular hardware by which the solutions are produced. A large number of Marr's innovations stem from focusing sharply upon the theory of visual (or more accurately, optical) computation.

The brain is conceived as operating a system of symbols that represent elements or features of an image in order to construct descriptions which, by a series of computational operations upon the symbolism, can, at the final stage of the visual process, yield a description of shapes of objects, their distance and orientation, and indeed an identification of them. The key to the computational theorist's problem at the high level of the theory of visual computation is the choice of the series of representations which can represent explicitly the informational input and transform it by means of specified algorithms into a final description of what is seen. Marr's proposal involves three primary types of representation successively richer in descriptive content. The first is the *primal sketch* which describes the light-intensity changes in the image, i.e. not a set of light-intensity values for every point in the image, but rather an array of values representing the directions, magnitudes and spatial extents of intensity changes at points in an image that are places of locally high or low intensity. The relative positions of these points is also made explicit in the primal sketch. The production of this 'grey-level' representation involves various phases, from the raw primal sketch, which consists of a set of statements about edge segments, bars and blobs, to the full primal sketch which provides a fuller description of the image, associating properties like length, width, brightness, etc., with positions in the image. The second representation is the *2½D sketch* which represents the surface orientations in a scene. From the texture, contour and shading descriptions present in the primal sketch, as well as information about discontinuities in depth signalled by stereopsis mechanisms and information about occlusion specified by occluding contours in the primal sketch together with discontinuities in patterns of motion, the brain is conceived to compute a viewer-centred description of the layout of structures in the world. The third and final representation is a *3D model representation*. An image-space processor is conceived to operate upon the viewer-centred axes of the 2½D sketch and to translate them into object-centred co-ordinates of an axis-based structural description. This process involves access to a stored catalogue of 3D model descriptions of objects, matching with which constitutes recognition.

This brief account of Marr's theory does not do justice to the imaginativeness and ingenuity of his programme. My concern, however, is not with the details, or even with the central elements, of his theory. Its fruitfulness and coherence as a computational theory for artificial-intelligence research is a matter for evaluation by computer scientists. Whether it does or does not provide the basic framework for advances in 'machine-vision' is something that will doubtless emerge from their work. My sole concern is with the question of whether his theory is (as it purports to be) a theory of vision, in particular of human vision, or indeed whether it even provides a coherent framework for such a theory. More precisely, I shall investigate its conceptual presuppositions in order to show not that it is a false empirical theory which fails to match known facts about vision and the neural mechanisms that make it possible, but rather that as an explanatory theory of vision it is a non-starter since as such a theory it is not conceptually coherent. To show that this is so it is not necessary to explore the adequacies of the various supposed levels of computational representation for the production of a symbolic representation of what is seen; what is necessary is to examine the conceptual or philosophical presuppositions of the theory. Marr was perfectly explicit about these:

> From a philosophical point of view the approach ... is an extension of what have sometimes been called representational theories of the mind ... according to which the senses are for the most part concerned with telling one what is there. Modern representational theories conceive of the mind as having access to systems of internal representations; mental states are characterized by asserting what the internal representations currently specify, and mental processes by how such internal representations are obtained and how they interact. This scheme affords a comfortable framework for our study of visual perception, and I am content to let it form the point of departure.[5]

It is characteristic of philosophical confusions in general that they are embedded in the very point of departure. They are liable to run unnoticed through an elaborate and sophisticated empirical theory precisely because these conceptual incoherences are present in the very form of the questions the theory addresses. I shall suggest that precisely this occurs in Marr's work. 'What are the problems that the brain solves when we see?',[6] 'How [does the visual system] extract from images the various aspects of the world that are useful to us?',[7] '[What is] the nature of the internal representations by which we capture this information and thus make it available as a basis for decisions?',[8] 'How does one obtain constant perceptions in everyday life on the basis of continually changing sensations?'[9] are just such incoherent questions. Far from Marr having created a new discipline which will uncover some of the 'mysteries' of the brain, he has created a new version of an old mythology. Modern representationalist theories of the mind differ from classical representationalist theories, but they suffer from very similar conceptual confusions.

VISION

Marr opens his book with the following paragraph:

> What does it mean to see? The plain man's answer (and
> Aristotle's too) would be, to know what is where by looking.
> In other words, vision is the *process* of discovering from images
> what is present in the world, and where it is.[10]

The putative plain man's answer, rough and ready as it is, is not far
off the mark (although, of course, a person can see an object without
knowing what it is and can look at an object without seeing it). But
to claim that to see is to know what is where by looking is manifestly
not the same as to claim that vision is the process of discovering from
images what is present in the world. The former claim is roughly
correct, the latter is mistaken. To see something is not to discover
something *from an image*, not all seeing is discovering, and seeing is
not itself a process.

In the first place, the concept of discovering from *a* that *b* is the case
requires some scrutiny. For a person to discover from an array of data
that such-and-such is the case requires that the data be known to the
person. Sherlock Holmes can discover that the murderer was over
6 foot tall, smoked Turkish cigarettes, was left-handed, etc., from the
evidence of his footprints, fingerprints, cigarette-ash, etc., but only
on the condition that Holmes *knows* the evidence.

In a perfectly ordinary sense of 'image', there is indeed such a
thing as discovering from an image facts about what is present
in the world. From a photograph of a certain garden, one can
discover what flowers were in bloom and where they were when
the photograph was taken. But this is only possible if the image,
photograph or picture is perceived and apprehended for what it
is. In this common-or-garden sense, discovering facts from images
presupposes vision and cannot explain it. And it is evident that this
is not what Marr has in mind.

In some of Marr's explanations it seems that the image from which
a perceiver is alleged to discover facts about the world around him is
the retinal image. This is intimated by the curious claim that 'exactly
the right question' is 'How does one obtain constant perceptions in
everyday life on the basis of continually changing sensations?' The
latter claim is obscure, since it is unclear what Marr considers to be
the 'continually changing sensations' from which 'perceptions' are

obtained. If they are not the constantly changing retinal images, there does not seem to be any candidate for the office, and if they are retinal images, it is misconceived to think that retinal images either are or produce sensations. Sensations are felt (one feels pain, giddiness, nausea) in particular locations (in one's tooth, head, stomach) but one does not *feel* one's retinal images, one is not aware of them, and they are not objects of attention.

Although, as we shall see, Marr does not conceive of the retinal image as the 'image' from which we discover what is where in the world, it is still worth chasing this hare for a while. Retinal images are not visible to the person on whose retinae they are formed. The perceiver cannot be said to discover from his retinal image what is in the world since it is not available to him as a collection of evidential data from which to infer what is around him. Seeing an object is not a cognitive transaction with retinal images from which information is derived about what the images are images of. Of course, it can be said that unless there were an image on my retinae of what I see, I would not see what I see. But a causally necessary condition of the possibility of seeing an object is not thereby a datum from which information about what is seen is derived (in the ordinary sense of these terms). Moreover, the presence of a retinal image is, in an obvious sense, incidental to the neural processes necessary for a creature to see. For the presence of a retinal image depends upon the fact that the retina happens to be a reflective surface. In the case of insects with convex retinae, no image is formed. It is not the retinal image that produces the retinal responses that are transmitted along the optic nerve, but rather the pattern of light irradiation that falls on the retinae.

It seems that it is the latter – the pattern of light radiation as it affects the retinal cells – that Marr misleadingly refers to as 'the image'. This is indeed the (animal) visual-analogue of what is referred to as 'an image' in the theory of machine-vision, where the 'image' is acquired by a sensor (typically a television camera) and converted into the machine (electrical) correlate of an array of brightness values (pixels) at a grid of points. The 'image', in this sense of the term, is not an image in the sense in which a picture is an image, although it can be converted into one. (Hence the 'primal sketch' does not provide a set of 'statements' about edge segments, bars and blobs, etc., *of the image*, since there are no edge segments, bars and blobs in the image, i.e. light array. Rather, it provides a coded set of light intensity values from which one can *construct* an image of a crude sort of what is in view.)

Can one then say that vision is the process of discovering, from patterns of light irradiation that fall upon the retinae, what is in the world? That would be misleading. Rather, one sees what one sees as a result of light falling upon one's retinae, but one does not discern, let alone discover, what is in the world around one *from* an 'image' in this sense. One does not *derive* what it is that one sees from such an 'image', since the image is not something available to the seeing person as a datum, i.e. as a piece of information (in the ordinary sense of the term) from which one can derive or infer anything. One sees whatever one sees only if there is light – that is a condition of visibility; a visible object can be seen by the use of one's eyes, and that requires that patterned light fall upon the photosensitive retina. But what it is that one sees – *a fortiori* a description of what it is that one sees – is not derived from an 'image', let alone from a representation of an 'image', which one does not even see. (We shall revert to the matter of 'descriptions' below.)

Second, it is worth noting *en passant* that it is false that all seeing is discovering. If I am looking for a thimble and, peering under the sofa, see it lying there, I might be said to have found or discovered the thimble. But if, while conversing with you, I look at you and see you, I cannot be said to have *discovered* that you are still with me. If you smile or scowl at my remarks, I will see your responses and note them, but I cannot be said to be discovering that you are smiling or scowling. Still less, when I read over what I have just written, can I be said to be discovering what I have written, unless I discern an inadvertent error. Only in special circumstances, against specific kinds of context, can seeing be said to involve discovering.

Third, is it correct to characterize vision as a process? Marr explains that 'the term *process* is very broad. For example, addition is a process, and so is taking a Fourier transform. But so is making a cup of tea, or going shopping.'[11] This is already to start on the wrong foot. Addition is not a process, but an operation: '+' is a sign for addition, and it does not symbolize a temporal process. '2 + 3' does not signify something going on in time, as does 'John is making a cup of tea', rather it signifies the number five (as the sum of 2 and 3). Nor does '+' in '2 + 3' signify a process, as does 'making a cup of tea'; it signifies a function mapping pairs of numbers onto a number. Is adding then a process? If we bear in mind that it is an essential feature of our concept of a process that it goes on in time, consists of sequential phases, and hence can be interrupted prior to completion when only half or a quarter of the process has been completed, it is evident that adding sometimes is a process (or activity) and sometimes is not. Adding up a long shopping list can be said to be a process (it is interruptible, has phases, can be half-completed – as when one has added the first column of digits), but adding 2 and 3 is not a process.

Having noted that 'process' is a 'broad' term, Marr restricts his attention, he says, to its meaning in application to machines carrying out information-processing tasks. Further,

> In the theory of visual processes, the underlying task is to reliably derive properties of the world from images of it; the business of isolating constraints that are both powerful enough to allow a process to be defined and generally true of the world is a central theme of our inquiry.[12]

This, I suggest, begs all the crucial questions. Let us take, as Marr does, a simple example of a cash-register. Whether mechanical or electrical, doubtless a considerable number of events must take place between registering '£2', '£3' and '+', and the machine's displaying '£5'. These sequential events can doubtless be interrupted. Does it follow that the machine can be said to have carried out half the process of adding £2 and £3? Surely not; rather, the machine has gone through half the mechanical or electrical phases requisite for mechanically computing the sum of £2 and £3. (We may, for present purposes, disregard the fact that machines do not add in the sense in which human beings do, i.e. there is no question of a machine understanding what addition is or what numerals are used for.) But to have gone through half the mechanical or electrical phases necessary for the cash register to display '£5' is not for the cash-register to have gone through half the process of adding £2 and £3, since adding £2 and £3 is not a process. One cannot ask here 'How much has it added so far?', 'Has part of the sum been added yet?' or 'What are the results thus far?'. We have already argued that vision is not a matter of deriving properties of the world from images of it. It should now be observed that vision, seeing, is not a process at all.

The theory of *neuro-visual* processes is the explanation of the generation and transmission of electrical impulses along neural pathways to the 'visual' striate cortex and beyond. A causal condition for an animal to see is the occurence of such complex electro-chemical processes. But it does not follow that seeing is a process. (The point is a logical, not a biological, one: a multitude of mechanical or electrical processes are requisite for a clock to keep time accurately, but it does not follow that telling the time is a process.) To be able to see (i.e., not to be blind) is to possess a perceptual capacity which is exercised by the use of the organs of sight. It is exercised in a large variety of ways which we subtly discriminate in our rich vocabulary of vision, e.g. to see, spot, glimpse, peep, glance, peek, catch sight of; to watch, look at, look for, stare at, gaze, observe; to examine, scrutinize, inspect, scan, survey; to discern, make out, descry, recognize. Some of these are, or are at least akin to, processes or activities. Thus visually to examine an artefact, inspect a room, scan a scene, survey a landscape are visual activities that take time, have phases, can be interrupted or completed. Others, though they may be protracted, need have no phases or completions, e.g. to look at, watch, gaze, stare at. Yet others are not process-like or activity-like, but are rather akin to achievements, e.g. to discern, make out, descry, spot. And doubtless many further distinctions can be drawn which may supplement, cut across or further discriminate between these relatively crude ones.[13] Clearly none of these exercises of one's visual capacity is possible unless one also *sees*. Some of these exercises of sight are, as noted, activity- or process-like and, like the others, they involve seeing. But seeing itself is not a process or activity. One can watch, observe, scrutinize, survey or scan something deliberately or carefully, but one cannot see something deliberately or carefully. 'I am watching, looking at, looking for, observing, examining X' may be answers to the question 'What are you doing?' but 'I am seeing' cannot. One may see or hold in view an object for a time, but one is not 'seeing it' throughout the time, although at any moment of the period in which one holds it in view, one sees it. ('I can still see it', one might say, but not 'I am still seeing it'.) As Aristotle already remarked, and Ryle emphasized, if one is in a position to say 'I see it' one can also say 'I have seen it'. Not only is seeing itself not a process, but many exercises of the sense of sight are *not* activity- or process-like, e.g. to glimpse, spot, discern, recognize, make out. It is a conceptual mistake to conflate the neural processes which are requisite for an animal to see something before it with phases in a process of seeing, for seeing is no process nor is it the final link in a chain of phases constituting a process. From this initial confusion a multitude of further incoherences flow.

Before moving on to examine these, however, further conceptual clarification of vision as opposed to machine-vision is appropriate. For not only is it muddled to characterize vision as 'the process of discovering from images what is present in the world', but even the thin characterization of vision as 'knowing what is where by looking' is far too small a canvas upon which to sketch a theory of vision. The conceptual network within which the concept of vision (and concepts of the perceptual faculties) is embedded is rich and closely woven. We are all familiar with it, for it constitutes the backcloth which makes intelligible our constant use of our perceptual vocabulary. If we totally disregard it while pursuing an empirical theory of vision we are likely to overlook conceptual reticulations which are essential for the theory we construct to constitute a theory of *vision* at all. It is an unquestioned presupposition of Marr's work, and of others working in artificial intelligence, that machine-vision is a species of vision, and hence that the theoretical principles requisite for the design of appropriate industrial robots can be extrapolated without more ado to the study of animal (and human) vision. It is precisely this supposition that will be challenged in this chapter, but some preliminary indication of the very general conceptual grounds for challenging it may aid the understanding of subsequent more detailed scrutiny.

Vision, like hearing, taste or smell, is a perceptual capacity possessed by creatures with a wide range of other capacities. A creature that can see is also characterized by a multitude of other features that are essentially (conceptually) connected with its possession of further perceptual and non-perceptual faculties. We learn and teach the use of the vocabulary of perceptual verbs and cognate expressions only in application to such creatures as they display a complex and variegated behavioural repertoire against a rich context of their environment. Hence the meaning of 'to see', 'to smell', 'to hear', etc., and the conditions of application of these expressions are logically bound up with the applicability to the subject of such predications of a host of further psychological verbs. A creature that can see can also look around it in search of what it wants, look for things it likes, look at objects that interest it, glance at items that capture its attention for a moment, pursue those it desires and disregard others, flee from those it perceives as threatening and which it fears. It may be fascinated or mesmerized by what it sees, be surprised, delighted or bored by what it holds in view. For human beings in particular, the perceptual faculties (especially taste and smell) are *also* hedonic faculties, hence we may enjoy looking at, take pleasure in seeing, a scene, a painting or a view. The behaviour of such creatures which licenses us (logically or grammatically) to say that they see (watch, look at, glimpse) is also behaviour which licenses us to say that they want, like, fear, are interested or uninterested, attend to or disregard things, have purposes and goals. It is the possibility or intelligibility of predicating such things of different creatures that constitutes, as it were, the grammatical habitat of verbs of perception in general and of vision in particular. The denser the range of such predications, the firmer the grip which perceptual concepts have in application to a subject; the thinner the range, as with insects or light-sensitive unicellular organisms, the greater the slippage. Remove them altogether, as in contexts of discourse about machine-vision, and one is no longer talking of vision in the ordinary sense of the term, but in a secondary or derivative sense. (One can marry money, be wedded to one's work, or mystically married to Christ, but these expressions are parasitic upon the institution of marriage.)

Some creatures that can see, namely human beings, can now build machines that relieve them from difficult or tiresome visual tasks, just as they can build machines that relieve them of calculating tasks. It is useful (and time-saving) to use a pocket calculator instead of carrying out a complex computation on paper. By using one, a person avoids the labour of calculating himself and finds out the result of computation *without* calculating. Does it follow that *something else*, i.e. the machine, does the calculating?[14] No – not in the same sense. The pocket calculator does not know what numbers are or what numerals are used for (nor is it ignorant!); it does not know what 'addition' or 'subtraction' signifies, and it does not understand (or misunderstand) the signs it displays; it does not believe or disbelieve that the sign it produces is the correct result of a computation, but that is not because it knows or is absolutely certain that it is right. If its display panel were removed it would (appropriately adjusted) continue to pass electrical current through its circuitry in precisely the same way, although it would not – as you or I might, if we remained silent after calculating – have been doing mental arithmetic. If its output were connected with an electric piano, it would be a (rather bad) music-making machine, not a calculator – no matter what was written on its buttons – even though the gadget would not have changed at all in its essential processes. It is, of course, natural to say that the calculator calculates, and there is nothing wrong with saying so, save that it is immensely misleading unless one notes that this is a secondary use of the term 'to calculate', a use in which the expression has been ripped out of its natural grammatical habitat and relocated in a position in which it has a different meaning that is nevertheless essentially parasitic on its primary meaning. This essential parasitism is evident if we consider what significance the expression would retain if the *primary* meaning were defunct, or ceased to have any genuine applications. If all human beings were destroyed, but their computers and calculators remained, and if a tribe of baboons pressed appropriate buttons on these devices, would the machines be calculating even though no one any longer knew what calculation is, what numerals are for and what arithmetical functions mean? Numerals and signs for arithmetical operations are symbols only in so far as they have a use in making calculations for the description and transformation of empirical statements about magnitudes or numbers of objects, stuffs, quantities and spatial relations. Lacking any such roles, they are just marks on paper or electronic displays signifying nothing, and the machines we build in order to save ourselves the labour of calculating are, if deprived of their roles in our lives, just piles of gadgetry producing meaningless marks.

Something similar applies in the case of machine-vision. It is useful in industrial processes to have machines that can scan objects and respond to, for example, hair-cracks in metal, defects in shapes of castings, orientations and misorientations of objects in array. It is labour-saving and often more efficient than employing a person to do the job. Indeed, if X-ray devices are used, the machine can do things a human being cannot – unless he uses an X-ray device.[15] Does it follow that the machine can *see*? Again – no, not in the primary sense of the term. It is not incorrect English to talk metonymically of machines 'seeing', but it is immensely misleading and has misled countless people, including Marr. Application of perceptual predicates to machines is essentially a secondary use of the terms 'to see', 'to hear', 'to smell', 'to taste'. It is parasitic on the primary use in application to animals and human beings. This is not because they 'have minds', nor is it because animals and men are biological structures and industrial robots are not. It is rather because our uses of these expressions (and so their meanings) are bound up with the highly complex behavioural repertoire of creatures in the rich environment of the world they inhabit, and systematically interwoven with a host of further psychological predicates the application of which is licensed by the same forms of behaviour.

Of the industrial robots we build we can say that they perceive only in a secondary sense. If food manufacturers were to design a tasting machine for purposes of monitoring food-processing they would not have made a gourmet, and if museums used an infallible Rembrandt-identifier they would not thereby have an art connoisseur on their staff. Creatures that can see can have good or poor vision, they may be short- or long-sighted and they can go blind. But a machine is neither short-sighted nor long-sighted even if it is built to focus only on objects 2–6 feet away or only on ones 100–500 yards away. If a 'seeing-machine' is damaged, it has not gone blind, and repairing its sensor is not curing its blindness, any more than if a calculator has a defective connection it has forgotten how to calculate (and shaking it is not jogging its memory!). That we do not say such things is not an insignificant fact about ordinary usage, but a reflection of our awareness of a metonymical or derivative use. As in the case of the calculators, similarly in the case of seeing machines – if all living creatures were wiped out, but some automated factories continued to function and the 'visual' sensors etc. of their robots continued to operate, there would nevertheless be no seeing creatures in the world. An analogy may illuminate the point: if all financial institutions and coinage etc. were abolished, but children continued to play Monopoly, there would nevertheless be no money, no buying and selling, or going bankrupt.

So much for preliminaries and for the general background of the criticisms I wish to bring against Marr. The more detailed conceptual criticisms that follow will, I believe, confirm that the application of perceptual predicates to machines is, as argued, a secondary use of these terms. Hence the naïve extrapolation of principles of machine vision to human vision is illegitimate. The fact that the conceptual structure creaks and jams at every significant point exemplifies the illegitimacy of the analogy.

REPRESENTATIONS

In the second paragraph of his book, Marr declares that

> if we are capable of knowing what is where in the world, our brains must somehow be capable of *representing* this information . . . The study of vision must therefore include . . . also an inquiry into the nature of the internal representations by which we capture this information and make it available as a basis for decisions about our thoughts and actions.[16]

Marr gives no reason for the astonishing claim that if we are capable of knowing by looking around us what lies before us, *it follows* that our brain must be capable of representing this information. It is not merely a *non sequitur*, but is actually incoherent, since *there is no such thing* as a brain having the capacity to represent information in the ordinary sense of this expression (and as we shall see, it is important for Marr's account that it is – also – the ordinary sense of 'representing information' which is being deployed). Before trying to show that this is incoherent, however, it is worth pausing to reflect on what might lead one to the bizarre thought that the possibility of coming to know how things are in one's environment requires that the brain be capable of representing things.

It is fortunate that others have stepped in to fill the lacuna in Marr's argument. I shall take as an example J. P. Frisby's discussion in his book *Seeing: Illusion, Brain and Mind*, not because there is any reason to suppose that Marr would or would not have pursued a similar argument, but rather because Frisby, who is both a distinguished experimental psychologist of vision and an ardent admirer of Marr's work, exemplifies a pattern of reasoning that nicely demonstrates the pitfalls of Marr's type of approach to the study of vision. Frisby argues as follows:

> there must be symbols inside our heads for the things we see, symbols which themselves are unlike the things they represent. Upon opening up a patient's head for a brain operation, the surgeon does not find there a miniature stage-set of the world! All he finds is a pink blancmange-like mass of brain cells. So it is an inescapable conclusion that there must be a symbolic description in the brain of the outside world, a description cast in symbols which stand for the various aspects of the world of which sight makes us aware. In fact, when we began by asking 'What goes on inside our heads when we see?' we could as well have put this question as 'When we see, what are the symbols inside our heads that stand for things in the outside world? . . .
>
> The idea of visual experience as a symbolic process may seem a strange one. The likely reason for this is that the world we see . . . is so very clearly 'out there' that it can come as something of a shock to realize that somehow the whole of this world is tucked away in our skulls as an inner representation which stands for the real outside world. It is difficult and unnatural to disentangle the 'perception of a scene' from 'the scene

itself', but they must be clearly distinguished if seeing is to be understood. When the difference between a perception and the thing perceived is fully grasped, the conclusion that seeing must involve a symbolic description sitting somewhere inside our heads becomes easier to accept.[17]

The distinction between a perception, e.g. seeing a magnolia, and the thing perceived, viz. the magnolia, is not difficult or unnatural to disentangle, since it is no more possible (intelligible) to mistake one for the other than it is possible to mistake a railway coach for a railway company. One may confuse or fail to distinguish a magnolia from a mulberry tree, but one cannot mistake a magnolia for seeing a magnolia any more than one can hitch a railway company to a railway engine. But one can, of course, be confused about the *concept* of a company or of a perception. Once we distinguish the concept of the objects of vision from the concept of seeing, it does not follow that seeing must involve a symbolic description inside our heads.

Not only does it not so follow, but also it is not even intelligible, as is evident from reflection upon what is called 'a description' or 'a symbolic description'. A description, in the primary sense of the expression, is a form of words or symbols, a sentence expressing a proposition which specifies an array of features of an object, event or state of affairs. It may be true or false, accurate or inaccurate, detailed or rough and ready. Descriptions are typically contrasted with other objects of speech-activities such as prescriptions, questions, recommendations, justifications or exclamations. In an extended sense of the term we sometimes also refer to maps, plans or blueprints, and diagrams as descriptions. We would, however, be pushing beyond the rough boundaries of the concept of a description if we were to call pictures 'descriptions'. A photograph of a person, a painting of a building, a television picture of an event are not properly said to be descriptions of that of which they are photographs, paintings or pictures, although a description of a given pictorial representation will typically also be a description of what is represented, and hence a pictorial representation may serve much the same purpose as a description. If they are to be called 'descriptions' in a loose sense, at any rate they cannot be said to be symbolic descriptions, since a picture, though it may be a symbol, is not a symbol of that of which it is a picture. A pictogram of a fish may be a symbol for a fish, but is not a description of one. A picture of a fish may be a symbol of Christ, but is not a symbol of or for a fish.

A 'symbolic description' therefore is expressed by a form of words or symbols. It may be spoken or written down; it may be encoded for rather special purposes, e.g. concealment, as in the case of a cipher, or transmission, as in the case of Morse code. One can find descriptions in books or newspapers, or hear them in discourse or on the radio. What would it be to find a description inside a person's head? Barring the distasteful thought of finding an inscribed piece of paper inside someone's skull, there is no such thing as a description located in the brain. Cannot a pattern of neural firings that corresponds causally to a given stimulus in the visual field not constitute a description of the stimulus or of its cause? No, for patterns of neural firings are not symbols (any more than electrical impulses moving along telephone wires are symbols, even though one may sometimes recover symbols from them). For something to be a symbol it must have a *rule-governed use*, there must be a correct and an incorrect way of employing it. It is employed correctly when it is used in accord with accepted explanations of its meaning, explanations that are accepted as correct by other users of the symbol, other speakers of the language of which the symbol is an element. It must have a grammar which is given by the explanation of its use. An agent employs a symbol only if in using it he follows, knowingly conforms with, the rules for its use, if he knows what it means and can, in some way or other, explain what it means or what he means by it. But brain cells do not know (nor are they ignorant of) what any symbols mean; they cannot be said to follow (nor to fail to follow) rules for the use of symbols. They cannot be said to use a symbol correctly, nor can they be said to use a symbol incorrectly, since it makes no sense whatever to talk of brain cells *using a language*. It makes sense to say of someone who has mastered the technique of using a language that he means by a symbol 'S' precisely what 'S' means (i.e. that he uses it correctly), and it also makes sense, if his mastery of the language falters, to say that by 'S' he meant 'R', even though 'S' does not mean 'R'. But neurons do not mean or fail to mean something by their electrical activities (although, of course, that a certain neuron fires may mean that a certain retinal cell has been stimulated, just as black clouds on the horizon may mean rain tomorrow, and smoke may mean fire). Brain cells cannot be said to do anything intentionally or unintentionally, and *a fortiori* cannot be said to employ symbols and in so doing to mean something by them. It makes no sense to conceive of a pattern of electrical activity in the cortex as constituting either a description or a misdescription of a perceived object any more than it makes sense to conceive of it as a prescription, request or entreaty.

Frisby is surely right to reject the idea that to perceive involves having a 'miniature stage-set of the world' in the brain (or indeed a picture on the pineal gland). But there is no good reason for thinking that the 'inescapable alternative' is that there be a symbolic description of the world in the brain. Indeed, this supposition is literally unintelligible. It is true that a language-user who looks around him can describe what he sees. But that he is able to do so does not imply that there is a description of what he sees 'tucked away in [his skull] as an inner representation which stands for the outside world'. That incoherent supposition turns on the idea that the brain must, as Marr puts it, be capable of representing information by means of internal representations. The confusion implicit in that idea has already been partially unpacked, but it merits closer scrutiny in the context of Marr's theory of vision.

A *representation*, Marr explains,

> is a formal system for making explicit certain entities or types of information, together with a specification of how the system does this ... the result of using a representation to describe a given entity [is] a *description* of the entity in that representation.[18]

According to this explanation, a representation is a *method* of representing or describing something by means of a (rule-governed) symbolism. Marr's confusions become evident in his illustrative applications of the term. Different numeral systems (Roman, Arabic, binary)[19] are, he claims, formal systems for representing numbers. Second, a musical score of a symphony provides a way of representing a symphony. Third, information-processing machines work by using symbols to stand for, i.e. represent, things.

To take his applications in turn: first, while a numeral system can be said to be a method of representation, it is not a method of representing or describing numbers, but rather for describing the numbers, dimensions, proportions, etc., of objects (stuffs, quantities etc.) around us in empirical statements that are about objects (stuffs, quantities, etc.) not about numbers. '37', 'XXXVII', '100101' are not descriptions of thirty-seven, but symbols in different notations of thirty-seven. A numeral is no more the description of a number than ' $\sim (\xi)$' or 'FT(p)' are descriptions of negation (in the notation of *Principia* or in the T/F notation of the *Tractatus* respectively). Indeed, it is doubtful whether anything can legitimately be called 'a description of a number'. (The reasons for this run deep: numbers are not kinds of entities; their internal properties *define* rather than describe them; and we do not, with good reason, think of numbers as having external properties.)

Second, a musical score of a symphony is not, according to Marr's definition, a way of representing a symphony, *if* that means that the score is *a representation* of the symphony. For his definition restricts 'representation' to a *method* or *system* of representing. On that specification it is the musical notation (together with its rules) which is the representation of any piece of music. A particular score *in* a given representation is a description (in an extended sense) of the particular piece of music of which it is the score. (Why 'in an extended sense'? – because, *inter alia*, it is more appropriate to think of a score as a *recipe* or *prescription* for playing that piece of music.) However, it is not surprising to find Marr wavering between using 'representation' to signify a method of representing, and using it to signify a description in the symbolism of a given method of representation. For if a primal sketch or 3D model representation is a 'representation', then a representation is a description not a system or method of representing or describing entities.

Third, it is thoroughly misleading to say that information-processing machines work by using symbols to stand for things. Rather, we so build machines that certain operations in the machines correspond in predetermined ways to symbols that we use to represent things. Only a creature that understands a symbolism can, for reasons elaborated above, literally be said to use symbols. Machine 'languages' such as 'BASIC', 'PASCAL', 'FORTRAN' are not languages machines speak or understand; indeed, they are not, in the sense in which English or German are, languages at all.

Marr contends that the mind 'has access to systems of internal representation'. Bearing in mind his equivocation over 'representation', this is a claim that requires scrutiny. If 'a system of representation' signifies a set of symbols together with combinatorial rules for their use in describing objects, states of affairs, etc. (i.e. in 'making explicit certain entities or types of information') then for the mind to 'have access' to such a system might mean that 'the mind' has mastered the techniques of employing such a symbol-system in rendering (*inter alia*) empirical descriptions. But for 'the mind' to have mastered the use of a symbol-system (a grammar and vocabulary) is for the *person* to have acquired these skills. The criteria for whether a person has done so consist in his correctly employing the symbols in speech, in his correctly responding (i.e. in his responding with understanding) to the use by others of such symbols, and in his giving correct explanations of the use of these symbols when asked what they mean or what he means by their use in a given context. The only symbol-systems human beings thus master are human languages and related symbolic notations.

If, on the other hand, 'a representation' signifies not a method of representing or describing, but rather a description expressed by means of a given method of representation, then to have access to representations or descriptions must simply mean that there is available to a person an array of intelligible descriptions. A creature that has a mind can indeed describe a multitude of things; but to be able to describe is not to have access to descriptions. One has access to descriptions if, for example, one has access to books that contain the relevant descriptions couched in a language one knows.

However, neither sense of 'having access to representations' is at all relevant to the explanation of vision. Far from the skills involved in having mastered a technique of representation (having 'access' to systems of representation) being a prerequisite for vision, their acquisition typically presupposes vision (or other perceptual modalities). The learning and use of a symbol-system requires that the speaker or user of the symbolism can perceive the symbols he uses or apprehends. Lack of mastery of a symbol-system is not a criterion for blindness or deafness; neither animals nor small children are held to be blind or deaf on the ground that they have not mastered any method of representation.

All this is clearly irrelevant to Marr's concerns. His claim is that the mind has access to *internal* representations. What can this mean? If a representation is a description given by means of a certain method of representation, then presumably an 'external representation' is one which is written, uttered or otherwise displayed in communicative acts. And, *pari passu*, an 'internal representation' is a description that one has in mind when one thinks or imagines that something is thus-and-so. Of course, if I can think or imagine that p (where 'p' is or incorporates a description), then I can also express what I think or imagine aloud. There is no such thing as an 'internal representation' in this sense which cannot be manifest in an external one. (A mental image, if it is confusedly to be called 'a representation' is not a symbolic one unless what one imagines is a symbol; moreover, what I can imagine I can also describe, draw or otherwise construct for others to apprehend.[20]) If, on the other hand, 'a representation' signifies a system (a grammar and vocabulary) of representing things, it is wholly opaque what it is for a representation to be 'internal' as opposed to 'external'. Are natural languages, constructed (formal logical) languages, arithmetical or musical notations 'external' systems of representation? It is doubtful whether the question makes sense, since it is doubtful whether the dichotomy of 'internal'/'external' has any application to systems or methods of representation.

It seems, from Marr's discussion, that 'internal representations' are representations *belonging to the brain*. The 'internality' of the representations presumably signifies that they are 'in the brain'. The plural 'representations' must signify either different symbolic systems or the different methods by which, for example, the primal sketch, the $2\frac{1}{2}$D sketch or 3D model are allegedly presented, or alternatively it must signify these different 'descriptions' or 'representations' themselves. If that is so, incoherence breaks out at three different levels.

First, if 'representation' means the method (i.e. the symbolism and its grammar) of representing light-intensity values, or $2\frac{1}{2}$D contours etc., then the method of representation is the appropriately adapted symbolism and techniques of higher mathematics. This *form of representation* is not in the brain, or anywhere else. It is used by computational theorists to map one array of values onto another, and it is a matter of conjecture that there is a pattern of causally connected features in the brain that exemplify the functional relationships expressed in the appropriate mathematical symbolism. If, however, 'representation' means a symbolic description in a given (method of) representation, then, of course, no such thing is to be found in the brain for reasons specified. Even if there are functionally correlated arrays of neural activity (e.g. between retinal responses and neural activity in the hypercolumns of the 'visual' striate cortex) which can be described by a neurophysiologist as correlated with a visual scene, it does not follow that the patterned array of neural reactions constituted a symbolic description. Indeed, the very suggestion is incoherent.

Second, the supposition that the mind has 'access' to a system of internal representations must signify that the mind has access to the alleged representations (symbolism) of the brain. This makes no sense. Even if it were intelligible to suppose that the brain has mastered, understood and used a symbolism, it would remain unintelligible for the mind to 'have access' to it or to its use in giving descriptions. The picture underlying this idea is a venerable one: Locke charmingly described the brain as 'the mind's Presence-room' to which ideas are conveyed through the conduits of the nerves,[21] and more recent analogies compared the brain to a central telephone exchange with the mind as the telephone operator. We find these old images comic – the new one is no less so. Does the mind *read* these 'descriptions' with mental eyes? Or does it hear the brain speak them? And in what language, familiar to the mind, are they written or uttered?

Third, it might be suggested that Marr's use of 'representation' is a special technical one, wholly detached from symbolisms and their use; consequently these criticisms miss the point altogether. But this is not so: Marr claimed that numeral systems are representations, that 'a representation for shape would be a formal scheme for describing some aspects of shape, together with rules that specify how the scheme is applied to any particular shape',[22] that a formal scheme 'is a set of symbols with rules for putting them together',[23] that

> a representation, therefore, is not a foreign idea at all – we all use representations all the time. However, the notion that one can capture some aspect of reality by making a description of it using a symbol and that to do so can be useful seems to me to be a powerful and fascinating idea.[24]

This is indeed true; we all talk, use a language, describe things, issue orders, pleas, requests, pronounce verdicts, exclaim, proclaim and so on through indefinitely many other acts of speech, in which we employ a symbolism and evince our mastery of a method of representation. (Although animals, which can see as well as or better than we, do not.) The idea is hardly novel; what is novel is the supposition that our brains engage in similar activities. That idea may be fascinating, but far from being powerful, it is incoherent.

SEEING, REPRESENTING AND DESCRIBING

Vision, Marr contends, is 'first and foremost an information processing task'. In an animal, this task must be carried out by the brain. What it must do is derive properties of the world from images of it. At the final stage of visual information-processing an axis-based structural description must be matched with a stored catalogue of 3D model descriptions or templates to enable *recognition*. The output of the visual process, Marr claims, is the production of a *description* that is useful to the viewer.[25] Marr understandably hesitates over this extraordinary claim: it is, he observes lamely, rather nebulous. Unlike the input, the result of vision is much harder to discern, let alone specify precisely.[26] Nevertheless, he claims, his new approach makes quite specific proposals about this: 'the quintessential fact of human vision [is] that it tells about shape and space and spatial arrangement. Here [lies] a way to formulate its purpose – building a description of the shapes and positions of things from images.'[27]

It should first be observed that in the ordinary sense of 'information' to see something is not to process information, although *sometimes* seeing involves acquiring information. To see a tree in the quad is not to be given any information; rather, to be *told* that there is a tree in the quad is to be given information. To see a tree in the quad is, if one did not know that there was a tree there, to acquire a piece of information – but it is not to 'process' information. And if one has been daily looking out of one's window at the tree for years, to see it yet again is not to acquire information at all (*ceteris paribus*). Nor is it the case that if one sees X one thereby becomes informed about X, not only because one may already know everything about X that one can see, but also because one may take X to be Y and hence become misinformed (as when I see N.N. in the distance and take him for his twin).

It may be said that the neural processes requisite for an animal to see are, in a technical sense of 'information', information-processing tasks. Maybe so – but if one makes this more modest claim one must beware of conflating two quite different senses of 'information'. In this sense of 'information' seeing does not give an observer information about what is in the world and where it is.

To be sure, the input of the neuro-visual process is a pattern of light irradiation falling upon the retinae, but can the brain be said to construct from this a representation of anything, in particular a 'grey-level' representation? That depends upon what one means by 'representation'. If it is found that a selective array of cells responds in a systematic way to the light intensities falling on the retina, one might – misleadingly – call the pattern of responses 'a representation' of the light intensities (or an image). But note that here 'a representation' simply signifies an array of items systematically projectible onto another array. This notion of a representation is not one which we 'use all the time' in our linguistic activities. It is not a description of anything, and it does not consist of symbols used in accord with rules, although the theory that describes the functional correlations between the arrays will be expressed in a symbolism and will incorporate descriptions of arrays of elements. The conjectured grey-level representation in the brain does not consist of a set of statements, since a set of statements can be made only by the use of a symbolism in accord with its conventional grammar. But neural firings are not symbols, do not have definitions or rules of syntax, are not employed by symbol-using creatures, cannot be used correctly or incorrectly, cannot be grammatical or ungrammatical and are not part of a language.

According to Marr, the visual process is a mapping of one representation onto another, the initial representation being arrays of light-intensity values as detected by retinal photoreceptors. An intensity value at co-ordinate (x, y) is, he explains, denoted by a symbol of the form $I(x, y)$ each value of which specifies a particular level of grey at a point or region. A whole array of such picture-elements (pixels) is held to be a representation. We may concede that an ordered array of specifications of intensity values at points would be a symbolic representation of a pattern of light irradiation (or, for that matter, of a picture). It would be a description, in a conventional notation, of 'greyness' of points or regions in an array. But the differential reactions of photoreceptors or other cells do not constitute, individually or collectively, a symbolic representation of a light-intensity array or of anything else. The photoreceptors do not find out or describe the intensity of light at given points, they react to it. Their reactions are no more symbols than are the reactions of points on a photographic film to a pattern of light irradiation. The $I(x, y)$-notation is indeed (part of) a method of representation – one adopted by scientists in their theory-construction. But it is no more 'available' to the retina or brain than the notation of isobars is 'available' to the weather. A description in the $I(x, y)$-notation is a symbolic representation of a pattern of light irradiation, but no such description could intelligibly be found in or used by a brain.

In the case of machine-vision the penultimate stage of the work of the (computer) *processor* involves matching, in which the 'image' of the object (a coded array of pixels) is matched with a stored reference 'image'. Much of the importance of Marr's work consists in his ingenious reflections on how to generate a '3D model representation' from a '2½D sketch'. Identification of the object must then proceed via matching with a stored 'catalogue' of

3D model 'descriptions'. The question that must concern the psychologist who is studying animal or human vision, or the philosopher investigating the concept of vision, is the intelligibility of employing the analogy between machine-vision and vision proper at this point. It seems obvious that the analogy breaks down. Even if it made sense for the brain to contain a 'stored catalogue' of '3D model descriptions', how could it do so without the animal or person ever having seen an object of the given type before? Or are we to assume, *mirabile dictu*, that animals and men alike are innately equipped with such a 'catalogue'? The simple fact is that both animals and men can see things they have never seen before, so neural matching (if it were intelligible) cannot be a condition of seeing. Furthermore, human beings can *recognize* things they have never seen before, viz. on the basis of antecedent non-visual information ('Magdalen College is the first gothic college you will see as you enter Oxford from the east'). And finally, it is false that all recurrent seeing involves recognizing. I look at the clock and see that it is 6.15 p.m., but I do not *recognize* anything; I see my wife across the table at dinner, but it is mistaken to suggest that I recognize (or fail to recognize) her; I see the words on the page before me, but it is wrong to claim *in this context* that I recognize them – that would be in order after a cataract operation, or if I saw them plagiarized in a nefarious colleague's paper. Only in special contexts, against a range of background presuppositions of normality, does it makes sense to characterize seeing the familiar as recognizing.

Matters are in fact even worse than this. It makes sense to talk of a person matching a description to items in a catalogue. For a person to do so, he must be able to *perceive* and *know how to use* the catalogue as well *understand* the description. In *this* sense of 'identifying an object by reference to a stored catalogue' it is obviously incoherent to suppose that the brain or any part of it should do so. For neither the brain nor its parts can perceive (or fail to perceive), know how to do something (or be ignorant), understand anything (or fail to understand). In so far as the hypothesized 'matching' can intelligibly be said (whether truly or falsely) to occur in the brain, the postulated correlated arrays are neither descriptions nor catalogues. The supposition that a person sees an object A only if the brain identifies a 'description' by reference to a stored 'catalogue' and recognizes A is doubly incoherent. Neither a brain nor its parts can be said to *identify* anything or to recognize objects, either by acquaintance or by description, even in the metonymical sense in which a machine can be said to do so. Moreover, a person can see A and know it to be A, even though it would be wrong to say that he recognizes A (as when one sees one's wife across the breakfast table). A person may see A, but misidentify it, taking it to be B (e.g. A's twin); or he may see A, but not recognize it at all. To think that all seeing involves recognition which in turn consists in neural 'matching' of description and catalogue is a serious confusion.

The final stage of the visual process, indeed the *output* of the process, is, according to Marr, the production of a useful *description*, a description of shapes and positions of things in one's environment. This description is allegedly embodied in an internal representation which is *made available as a basis for decisions*.[28] (This characterization is, yet again, derived from machine-vision, since the processor's 'identification' of the object or feature triggers, in a predetermined way, the robotic 'decision'. And for this to occur *vision is not necessary* – which is why we use these machines instead of workers.) Here too the computer analogy upon which is based the extension of Marr's work from 'artificial intelligence' to animal or human vision manifestly crumbles. The output of the neuro-visual process, if it can be said to have 'an output', is *that the creature sees* whatever it sees. But to see something is not to construct or produce a description of anything; indeed, it is not even to be *able* to produce a description. Animals and pre-linguistic children indubitably see things around them (unless they are blind), but they cannot describe what they see. Only a creature that has mastered a language can describe anything. A language-user may produce descriptions of what he sees, as indeed he may produce misdescriptions, despite having excellent vision. Seeing is not describing. (Nor, for that matter, is hearing, smelling, or tasting; to hear Beethoven's 9th is not to describe or even to be able to describe it!) And, as we have seen, the idea that the *brain* might produce a description (or 'internal representation') and make it available to the mind, and that this transaction is constitutive of seeing, is doubly incoherent.

Finally, is it correct to say that the quintessential fact of human vision is that it tells about shape and space and spatial relations? Strictly speaking, vision does not *tell* anything; rather, a person who sees can tell *that*, indeed *see that*, things are thus and so in his vicinity, and hence, if he has mastered the use of language, can tell others what he sees. One who can see can find his way around his environment without bumping into things, apprehend objects in the distance, follow the movement of an object with his eyes, and so forth, while those who are blind cannot. (These, be it noted, are grammatical, not empirical, observations; they are elements of an explanation of what 'to see' *means*.) If Marr simply has in mind that *what* we see are shapes and spatial relations of objects, then one would not wish to quarrel with this claim, if it is appropriately qualified. But it needs to be qualified in order to ward off potential misunderstandings. First, we see many things and categories of things other than shapes, surfaces and spatial relations of objects. For we see colours and movement; also light (and that in many different senses), flashes, glows and glimmers. We see events, states and processes; also materials (stuffs in contrast to things), 'disturbances' such as knots, holes or gaps. Second, it would be quite wrong to suppose that whenever we see whatever we see, we necessarily see a shape, surface and spatial relation. For these are not proper objects of vision in the sense in which sounds are proper objects of hearing. If A hears X, it follows that A heard a sound; but if A sees X, it does not follow A saw a shape, a surface or a spatial relation. Holes are visible, but have no surfaces; one may see a cave, but its surface and shape may be enshrouded in gloom; one may see an explosion, but an explosion has neither a shape nor a surface, any more than does the sky, in the colour of which one may 'visually immerse' oneself. One may see the water in the glass, the sand on the beach or the mist on the moor, but none of these stuffs has a shape. Third, one must beware of an equivocation on 'shape' and 'surface'. In one sense, every material object has a shape and surface, i.e. contour and area which, if illuminated, is visible. (But note that we see many things which are not material objects.) In this sense of 'surface' it is not an empirical truth that whenever one sees an object, one sees its surface (and, perhaps, typically its shape). That is simply part of what is meant by 'seeing a material object', for 'surface' amounts to no more than what is visible of the object. But in another sense, there are many objects, particularly animate ones, of which it makes scant sense to talk of seeing their shape. Does a person's *shape* change as he sits down, lies down, walks or runs? We may or may not see the contours of his body, his silhouette, from this or that position, but only in special circumstances (e.g. when talking of his figure or posture) do we talk of seeing his shape. Similarly, if the claim that we see surfaces of things is meant to be an empirical statement, then of course we often do not see surfaces of things, for example when one sees a peeled orange, a slice through a tree trunk, or a dissected corpse. Hence, finally, it would be wrong to suggest that whenever we see X, we identify it as X by reference to its shape. We see many things and know what they are without identifying them (e.g. one's wife across the dinner table, one's hand or leg); some visibilia we see and identify, but not by reference to their shape (e.g. blood, water, gold); and others we may see and fail to identify, whether or not we see their shape, and whether or not we identify it.

REPRESENTATIONAL THEORIES OF THE MIND

It was noted in the opening section of this chapter that Marr characterizes his approach from a philosophical point of view as an extension of representational theories of the mind. He briefly earmarks such a view as claiming that 'the senses are for the most part concerned with telling one what is there', and distinguishes modern representational theories as conceiving of the mind as having access to systems of internal representations, and of mental states as being characterized by asserting what the internal representations currently specify and mental processes by how such internal representations are obtained and how they interact. Marr declares this scheme to be a 'comfortable framework' for the study of vision. It will be evident from the arguments I have rehearsed that, far from being a comfortable framework, it is an altogether disastrous one. The subject of representational theories of the mind is a large one, and its confusions and incoherences manifold. All I wish to do here is to conclude with a few remarks on Marr's observations, and briefly to relate his modern representationalism to its classical forebears.

In most contexts it is quite harmless to say that the senses are concerned with telling one what is there. We speak quite freely of believing or disbelieving our eyes or ears, of being deceived by our senses, of having little faith in our sense of smell or taste. These are picturesque metaphors. Metaphors, however, can mislead. This particular array of metaphors is built upon the picture of the sense-organs as information-transmitters, and its deployment by an information-theorist is potentially deceptive. For, of course, our eyes do not see things and tell us what they see, nor do our ears hear things and inform us what they hear. The sense-organs are used by us to find out, observe, apprehend what is in our environment. The sense-faculties are capacities for apprehending how things are in the world by the use of the organs of sense. The senses are not information-transmitters, even though it is true that we acquire information by their use. They do not transmit to us 'internal representations' nor do they make available to the mind symbolic descriptions.

The expressions 'state', 'process', and also 'act', 'event' and 'activity' are very general and also exceedingly vague and flexible. We talk of different states of matter (solid, liquid, gaseous), of the state of the room (neat and tidy) or garden (neglected and disorderly), of the state of the nation. Very roughly, states consist of patterns of relationship between elements that *obtain* at a time: they may be momentary or persistent. Processes, on the other hand, are dynamic: they go on for a time, and consist of sequential transformations of states. These concepts, however, are not precise, although they may be given a precise use in special contexts (e.g. in physics).

We speak not only of physical, political or economic states and processes, but also of mental states and processes, as indeed we speak of mental acts and activities. The extension of these categorial concepts to the mind from their primary use in application to the non-mental is natural. But like all such extensions, it involves subtle modulations in meaning (a flash of inspiration involves no light, the light-hearted who have shed a burden of supposed guilt do not weigh less, the waves of depression that beset one have no wavelength). We do indeed speak of mental states, paradigmatically in connection with emotions and moods. Someone is said to be in a state of excitement, intense agitation, depression or anxiety. These characteristically persist for a time. Are they 'characterized by asserting what the internal representations currently specify'? It is difficult to make sense of the question. Such mental states are characterized primarily by patterns of behaviour and behavioural disposition in certain circumstances. It is true that emotions have objects: one is angry about something or with someone, delighted at something or other, envious of someone. But it would be confused to call the directedness or intensionality of emotional states 'having an internal representation'. And moods, of course, typically lack any specific object. The concept of a mental state can be applied beyond the limits of moods and emotions. We talk of people being in a state of intense concentration. Some might find it acceptable to characterize having a headache or toothache as being in a mental state, while others may find it unnatural and jarring. But if to have a persistent headache is to be in a mental state, it certainly is not characterized by asserting 'what the internal representations currently specify', but rather as throbbing, dull and at the back of the head. On the other hand, one would not conceive of having a sudden twinge of pain, feeling a tickle or itch as being in a mental state. These might be thought of as mental events rather than states. They happen or occur rather than obtain. Note that mental states (depression or headache), unlike non-mental ones, do not in the same sense involve a 'static' relationship between elements. Moreover, mental states obtain *for a time*: to suffer a pang of anxiety is not to be in a state of anxiety. Finally, verbs of perception, especially the primitive concepts of seeing, hearing, smelling, etc., do not signify mental states. To be alert or watchful may be a mental state; to see X or to hear Y is not.

The notion of a mental process, which must not be confused with a neural process, is even more restricted and nebulous. We employ it primarily in the cognitive rather than conative or emotive domains. We talk of thought processes, of the process of thinking a problem through, of the creative processes of the artist; but also of the difficult process of becoming accustomed to new situations (the loss of a loved one). The notion of sequential development is involved here, as it is in the case of non-mental processes, but not or not necessarily that of a sequential transformation of states. If thinking a problem through is conceived of as a process, it suggests thinking first of A, then of B, later of C; but thinking that such-and-such is the case and hence that so-and-so, is not a transformation of states but rather, if anything, a transformation of propositions. It would be misguided to characterize mental processes, whether thinking a problem through or becoming adjusted to grief, as a matter of obtaining 'mental representations', let alone of the mental process as the interaction of mental representations. Note again, that perceiving is not a mental process, although as noted, some exercises of perceptual faculties – e.g. scanning, scrutinizing, examining – are activity-like.

The study of perception in general, and human perception in particular, is not an investigation into representations and their relationship to what they are representations of. That is the study of symbol-systems, languages, notations, pictures and other (para-digmatically social) artefacts employed by concept-using creatures. To perceive something is not to represent anything, although it is true that perceivers who have mastered a language can describe (or represent) what they perceive. But, of course, the fallacy that perceiving is in some sense representing is an ancient one.

Seventeenth-century representational theories of perception were propounded by representational idealists led by Descartes on the continent and Locke in Britain. They argued that the world around us is never perceived directly but only mediately, that what we directly perceive are not what we ordinarily take ourselves to perceive but rather *ideas*, and that we never apprehend the world as it is, independent of our perception of it. The ideas which we directly perceive, on this view, represent the objects that give rise to them, but only in certain respects. This confused conception was extensively debated and criticized by philosophers in the following centuries. Very briefly, if there is no such thing as direct perception, there can be no such thing as indirect perception either. The only intelligible employment of the notion of indirect perception is to vision, and there it applies paradigmatically to seeing things in mirrors or periscopes – i.e., to cases of a break in the direction of sight – and is contrasted with seeing things without the aid of such devices. Further, if 'ideas' are mental items such as after-images, sensations or feelings, then they are not perceived at all, but rather *had* by a person. One neither perceives nor misperceives one's pains, and one does not see or fail to see one's after-images (if one does not 'see' it, there is no after-image – but not because one's 'eyesight' is so good). What we see are not ideas in the mind, but objects, events, or states of affairs, etc. in the world around us. What we taste when we eat an apple, is the apple, not an idea of the apple; when we feel the roughness of sandpaper, it is the sandpaper that we perceive to be rough, not a mental 'representation' of it; and when we listen to music what we hear are musical instruments playing, not noisy ideas in the mind.

One primary motivation for the curious conception of classical representationalists was the misguided belief that the world as it is independently of our perception of it is a colourless, odourless, tasteless, soundless array of material space-occupants qualified only by 'geometrical' properties of shape, size, motion or rest, solidity and number. So-called 'secondary qualities' of colour, sound, smell, taste, textures, heat or cold as we normally conceive of them were thought to be mere effects of objects upon our sensibility. Given this confused belief (a confusion which persists in many scientific quarters to this day), some form of representationalism or even pure idealism (as in Berkeley, Hume and later Mach) seemed unavoidable.

A second motivation was provided by a rudimentary, and at that stage wholly speculative, causal theory of perception. Corpuscular action was held to impress itself upon our sensory organs, stimulating the animal spirits in the nerves, which, transmitting the agitation to the brain, generated in an inexplicable manner an idea or sensation in the mind. To perceive was thought to be a matter of apprehending the idea thus produced, and 'veridical' perception was thought of as perceiving an idea which – in appropriate respects – accurately represented the object which caused it. This account was a mixture of ingenious and ultimately fruitful empirical conjecture and conceptual confusion. The speculative causal theory of perception split in due course into two components, an empirical theory of physiological psychology and a purely philosophical causal theory of perception. The former, since the great work of von Helmholtz, has made substantial strides forward, although it is all too frequently beset (even in Helmholtz's writings) with a residue of philosophical confusions.

Marr's modern representational theory is not motivated by the first kind of consideration. There is no suggestion in his writings that what we perceive is a surrogate (idea, sense-datum, impression) for the objects in the world around us. But something very similar is evident in his theory. For the classical theorists the 'output' of the neuro-visual process was that the agent perceives an idea, for Marr it is that the agent constructs a description. For the classical theorist the end-product of light entering the eyes is the availability of a mental 'representation' of a pictorial kind, for Marr it is the availability of an 'internal representation' of a symbolic kind. Both are confused on purely *a priori* grounds. To see is not to perceive an idea in the visual mode, nor is it to describe anything. It is not to represent something to oneself, either pictorially or symbolically, although what one sees one may also imagine or describe (if one has mastered a given method of representation). The criteria – the logical grounds – for judging a creature to see are independent of the criteria for its having ideas and mental images, and also independent of the criteria for its having 'constructed' a description in its mind (if it is a creature with a mind), let alone (absurdly) in its brain.

The second kind of consideration does play an overt role in Marr's theory: both electrical processes in machine-vision and neuro-visual processes in the brain are causal. The insoluble difficulty encountered by classical representationalists was to explain the transition from hypothesized causal transactions of the 'little fibres' in the nerves ('les petits filets' as Descartes put it) to the *seeing* effected, it seemed, by the mind. How can causal chains in the brain terminate in what appears to be the conscious mental act of seeing? To postulate a causal interaction between mind and brain in the pineal gland (as Descartes did) or in the 'liaison brain' (as Sir John Eccles does) is merely to dress up a conceptual puzzle in the guise of a pseudo-empirical solution. As we have seen, Marr encounters a precisely parallel problem. Even if it made sense for the brain to contain descriptions in neurally coded form of what is seen, how could it make these putative 'internal representations' available to the mind? The 'problem' has and can have no empirical solution, for it is not an empirical problem but a conceptual confusion. Seeing (or otherwise perceiving) is not the final link in a neural causal chain, and it does not consist in the occurrence of any putative mental event of having (let alone perceiving) ideas or constructing descriptions. It is, very crudely speaking, the exercise of a capacity for apprehending how things are around us by the use of the eyes. Visibility, and hence illumination or luminosity, is an opportunity condition for seeing, and the proper functioning of the appropriate neural mechanisms is a causal prerequisite for an animal to exercise its visual powers. But seeing an object is not the terminus of a neural causal chain, since 'to see', like other perceptual verbs (and indeed the whole gamut of psychological verbs), is predicable of the animal as a whole, not of a part of it. Seeing is a function of – i.e. dependent on – the neural activities of the brain, but it is not an activity of the brain but rather of the animal (and it is mischaracterized as an *activity*). It is the activity *of the animal* in light (or in relation to luminous objects in the dark) that constitutes the logical ground for determining whether (and what) it sees. But its seeing is neither an event in the brain (even though a multitude of brain events are causal preconditions of seeing) nor an event in the mind (even though various things may cross one's mind when one sees – if one has a mind).

Not only does Marr's theory of vision run aground on the reefs that wrecked classical representational theories, it also recapitulates a feature which has characterized the whole history of visual theory, namely that the primary explanatory device in the various successive theories manifestly fails to explain *vision*.[29] Ancient Greek visual theorists, puzzled by the idea of perception without contact, adopted an intromissionist conception of vision and conceived of the corneal reflection as guaranteeing the apparently requisite contact by means of an emanation or image transmitted from what is visible, this image serving as a surrogate of the visible scene that would explain the possibility of vision. What the theory *prima facie* satisfied was their *a priori* demand for a form of contact; what it failed to satisfy was the requirement for an explanation of the possibility of vision. For either what we see is in fact the picture (image) on the cornea, in which case vision is not explained, or what we see is the visible scene, in which case the presence of a corneal reflection merely raises the question of how that contributes to vision – which has in no way been explained. Kepler, following Alhazen's lead, dispensed with the traditional conception of the eye as an image-receptor and conceived of it as an image-assembler. For he correctly identified the mechanism by which an inverted image is produced on the retina by the refraction of light passing through the lens. But, again, the question remains, how does the presence of a picture (reflection) on the retina explain vision? Evidently the deeper explanation must lie 'further back' in the brain – in what is *done* with this surrogate. Descartes pushed further back, developing a mechanistic theory of vision. He conceived (wrongly) of the retinal *image* (rather than the pattern of light irradiation) as stimulating the optic nerves so as to generate such motions as will cause a picture (only partially resembling the visible scene) to be assembled on the pineal gland. But, assuming that there is such a picture, how will it solve the 'mystery' of vision? How will it enable the person to *see*? At this point Descartes bluntly insisted that the image on the pineal gland *causes the mind to see*. The 'mystery' has just been pushed further back, from corneal reflection, to retinal image, and then to pineal gland!

It is obvious that Marr's theory of vision conforms to the pattern of his august predecessors. Of course, he dispenses with images on the pineal gland. Instead he offers us 3D model descriptions elsewhere. But, granting him greater leniency than we need grant Descartes,[30] even if there were something that might be called 'a 3D model description' in the brain, how would it explain *seeing*? To say that the mind 'has access' to the 'internal representations' produced by the brain is as least as mysterious as the claim that an image on the pineal gland causes the mind to see. And if Marr or his followers wish to dispense with the mind, or, more cogently, to insist that it is not the mind but the animal or person that sees, how is the transition from the presence of an encoded 3D model description in the brain to the experience of seeing what is before one's eyes to be explained? The apparent 'mystery of vision' is as elusive as ever, for, yet again, it is merely pushed further back. But the appearance of mystery is no more than the shadow cast by conceptual confusions. For seeing something is the exercise of a capacity, a use of the visual faculty; and the most an empirical physiological theory (or the abstract computational model for such a theory) could intelligibly do is to explain the causal prerequisites for possession of the capacity and the concomittants of its exercise. Any attempt to reduce a capacity to its vehicle or the exercise of a capacity to changes in the structure of its vehicle will inevitably violate the bounds of sense. Seeing an object is not a neural event, and that is a grammatical or conceptual truth, not an empirical hypothesis.

I wish to conclude with a few caveats to ward off misunderstandings. I have not suggested that Marr's work is valueless; on the contrary – it is an ingenious development in the theory of machine-vision. Similarly I have not suggested that *some* of the analogies between the mechanisms of machine-vision and neural mechanism of animals (including humans) may not prove fruitful for neurophysiological research. That an analogy does not stretch as far as one hopes does not imply that it is altogether useless. What I have suggested is that Marr's employment of the analogy at the global level is incoherent, that the conceptual framework which he adopts as a consequence of using this analogy is wholly inadequate. It is an inappropriate framework for the investigation of vision proper since it involves far-reaching conceptual confusions in the characterization of the phenomena to be studied. For seeing cannot involve the symbolic manipulation of 'internal representations' by the brain, it makes no sense to speak of the mind's having access to the brain's internal representations, and it is absurd to suppose that seeing consists in constructing descriptions. These confusions are not empirical. They are not bold hypotheses that may or may not be borne out by future experiments any more than were the representational theories of the seventeenth and eighteenth centuries. They are conceptual confusions that can be clarified only by careful scrutiny of the logical character of perceptual concepts. The philosophical foundations of modern representational theories of perception are as flawed as those of classical representationalism.

NOTES

I am indebted to Dr J. Hyman for many illuminating discussions on this theme.

1   I. Rosenfield, 'Seeing through the Brain', review of David Marr's *Vision*, in the *New York Review of Books* 31/15 (11 Oct., 1984), 53.
2   Ibid., 56.

3   D. Marr, 'Visual Information Processing: the Structure and Creation of Visual Representations', *Philosophical Transactions of the Royal Society, London* B 290 (1980), 199–218, at p. 203.

4   D. Marr, *Vision, a Computational Investigation into the Human Representation and Processing of Visual Information* (San Francisco: W. H. Freeman, 1980), 3.

5   Ibid., 5.

6   Marr, 'Visual Information Processing', 189.

7   Marr, *Vision*, 3.

8   Ibid.

9   Marr, *Vision*, 29.

10   Ibid., 3.

11   Ibid., 22.

12   Ibid., 23.

13   For detailed discussion see G. Ryle, *The Concept of Mind* (London, Hutchinson, 1949), chs V and VII; F. N. Sibley, 'Seeking, Scrutinizing, and Seeing', *Mind* 64 (1955), 455–78; Z. Vendler, 'Verbs and Times', *The Philosophical Review* 66 (1957), 143–60.

14   I owe this point to Dr J. Hyman.

15   But note that there is no such thing as seeing through a solid object, only detecting, by X-ray devices, what lies behind or within such an object.

16   Marr, *Vision*, 3.

17   J. P. Frisby, *Seeing: Illusion, Brain and Mind* (Oxford: Oxford University Press, 1980), 8–9.

18   Marr, *Vision*, 20.

19   Note the cross-classification: Roman and Arabic numerals differ importantly, but both are decimal notations. Binary typically employs the Arabic numerals 'O' and '1' but is not a decimal notation.

20   It is striking that Marr takes mental images to be descriptions of objects. Both in *Vision* and in 'Visual Information Processing' he cites R. N. Shepard's work. Shepard presented people with pairs of drawings of a figure that differed in orientation, and claimed to have found that the time taken to recognize a pair of pictures as pictures of the same object was proportional to the angle of rotation. From this he inferred that this recognition involved rotating a mental image at constant velocity in mental space. (This is absurd, since there is no such thing as rotating a mental image of an object in one's mind – only imagining a rotating object. And one can imagine an image rotating at constant or variable velocity as one pleases – the imagined velocity is stipulated. It is no more determinable than the imagined weight of an object one imagines weighing is measurable or the gravitational field in one's imagination is observable!) Marr cites this work with approval. It shows, he suggests, that the notion of a (mental or internal) representation must be taken seriously. He piles absurdity upon absurdity by claiming that in these experiments a mental description is being adjusted incrementally in orientation (*Vision*, 10). But not only is a mental image not a rotatable object (any more than is a painted image on a canvas) but also it is not

properly speaking a description. One can indeed turn over (mull over) a description in one's mind – but not by 30°, at constant velocity.

21 J. Locke, *An Essay concerning Human Understanding*, II. iii.1.
22 Marr, *Vision*, 20.
23 Ibid., 21.
24 Ibid.
25 Ibid., 31.
26 Ibid., 31–2.
27 Ibid., 36.
28 Ibid., 3.
29 For a detailed and illuminating account, see J. Hyman, *The Imitation of Nature* (Oxford and New York: Basil Blackwell, 1989), ch. 1.
30 For though it is false that there are any images on or in the pineal gland, it at least makes sense to suppose that there are, whereas (for reasons previously elaborated) it is incoherent to suppose that the brain formulates 3D descriptions in the cortex.

6

THE HOMUNCULUS FALLACY

Anthony Kenny

In the *Philosophical Investigations*, Wittgenstein says: 'Only of a human being and what resembles (behaves like) a living human being can one say: it has sensations; it sees; is blind; hears; is deaf; is conscious or unconscious'.[1] This dictum is often rejected in practice by psychologists, physiologists and computer experts, when they take predicates whose normal application is to complete human beings or complete animals and apply them to parts of animals, such as brains, or to electrical systems. This is commonly defended as a harmless pedagogical device; I wish to argue that it is a dangerous practice which may lead to conceptual and methodological confusion. I shall call the reckless application of human-being predicates to insufficiently human-like objects the 'homunculus fallacy', since its most naïve form is tantamount to the postulation of a little man within a man to explain human experience and behaviour.

One of the first philosophers to draw attention to the homunculus fallacy was Descartes. In his *Dioptrics*, he describes how 'the objects we look at produce very perfect images in the back of the eyes'.[2] He encourages his readers to convince themselves of this by taking the eye of a newly dead man, replacing with paper or eggshell the enveloping membranes at the back, and placing it inside a shutter so as to let light through it into an otherwise dark room. 'You will see (I dare say with surprise and pleasure) a picture representing in natural perspective all the objects outside.' 'You cannot doubt', he continues,

> that a quite similar picture is produced in a living man's eye, on the lining membrane. . . . Further, the images are not only produced in the back of the eye but also sent on to the brain

... and when it is thus transmitted to the inside of our head, the picture still retains some degree of its resemblance to the objects from which it originates.

But he concludes with a warning. 'We must not think that it is by means of this resemblance that the picture makes us aware of the objects – as though we had another pair of eyes to see it, inside our brain.'[3]

To think of the brain as having eyes and seeing the retinal image would be one way of committing the homunculus fallacy. But in spite of warning us against the fallacy at this point, Descartes himself commits it when he comes to discuss the relationship between the soul and the pineal gland:

If we see some animal approach us, the light reflected from its body depicts two images of it, one in each of our eyes, and these two images form two others, by means of the optic nerves, in the interior surface of the brain which faces its cavities; then from there, by means of the animal spirits with which its cavities are filled, these images so radiate towards the little gland which is surrounded by these spirits, that the movement which forms each point of one of the images tends towards the same point of the gland towards which tends the movement which forms the point of the other image which represents the same part of this animal. By this means the two images which are in the brain form but one upon the gland, which, acting immediately upon the soul, causes it to see the form of this animal.[4]

To speak of the soul encountering images in the pineal gland is to commit the homunculus fallacy; for *pace* Descartes, a soul is no more a complete human being than a brain is. In itself, there is nothing philosophically incorrect in speaking of images in the brain: Descartes himself is anxious to explain that they are very schematic images and not pictures except in a metaphorical sense:

No images have to resemble the objects they represent in all respects ... resemblance in a few features is enough, and very often the perfection of an image depends on its not resembling the object as much as it might. For instance, engravings, which consist merely of a little ink spread over paper, represent to us forests, towns, men and even battles and tempests.[5]

There would be nothing philosophically objectionable in the suggestion that these schematic images might be observed by a brain
surgeon investigating the gland. What is misleading is the suggestion
that these images are visible to the *soul*, whose perception of
them constitutes seeing. What is wrong is that exactly the same
sorts of problems arise about Descartes' explanation as about his
explicandum. To the Aristotelians who preceded Descartes, seeing
necessitated a non-mechanistic phenomenon taking place in the eye.
Descartes introduced new mechanisms, but in his system the non-
mechanistic event in the eye is replaced by a new non-mechanistic
reading of patterns in the pineal gland. The interaction between mind
and matter is philosophically as puzzling a few inches behind the eye
as it is in the eye itself.

One danger, then, of the homunculus fallacy is that in problems
concerning perception and kindred matters it conceals what is left to
be explained. In the case of Descartes, we are put on our guard by the
quaintness of some of the physiology, so that we have no difficulty in
discovering the gaps in his account; but the philosophical hiatus can
co-exist with much more sophisticated physiological information.

A contemporary expert on perception, Professor R. L. Gregory, at
the beginning of his book *The Eye and the Brain*, echoes Descartes'
warning against the homunculus fallacy:

> We are so familiar with seeing, that it takes a leap of imagination
> to realize that there are problems to be solved. But consider it.
> We are given tiny distorted upside-down images in the eyes,
> and we see separate solid objects in surrounding space. From
> the patterns of stimulation on the retinas we perceive the world
> of objects, and this is nothing short of a miracle.
>
> The eye is often described as like a camera, but it is the
> quite uncamera-like features of perception which are most
> interesting. How is information from the eyes coded into
> neural terms, into the language of the brain, and reconstituted
> into experience of surrounding objects? The task of eye
> and brain is quite different from either a photographic or
> a television camera converting objects merely into images.
> There is a temptation, which must be avoided, to say that
> the eyes produce pictures in the brain. A picture in the brain
> suggests the need of some kind of internal eye to see it but
> this would need a further eye to see *its* picture . . . and so
> on in an endless regress of eyes and pictures. This is absurd.

What the eyes do is to feed the brain with information coded into neural activity – chains of electrical impulses – which by their code and the patterns of brain activity, represent objects. We may take an analogy from written language; the letters and words on this page have certain meanings, to those who know the language. They affect the reader's brain appropriately, but they are not pictures. When we look at something, the pattern of neural activity represents the objects and to the brain *is* the object. No internal picture is involved.[6]

The warning against the fallacy is excellent; but the fallacy is itself implied in the suggestion that the brain knows a language and that it has an object like the objects of perception. A converse fallacy is committed when it is said that we are given tiny, distorted, upside-down images in the eyes and that we perceive patterns of stimulation on the retina. Here it is not a bogus subject of perception which is being supplied, but a bogus object of perception.

The reader may feel that this is completely unfair criticism. The words I have criticized are taken from the first page of a popular book. What is the harm in personifying parts of the body in order to dramatize scientific information which can be stated in completely neutral metaphor-free language?

Whether dramatization is good pedagogy depends on whether the important events happen on or off stage. The overall psychological problem of perception could be stated as follows: how does a human being cope with the available sensory information, and how does he act on it? Or, in one of Gregory's own formulations, how does information control behaviour? Now this is a problem which would still remain to be solved even if we knew every detail of the process of collection and storage of information; and one crucial aspect of it is the same whether the information is in the world, in the retinas, or in the central nervous system. The problem is this: what is the relation between the presence of information in the technical sense of communication theory and the possession of information in the non-technical sense in which one can acquire information about the world by looking?

For if having information is the same as knowing, then containing information is not the same as having information. An airline schedule contains the information about airline departures; but the airline schedule does not *know* the time of departures of the flights. The illiterate slave on whose shaven scalp the tyrant has tattooed his state secrets does not *know* the information which his head contains.

A category difference is involved here. To contain information is to be in a certain state, while to know something is to possess a certain capacity. A state (such as being a certain shape or size, or having a certain multiplicity or mathematical structure) is something describable by its internal properties; a capacity (such as the ability to run a four-minute mile or to speak French) is describable only by specification of what would count as the exercise of the capacity. States and capacities are of course connected: in the simplest case there is an obvious connection between being a round peg (state) and being able to fit into a round hole (capacity). But the connections are not always (as in that case) analytic; and many forms of expertise consist in knowing which states go with which capacities (e.g. what types of mushroom are poisonous, which alloys will stand which strains).

Knowledge is not a state but a capacity, and a capacity of a unique kind. The state of containing certain information is no doubt connected with the capacity which is knowledge of a certain fact; but the two are not identical, as the earlier examples show. We may wonder what extra is involved in the knowing that p over and above containing the information that p. What is knowing a capacity to do, and what counts as an exercise of that capacity? Clearly, there is no simple answer. One cannot specify behaviour typical of knowing as one can specify behaviour typical of anger. One cannot even specify behaviour typical of knowing that p, for a given p; what behaviour the knowledge that p will lead to will depend on what one wants. For instance, knowledge that the window is open will lead to different behaviour in the case of someone who wants it open and in the case of someone who wants it shut. To be sure, the verbal utterance of 'p' is an activity which is uniquely expressive of the knowledge or belief that p; but even so, this does not at all mean that anyone who knows that p will ever say that p.

There is, then, no simple way of specifying how knowledge gets expressed in behaviour and why some pieces of knowledge do not seem to affect one's behaviour at all. Still, to know is to have the ability to modify one's behaviour in indefinite ways relevant to the pursuit of one's goals. It is because the airline schedule does not have any behaviour to be modified by what is written on it that it does not know what the flight times are.

Let us return from knowing to seeing. Seeing, when not illusory, involves knowing: vision might be defined, crudely, circularly, but not uninformatively, as the acquisition of knowledge in the visual mode. In the Aristotelian tradition, prior to Descartes, it used to be said that it was not the eye that saw, nor the soul, but the whole organism. This was because the normal way to discover whether an organism sees is not just to study its eyes, but to investigate whether its behaviour is affected by changes of light and colour, etc. Consequently, an explanation of seeing must be an explanation not only of the acquisition and storage of information, but also of what makes the containing of this information into knowledge – i.e., its relation to behaviour.

In his paper 'On How So Little Information Controls So Much Behaviour', Gregory well says:

> Perhaps the most fundamental question in the whole field of experimental psychology is: how far is behaviour controlled by currently available sensory information, and how far by information already stored in the central nervous system?[7]

But in that paper he presents a theory of seeing as selection of internal models without saying how the internal models are related to behaviour. He speaks of a model 'calling up the appropriate muscle power' for lifting a certain weight, and of models 'mediating appropriate behaviour',[8] but he nowhere shows how these metaphors might be turned into literal language. What he really explains is how information of a certain type might reach the brain.

Now let us suppose that his explanation of this proves completely correct. Even so, the crucial problem remains; and what is still to be done is masked for the reader, if not for Gregory himself, by the use of homunculus predicates of the brain and the use of intentional or representational or symbolic predicates of items in the brain. Consider the following passage:

> In general the eye's images are biologically important only in so far as non-optical features can be read from the internal models they select. Images are merely patches of light – which cannot be eaten or be dangerous – but they serve as symbols for selecting internal models, which include the non-visual features vital to survival. It is this reading of object characteristics from images that *is* visual perception.[9]

But even if this mechanism is essential for visual perception, it is not visual perception. Selection of internal models would be possible, as seeing would not, in an isolated optical system incapable of behaviour. This is not just the ordinary-language point – 'we wouldn't *call* such a thing seeing' – it is a methodological point concerning the nature of the problems to be solved and the reasonableness of extrapolations from acquired results. The illusion that what is described is visual perception is encouraged by the use of language such as 'features can be *read*' and '*symbols* for selecting'.

Later in the same paper Gregory writes:

> On this general view perception is not directly of sensory information but rather of the internal models selected by sensory information. Indeed the current perception is the prevailing set of models.[10]

Clearly, it is inadequate to explain what perception is by saying that it is perception not of X but of Y: if I wonder what *perception* is, how am I helped by being told that it is of Y rather than of X? Gregory senses this: that is why his first statement of this thesis is followed by 'indeed' followed by a statement of an incompatible thesis. Perception cannot both be *of* the models and be the models.

So far my objection to the homunculus model has been that it is pedagogically and methodologically dangerous, as helping to cloak the nature of problems to be solved. But there is a more dangerous effect of the model which alone really deserves the name 'fallacy'.

Let us suppose that we waive our objections to the use of human-being predicates for non-human-beings like brains. Let us allow it to be said that the brain is P, where P is some predicate whose natural application is to whole human beings. (It may, after all, be used in quotes. It usually is – the first time.) There is still an important temptation to be resisted: the temptation to argue from

This man is P
to This man's brain is P

or vice versa. Gregory does not always resist this temptation. At the beginning of the quoted paper he argues that learning or storing particular events is always ontogenetic. Naturally stored information, he says, has two origins: ancestral disasters, and previous experience of the individual stored as 'memory'.[11] To prove that storage of particular events is always ontogenetic, he says:

> What is certain is that information gained phylogenetically is always of the general 'skill' kind. We are not able to recall individual events experienced by our ancestors.[12]

And apropos of learning skills such as tennis and piano playing, he says:

We may be able to recall the odd particular games or concerts, but as skills it is not individual past events which are stored, but rather appropriate behaviour and strategies.[13]

Here the homunculus fallacy is committed thus: 'X remembers that *p*' is being treated as equivalent to 'X has stored the event that *p*'. The only reason given for saying that information about particular events is not stored phylogenetically is that we cannot recall individual events in our ancestors' lives. But this is to argue from 'This man is not *P*' to 'This man's brain is not *P*' which is fallacious, even if the man's brain's being *P* is a necessary condition for his own being *P*.

In another paper, 'Perceptual Illusions and Brain Models', Gregory considers whether the brain is best regarded as a digital or as an analogue device. He writes:

It is most implausible to suppose that the brain of a child contains mathematical analyses of physical situations. When a child builds a house of toy bricks, balancing them to make walls and towers, we cannot suppose that the structural problems are solved by employing analytical mathematical techniques, involving concepts such as centre of gravity and coefficient of friction of masses. It is far better to make the lesser claim for children and animals: that they behave appropriately to objects by using analogues of senses object-properties, without involving mathematical analyses of the properties of objects and their interactions. Perceptual learning surely cannot require the learning of mathematics. It is far more plausible to suppose that it involves the building of quite simple analogues of relevant properties of objects: relevant so far as they concern the behaviour of the animal or the child.[14]

Here the homunculus fallacy is committed in the sentence, 'Perceptual learning surely cannot require the learning of mathematics.' It is the child that is doing the perceptual learning; what, if anything, is supposed to be learning mathematics is the child's brain. It is implausible that a child building toy bricks should know advanced mathematics; but from this nothing at all follows about what information is contained in the child's brain.

I conclude that there is good reason to heed the warning of Wittgenstein with which this chapter began. The moral is not that the human-being predicates cannot have their use extended at all, but that they must be extended cautiously and self-consciously, and that if they are extended one may not argue from the application of such a predicate to a whole human being to the application of the transferred predicate to anything other than the whole human being.

POSTSCRIPT

In a brief postscript, I wish to clarify some of the points made above, and to disown some of the theses attributed to me by some of those who read that part of this chapter. First, I do not accuse Professor Gregory of mistaking mechanistic description for conceptual analysis; nor do I think that either the philosopher's answer or the neurophysiologist's answer to the question 'what is perception?' enjoys a privileged status. Second, I do not object to every extension of the application of a predicate from a sentient whole to its parts. Third, I took up no position on the general question whether conscious activities can be said to *be* (nothing but) the micro-structural processes postulated to explain them. I will expand each of these points, and then briefly restate why I call the homunculus fallacy a fallacy.

I do not think that Gregory is under any illusion that he is doing conceptual analysis. I think he is engaged in constructing, and testing experimentally, hypotheses about the mechanisms necessary to explain the phenomena of visual perception. But conceptual analysis is relevant to what he is doing in two ways. First, analysis of the concept of perception is necessary to delimit what are the phenomena to be explained; second, analysis of the concepts of sight and language show that such things as seeing and decoding cannot be done by brains unless we can attribute to brains certain types of behaviour which we can attribute to whole human beings. To attribute such activities to brains without suggesting how the relevant behaviour might be attributable to brains is, I maintained, to mask empirical problems which remain to be solved.

The moral of my chapter, I said, was not that human-being predicates cannot have their use extended at all, but that their use must be extended cautiously. Consequently, I am unmoved if it is pointed out that hands can grasp and hold: such extensions seem to me well within the bounds of caution. Moreover, my objection was not essentially to predicates of wholes being attached to predicates of parts, but to predicates belonging to human beings being attached to non-human beings. The same fallacy could be committed (though my name for it would not be apt) by the incautious application of human-being predicates to wholes of which human beings are parts, such as communities and states. Populations, like human beings, grow and shrink; but it would obviously be fallacious to argue that a human being was shrinking because the population he belongs to is shrinking, or that a population is growing because every member of it is growing. And states may have intentions which none of their citizens has.[15]

The question whether perception can be said to be identical with physiological processes seems to me to lack a clear sense, and I do not wish to answer it one way or the other. My complaint against Gregory's identification of visual perception with his postulated selection of internal models was not based on a general thesis that perception cannot be identical with a brain process. Though states and capacities are conceptually different, it need not be misleading to say (e.g.) that a peg's ability to fit into round holes *is* its roundness. In the same way, it may be that there is a physiological process – the acquisition of a physiological state – which can be said to *be* visual perception. But no one can claim to have identified such a process until he has brought out its connection with the types of behaviour which are the criteria for the occurrence of visual perception. And this Gregory has not done.

A fallacy, strictly speaking, is a form of argument which can lead from true premises to a false conclusion. The inappropriate use of predicates, not being a form of argument, is not strictly a fallacy, as I observed. But it leads to a form of argument, which I claimed to detect in Gregory's articles, which is fallacious in the strict sense of the word: the argument that because a certain human-being predicate attaches to a human being it attaches to his brain, or vice versa. The mere inappropriate use of human-being predicates may be called a fallacy in an extended sense, because it may suggest conclusions which are unjustified – notably the conclusion that more has been explained by a psychological theory than has in fact been explained.

Normally, in an adult human being, the ability to see carries with it the ability to say what is seen, though of course not everything which is actually seen is actually talked about. The use of language to report what is seen, like any use of language, is remarkably free from stimulus control – a point which has been repeatedly made, in general terms, by Chomsky. No account of human perception can approach adequacy unless it includes an explanation of this fact. Consequently, even if we knew every detail of the physiological processes by which visual information reaches the brain, and every detail of the physiological processes by which the linguistic utterance of visual reports is produced, the problem of the relationship between the input and the output would be completely untouched. This problem is a major part of the problem of the physiological explanation of perception, and its existence is masked by talk of the brain reading features of objects from images and calling up appropriate muscle power.

NOTES

1   L. Wittgenstein, *Philosophical Investigations* (Oxford: Basil Blackwell, 1953), § 281.

2   R. Descartes, 'Dioptrics', in *Philosophical Writings*, trans. and ed. E. Anscombe and P. T. Geach (Edinburgh: Nelson, 1954), 239–56, at 244.

3   Ibid., 245–6.

4   R. Descartes, 'Passions of the Soul', in *The Philosophical Works of Descartes*, I, trans. and ed. E. S. Haldane and G. R. T. Ross (Cambridge: Cambridge University Press, 1931), 329–429, at 348.

5   'Dioptrics', 246.

6   R. L. Gregory, *The Eye and the Brain* (London: McGraw-Hill, 1966), 7.

7   R. L. Gregory, in *Bionics Research Reports* I (April 1968), 1 (this paper was also published in C. H. Waddington (ed.), *Towards a Theoretical Biology*, II (Edinburgh: Edinburgh University Press, 1969), 236–46).

8   Ibid., 8.

9   Ibid., 5.

10 Ibid., 8.

11 Ibid., 1 (his quotes).

12 Ibid.

13 Ibid.

14 R. L. Gregory, in *Proceedings of the Royal Society* B, 171 (1968), 279–96, at 294.

15 Cf. L. Wittgenstein, *Zettel*, ed. G. E. M. Anscombe and G. H. von Wright, trans. G. E. M. Anscombe (Oxford: Basil Blackwell, 1967), 1–48.

7

VISUAL EXPERIENCE AND BLINDSIGHT

John Hyman

Philosophers and psychologists share a taste for the bizarre. Philosophers have been known to speculate about brain transplants, the destruction and reconstruction of a human being and even the existence of a twin earth, complete with the twin of every living creature on the planet we inhabit. By comparison, the curiosities one can encounter in psychological textbooks and journals seem small fry. Nevertheless, there is an analogy between the purposes served by philosophical and psychological studies of this sort, for in both cases the oddity is supposed to show something about the norm, whether this is the normal behaviour of a concept or the normal functioning of whatever processes underlie our possession and exercise of psychological capacities. This chapter will examine a psychological phenomenon which is sufficiently strange to have proved of interest both to psychologists and to philosophers. The phenomenon is known as 'blindsight'.

I

The term 'blindsight', originally part of 'a temptingly catchy title for a local seminar',[1] was coined by Professor L. Weiskrantz as a name for the ostensibly paradoxical visual capacity of a subject known as D.B. whom he tested repeatedly in the 1970s, in collaboration with Elizabeth Warrington and others. After the surgical removal of his right occipital lobe, D.B. was found by ordinary clinical tests to be absolutely blind in the left half of his visual field, except for a small crescent of fuzzy vision at the top. However, the tests subsequently conducted by Weiskrantz yielded curious results:

166

We decided to use more or less the same method that Cowey, Clare Passingham and I had been using with destriated monkeys – reaching towards the stimulus with the extended arm and hand. Even though D.B. could not 'see' the lights, his accuracy was quite remarkable. He was given no knowledge of results during the test, and when shown his results at the end of the experiment he was openly astonished – he thought he had been guessing. We went on to show that D.B. could discriminate between horizontal, vertical and diagonal lines and also between simple patterns, provided the stimuli were larger than a critical size and provided he was required to 'guess' on a forced choice basis.[2]

As well as establishing the precise characteristics of D.B.'s visual capacity,[3] Weiskrantz and his colleagues repeatedly asked D.B. to say what he thought he saw.

Soon after surgery he was not aware of stimuli in his blind field at all, except for vigorously moving stimuli in some regions of the field which he described as not actually moving but as producing peculiar radiating lines. Later he gradually came to say that with relatively salient stimuli – large, contrasting, moving – he was 'aware' of something, he 'knew something was there', and roughly where it was, but he did not in any sense 'see' it – about this he was absolutely firm. . . . But, even so, as the stimuli are made less salient . . . [or] if they are directed into the dead 'heart' of the field defect, he reverts to saying that he is not aware of anything and is 'just guessing'. At this level, as we have said, he can still perform with high reliability – well over 95%.[4]

Apart from the summary of experimental results, three major conclusions are drawn in the 1980 lecture. First, Weiskrantz remarks that 'one of the lessons of neuropsychology is that inferences about normal processing stem less from the study of dysfunction as such than from dissociations of dysfunctions.'[5] Second, he concludes that the phenomenon of blindsight involves two quite different types of dissociation. The first is between different perceptual abilities, which are distinguished in terms of what the subject is capable of perceiving, e.g. form, location, orientation, movement. The second

is of a different sort. It is between a visual discrimination and the commentary offered by the subject himself . . . [This] type of dissociation is not merely one of verbal disconnection. The discriminative response can be verbal ... or non-verbal ... – it is between reacting and monitoring.[6]

Visual capacity, Weiskrantz argues, normally goes hand in hand with 'monitoring', or 'awareness', which is 'a form of privileged access': 'As far as neural processes are concerned,' he adds, 'it is probably a minority privilege.'[7] In the case of blindsight, the privilege has been rescinded, because of the 'disconnexion of the monitoring system'.[8] Third and finally, Weiskrantz suggests that the phenomenon of blindsight exemplifies 'Luciani's distinction between mental and sensorial processing'.[9]

This distinction is expounded earlier in the lecture, where Weiskrantz quotes Luciani's interpretation of the results of vivisection in monkeys. Luciani asked whether extirpation of the visual cortical centres robbed monkeys of their visual perceptions and their visual sensations, or whether it was only the visual perceptions, which are the result of 'elaborat[ing] psychically the visual sensations',[10] that were lost. In a passage quoted by Weiskrantz, he gave the answer:

> When some time has elapsed after the extirpation, their visual sensations become perfect again; they are able to see minute objects, what they want is the discernment of things and a right judgement concerning their properties and their nature; they are deficient, in a word, of visual perception.[11]

Earlier experiments with dogs had yielded a similar result: in spite of 'the most extensive extirpation of the occipito-temporal area ... the animal [eventually] begins again to make use of sight in the search for its food, but is not able to distinguish meat from sugar by its visual impressions only'.[12] Luciani's interpretation, remarks Weiskrantz, 'must be right'.[13]

Weiskrantz refers to a distinction between different sorts of mental process whereas Luciani seems, on the whole, to have envisaged a distinction between different sorts of mental entity. Nevertheless, the recent experiments with monkeys that Weiskrantz describes are supposed to have settled in Luciani's favour a debate that took place in the last decades of the nineteenth century. The dogs and monkeys on which he experimented were not simply made amblyopic, i.e. their vision was not merely dimmed or blurred; rather, their capacity for visual perception was destroyed, but their capacity for visual sensation was not. And the case of D.B., together with similar cases that emerged in the 1970s, is supposed to have demonstrated, contrary to received opinion, that Luciani's analysis can be extended to cover the neuropsychology of human beings: 'Luciani's distinction between mental and sensorial processing first emerged in research with animals 100 years ago,' writes Weiskrantz, 'but . . . its application to the early stages of the cortical visual system of man took . . . very much longer.'[14]

The recovery of visual abilities demonstrated by monkeys after vivisection stood for the best part of a hundred years in puzzling contrast to the avowals of blindness made by human beings who had lost, through injury or surgery, (more or less) anatomically corresponding parts of the brain. William James, for example, acknowledged the existence of 'psychic blindness' in human beings ('psychic blindness' is the name that Luciani, following Munk, gave to the loss of visual perceptions alone),[15] but he considered that it was invariably the result of the 'interruption of the paths between the optic centres and the centres for other ideas':[16] the destruction of the occipital lobes in human beings, James averred, always causes 'total blindness, sensorial as well as psychic'.[17] 'But is man really so fundamentally different from the lower primates?' asks Weiskrantz:[18] the case of D.B. apparently entitles us to reply that he is not.

II

Weiskrantz's research, and the research of others in the same field, came under attack in an article by Campion, Latto and Smith, which was published with Open Peer Commentary in *The Behavioral and Brain Sciences*.[19] Campion and his co-authors argue first, that if the clinical syndrome that Weiskrantz and others describe, differing markedly from degraded normal vision, actually exits it may be 'open to alternative nonblindsight interpretations' (p. 424) – i.e. the residual capacity of these subjects may be mediated by spared cortex after all; and second, that in fact there is no such syndrome – as far as we can tell, blindsight does not exist. This may sound rather like a lawyer arguing that his client was severely provoked and has a cast-iron alibi – but this inconsistency alone does not entitle us to reject either line of argument *a priori*.

The first argument turns on the claim that 'the issue of striate versus extrastriate mediation of function can only be satisfactorily solved . . . by histological examination of the brain tissue since without such anatomical evidence it is impossible to compare blindsight with degraded striate vision' (p. 445). Hence, although 'we cannot prove that blindsight, defined as nonstriate vision, does not exist . . . parsimony should lead us to reject it on the present evidence' (p. 446).

This straightforward argument, Campion and his co-authors claim, is obscured by confusion between two senses of the term 'blindsight', for if we use the term both to denote a residual capacity within a scotoma and to mean a visual capacity that does not depend upon striate tissue, then shifting between one sense and the other will make it all too easy to avoid facing the question of what sort of evidence entitles us to suppose that a residual capacity within a scotoma does *not* depend upon striate tissue. Thus the authors contend that although 'blindness defined by perimetry does not represent, necessarily, all and only striate destruction . . . the converse of this is the (at least implicit) assumption behind all blindsight studies' (p. 481).

A confusion of this sort is certainly a serious matter.[20] But the confusion appears to have been introduced into the discussion of blindsight by Campion and his co-authors, and not by Weiskrantz. For whereas the latter wrote, 'we cannot prove that blindsight, *defined as nonstriate vision*, does not exist' (p. 446, italics added), Weiskrantz has consistently used the term 'blindsight' to mean a residual capacity within a scotoma which is exercised despite the subject's concurrent avowal of blindness. I shall continue to use the term in this way, to denote a residual capacity, whatever its physical vehicle.

It is, needless to say, reasonable to demand evidence in support of the claim that blindsight is mediated by non-striate tissue, but Weiskrantz does not shirk the demand for evidence, and cover this up with a terminological sleight of hand. Whilst acknowledging that a definitive judgement will have to await post-mortem examination, he advances the hypothesis that D.B.'s residual capacity does not depend upon degraded striate tissue, first, on the grounds that it is 'qualitatively different' from normal vision or degraded normal vision (double dissociation is considered to be strong, if not decisive, evidence),[21] and second, by analogy with animal studies. However, Campion and his co-authors dismiss the animal studies as 'largely irrelevant', arguing that 'the animal work . . . has nothing to say about the soundness or otherwise of the human data' (p. 479); and as we have seen, they also question the relevance of behavioural evidence: 'the issue of striate versus extrastriate mediation of function can only satisfactorily be solved ... by histological examination of the brain tissue' (p. 445). Regrettably, the authors are inconsistent on this point, or else undecided. On the one hand they claim, in conformity with the last remark quoted, that 'a functional dissociation between awareness and localisation performance ... is irrelevant to the more important issue of destriate function' (p. 481); on the other hand they accept that 'lack of awareness could imply a visual capacity that was qualitatively different from normal perception and would thus reinforce the notion of nonstriate mediation' (p. 435).

However, we can set this problem to one side, for as remarked above a second line of attack is intended to show that we have as yet no evidence that blindsight, considered simply as a clinical syndrome, exists. This is obviously the more radical of the two lines of attack, and it turns on two quite different considerations. First, it is argued that experimenters have failed to guarantee that stimuli within a scotoma were not scattering light outside it; and second, the authors claim that the dissociations purportedly observed by Weiskrantz and others were in fact manufactured by their experimental procedures, and hence the apparent difference between blindsight and degraded normal vision is illusory. Thus, even if the qualitative differences between blindsight and degraded normal vision described by Weiskrantz could be counted as evidence that residual capacity within a scotoma does not depend upon striate tissue, the latter hypothesis remains as yet unfounded: subjects may have been responding to stimuli outside their scotomata; and furthermore, 'despite extravagant claims both inside and outside the blindsight literature, complete dissociations are *never* seen in blindsight' (p. 481).

On the issue of scattered light, the authors later (in their replies to commentators) acknowledge that at least one of Weiskrantz's tests was safe in this respect,[22] and so I shall turn directly to the second claim, the claim that dissociations were manufactured by Weiskrantz's experimental procedures. The reader will recall that Weiskrantz distinguished between two kinds of dissociation, the first between different discriminative abilities and the second 'between reacting and monitoring'. Campion and his co-authors deny that either has been satisfactorily demonstrated, but the debate over the first kind of dissociation is unhelpful: Weiskrantz complains that

Campion and his co-authors have neglected vital evidence;[23] and they retort that 'no data at all were provided for the dissociation studies, which were described in 14 lines of anecdotal evidence' (p. 479). Their discussion of the second kind of dissociation is less abrupt and more interesting.

The dissociation 'between reacting and monitoring' is, of course, the crux of blindsight. 'The problem that has captured the interest of blindsight researchers . . .' Weiskrantz notes, arose 'directly from the study of the patients themselves and in their relation to behavioural and physiological evidence from animals. It was the disjunction between their verbal reports and their discriminative capacity that was surprising.'[24] As we shall see, Campion and his co-authors argue that blindsight research incorporates experimental procedures that are bound to manufacture evidence for a dissociation between visual capacities and visual awareness, and misrepresents the nature of the scotoma.

Initially, Campion and his co-authors do not dispute the evidence for a dissociation 'between reacting and monitoring' in blindsight studies. They simply wonder what the fuss was about, for 'it is a common observation that when detecting near-threshold stimuli, subjects are frequently unaware that their performance is better than chance' (p. 425). D.B.'s reaction to the results of the experiments was therefore only to be expected; and what has been called 'blindsight' is simply degraded normal vision, which is directly comparable to the visual capacity of the normally sighted in near darkness.

In order to test this analogy, we need to compare D.B.'s residual capacity in the scotoma with his capacity for forced-choice discriminations of peripheral stimuli in the intact field, which Weiskrantz has done:

> when we measured detection (presence/absence of a spot) at a far peripheral location (80°), he said that he did not see the light. With forced-choice guessing, however, he scored at 21/30 and 20/30 correct, scores that are above chance. . . . But they are well below the 90 to 100 per cent performance that D.B. can display with a variety of stimuli in his field defect which he also reports not seeing.[25]

Correspondingly, if the visual stimuli in the intact field and in the scotoma are engineered to yield, for example, the same statistical relationship between 'hits' and false alarms, D.B. still insists that he sees the stimulus in the intact field, but not in the scotoma.[26]

This settles the matter in Weiskrantz's favour, if the evidence for a dissociation in respect of stimuli within D.B.'s scotoma is unimpeachable. However, the authors' second objection to the proposed dissociation is that the experimental procedures in blindsight studies 'minimise the evidence for awareness and maximise the evidence for performance' (p. 481). 'By this argument,' they add, 'blindsight would simply represent the extreme end of a continuum of sensitivity varying from normal vision to complete blindness' (p. 482). This objection is fundamental, but even the paper's most sympathetic commentator (Professor R. Haber) concludes that it cannot be sustained, at least on the evidence presented. The objection obviously rests upon the assumption that perimetry, the technique used to plot a scotoma, 'defines an area of unawareness of a stimulus ... under conditions that enforce a *conservative* criterion' (p. 481, italics added): in other words, it is cogent only if perimetry 'is bound to underestimate visual sensitivity' (p. 425). However, as Haber notes, this assumption fails to take account of a subject's willingness or otherwise to acknowledge awareness of a barely detected stimulus. 'It is quite possible,' he remarks, 'and perhaps even likely, that a patient being tested in a perimeter has many reasons to set a very risky rather than a cautious criterion, thereby responding yes to the slightest hint of light' (p. 454). And if a subject is inclined to acknowledge awareness when he is uncertain, then evidence of blindsight will, of course, be suppressed rather than manufactured.

Campion and his co-authors might have mustered evidence for the claim that 'perimetry is bound to underestimate visual sensitivity' had they not been persuaded that the proposed dissociation between D.B.'s perceptual abilities and his awareness of a visual stimulus – 'between reacting and monitoring' – must in any case be rejected on *a priori* grounds. For their final objection to the proposed dissociation is simply that they doubt whether any psychological investigation which depends upon distinguishing between those occasions when a subject is conscious of a stimulus and those occasions when he is not can lay claim to scientific rigour: 'the unconscious aspect of blindsight ...' they remark, 'is impossible to treat scientifically' (p. 427); and in the concluding section of the paper, they argue that 'Consciousness is an elusive concept ... [and] it would therefore seem more productive to ignore it as an issue and concentrate on establishing empirical relations between neural structures and behaviour' (p. 446). 'Unconsciousness' (in this context at least) and 'blindsight' are terms 'that have no place in a scientific study of the brain' (p. 483).

I shall shortly consider how these behaviourist strictures bear on the problem of blindsight; but I do not propose to examine them in the general form they take here. For one thing, this general claim about the limits of scientific psychology is more or less withdrawn in the replies to commentary (p. 481, final paragraph); and for another, it is too imprecise for useful comment. Notice for example that there are two concepts of consciousness, which we distinguish in terms of the fact that used one way the word 'conscious' takes an object, and used the other way it does not.[27] Thus on the one hand a person may be conscious (or aware) of a dog barking or his teacher's disapproval; on the other hand, we may have occasion to say that he is conscious or unconscious *simpliciter* – if he has been knocked out or sedated, for example. So, what constraints are placed on the neuropsychology of anaesthesia, or sleep, by the proposal that we 'ignore [consciousness] as an issue'? And if the behaviour we are invited to correlate with 'neural structures' includes verbal behaviour, when is a subject's verbal behaviour merely verbal behaviour, and when is it an unreliable 'report . . . on his subjective experiences' (p. 435), beyond the pale of scientific enquiry?

However, these ill-defined anxieties about the place of consciousness in scientific psychology assume a more urgent and a more precise form when Campion and his co-authors discuss the nature of the scotoma. Perimetry, they argue, does not establish the boundaries of consciousness: it is 'an entirely arbitrary, but nevertheless clinically useful' method for determining an area of markedly reduced visual sensitivity (p. 481). Consequently, they are happy to accept Pöppel's claim that 'residual vision in areas of the visual field that are perimetrically blind is certainly a fact' (p. 459): 'what is not meaningful is to extend this definition of a scotoma so that it includes a definition of consciousness' (p. 481). The implication of this view is that 'using behavioural criteria alone [i.e., ignoring any evidence which bears on the question of what D.B. is aware of], blindsight would simply be taken to show that the subject was not blind' (p. 435).

Once again, therefore, Campion and his co-authors conclude that D.B.'s residual capacity is directly comparable to the truncated capacity of the normally sighted in near-darkness. However, the argument is based on a methodological principle, rather than an actual comparison of D.B.'s residual capacity within the scotoma and his sub-threshold capacity in the intact field. As we have seen, that comparison showed that the radical and systematic dissociation of D.B.'s visual capacity and his visual reports is not reproduced by peripheral stimuli in the intact field. But if all the evidence speaks against an analogy between blindsight and near-threshold vision, why protect it by methodological gerrymandering?

The critique of blindsight that we have examined failed to provide a single cogent challenge to Weiskrantz's experimental procedures or his results. The critique finally turns on the repudiation of a dissociation between 'reacting and monitoring', and this repudiation finally rests upon a methodological principle. We shall, in due course, examine the principle. For the moment, it is sufficient to note that even if one regards a subject's verbal commentary as an unverifiable report of a private experience – as Campion and his co-authors evidently do – it does not follow that the commentary can be ignored. For whatever its status *qua* report, the verbal commentary is an utterance, an ineradicable part of the complex response to a visual stimulus. The argument against regarding blindsight as a case of sub-threshold vision depends only upon the systematic difference between verbal responses to stimuli within D.B.'s field defect and peripheral stimuli in the intact field which have been engineered to yield a similar performance in the forced-choice tasks. It does not depend upon any dubious claims about D.B.'s private experiences.

III

There appears to be something paradoxical about blindsight. For it appears that we can only do it justice by tearing apart the language of vision. D.B. is not, after all, *absolutely* blind in the so-called 'blind' part of his visual field. And yet – how can we deny it? – *he sees nothing.* He says that he sees nothing, and it seems no less absurd to suggest that he is mistaken than it would be to suggest that what people say about their present thoughts and sensations can sometimes be mistaken.

Compare the case of sensations. It is not merely unlikely or implausible that anybody should mistake a stomach-ache for a headache, for there is no such thing as a mistake of this kind, just as there is no such thing as tasting the size of something, or smelling its weight. If I said one morning that the previous day I had – unusually – supposed myself to have a stomach-ache when in fact I had a headache, it would be wrong to call this a blatant falsehood; for it is, in fact, a rather curious sort of nonsense – not exactly gibberish, but not unlike the stuff of fairy tales and playful jokes.

But if it is absurd to imagine a mistake of this kind, is it less absurd to imagine a person mistakenly supposing that he cannot see? D.B. denies that he can see, and who are we to doubt him? And yet the experimental evidence is unequivocal. The paradox of blindsight lies in the fact that we want to deny that D.B. is blind *and* that he can see. In other words, the phenomenon seems to demand a nonsensical description. Hence its name.

The analogy between blindsight and sub-threshold vision was intended to dispel this air of paradox, by softening the harsh contradiction between discriminative capacity and verbal commentary.[28] Weiskrantz's own explanation of the difference between D.B. and the normally sighted is very different. He suggests that the ability to make visual discriminations, the ability to react to what is present in the visible environment, normally goes hand in hand with 'monitoring', which is 'a form of privileged access', but in D.B.'s case the monitoring system has become disconnected. And he also says that blindsight exemplifies Luciani's distinction between mental and sensorial processing. I shall discuss both of these suggestions, the first (in this section and in section IV) at considerably greater length than the second (in section V).

As far as monitoring is concerned, I shall argue that the idea of a monitoring system is not a scientific hypothesis, but the product of a philosophical picture of psychological experience, a picture which has influenced *a priori* and experimental psychologists alike since the seventeenth century, including both Weiskrantz and his detractors. This picture (it is too varied in its manifestations and too diffuse to be called a theory) can be constructed in two stages. First, imagine sensation – having an itch or a toothache – on the model of perception. It is not a matter of perceiving some feature of the environment, a house or a tree, but it is tempting to think of sensation as the perception of something inner, a private and ethereal object. Now imagine perception on the model of sensation, and it will seem that when we perceive a house or a tree, what we are *immediately* aware of is again a private phenomenon, although one which corresponds in a way that an itch does not to an actual physical object in our vicinity – the actual house or tree.

According to this picture, our ability to say what we think and desire, and what we feel and see, depends always upon our awareness of a private mental phenomenon; and this awareness (unlike our awareness of the physical features of our environment) has generally been thought to be infallible.[29] Descartes, for example, stated that

> our perceptions are of two sorts, and the one have the soul as a cause and the other the body. Those which have the soul as a cause are the perceptions of our desires and of all the imaginations or other thoughts which depend on them. For it is certain that we cannot desire anything without perceiving by the same means that we desire it.[30]

As this quotation shows, my perfect awareness of the present contents of my mind was thought of as a sort of perception. It could not of course be attributed to the use of a physical organ like an eye or an ear; but it was nevertheless assumed that we possess a quasi-perceptual faculty, an interior perceptual faculty which somehow always ensures that we have, in John Stuart Mill's words, 'the knowledge which nobody denies us to have, of what passes in our minds'.

However, there is an inherent instability in the idea of an introspective faculty. For, on the one hand, as long as I restrict myself to a description of how things *seem* to me, I cannot possibly be mistaken. And yet it is difficult to see how a faculty which is conceived on the model of our notoriously fallible perceptual faculties could be perfectly immune from error.

Descartes responded to this ticklish situation by claiming that the perception and its object are one and the same. One can see why. For if the perception and its object were independent of each other, one could exist without the other, which would imply that I could have the mere illusion of a painful sensation, or conversely, I could have an intense pain without knowing it. Nevertheless, if we conceive of self-knowledge on the model of a perceptual faculty, and yet we also claim that the experiences of which we are aware and our introspective awareness of them are one and the same, we take with one hand what we gave with the other: the perceptual model is no sooner invoked than exploded; and the obscure question of what enables us to know our own minds is left unanswered. Perhaps this is why Mill preferred to explain the infallibility of the introspective faculty by means of a dignified platitude: 'Whatever we are directly aware of, we can directly observe.'[31]

However it was accounted for, a faculty for introspection was from the outset an indispensable component of the broader philosophical picture. I shall shortly argue that the private phenomena which each of us is supposed to apprehend in his own mind are elements of a philosophical fantasy, and hence the idea of an introspective faculty is confused and redundant. And I shall argue that the idea of a monitoring system is a variation on the theme of a faculty for introspection. I shall begin by discussing the theme, and then return to the variation in section IV. Because the philosophical picture I have sketched is developed in the two stages mentioned, I shall begin by focusing on sensation.

The decisive arguments against this philosophical picture of the mind can be found in the writings of Ludwig Wittgenstein;[32] and the crucial insight which enabled Wittgenstein to dismantle it was that it ultimately rests upon a hidden and mistaken assumption about language.

In his *Philosophical Investigations*, Wittgenstein argued that the picture of the human mind as an interior world to which only its owner has direct access goes hand in hand with a conception of language as essentially descriptive. According to this conception, describing a battle or a landscape is one sort of description and describing a sensation or a perceptual experience is another, but the difference between these sorts of description consists simply in the difference between the sorts of things described. 'The Assyrian came down like a wolf on the fold' and 'My foot hurts' differ inasmuch as the subject-matter of the first comment is military and historical, whereas the second concerns only my present sensations, but the first comment describes the relevant historical fact in just the same way as the second describes the relevant psychological fact, and both comments are informative in virtue of their corresponding in this way to the facts.

In effect, Wittgenstein realized that the apparent analogy between these comments, their apparently common descriptive purpose, is both a major source of the analogy between a putative faculty for interior perception and the faculties of sight and hearing, and the indispensable prop that keeps it from collapsing. Being in severe pain does not force us to think in terms of an interior perceptual faculty, and neither does contemplating another's pain. But if we regard words such as 'pain', 'tickle' and 'itch' as names of sensations, words whose meanings are learned when they are associated with the corresponding sensations, and which are put to use when we describe our experience – 'My foot hurts', 'That tickles', and so forth – then some kind of faculty to perceive these features of our mental lives must exist, for how else could you 'read off what you say from the facts'?[33] And the unassailable confidence with which we make utterances of this kind will in consequence be attributed to the unerring accuracy of that faculty.

Wittgenstein urged that we 'make a radical break with the idea that language always functions in one way, always serves the same purpose',[34] and challenged the analogy between a remark describing, for example, an historical incident and a first-person, present-tense psychological statement – the type of utterance which has been called an 'avowal'. The challenge consists of an intricately woven fabric of argument which is designed to show that avowals do not serve a descriptive purpose at all; that words such as 'pain', 'tickle' and 'itch' should not be viewed as names of – as it were, labels attached to – psychological items; that the meanings of such words could not be determined by associating them with features of mental experience; and hence that this cannot be how we learn to use such words.

One of the central strands of Wittgenstein's argument begins by inviting us to suppose that a person, whom we may call A, decides to name a particular sensation 'S' so that he will be able, in future, to keep a record of its occurrence. A christens the sensation 'S', precisely by associating the sign and the sensation: he concentrates his attention on the sensation, and says 'S!'. But what, asks Wittgenstein, makes this performance an act of christening? For the mere concurrence of the utterance and the sensation will not give the sign a meaning. After all, I can gaze at the moon and say 'Tra-la', but I shall not thereby have given it a name.

We can approach an answer to the question by considering what the christening is supposed to achieve. This much is clear: if the performance actually christens the sensation and gives a meaning to the sign, then it will determine what is to count as a correct use of the sign, and what is not. For this is the difference between meaningful signs and meaningless ones: a meaningful sign, unlike a mere squiggle, can be used correctly or incorrectly. And we can employ the definition of the sign to confirm that its use on a particular occasion was correct, or incorrect, rather as one would use the sample of a fabric to show that a skirt was made from that fabric, or that it was not.

An actual christening, or the ceremony at which the President of the United States is sworn in, gives a child a name, or confers upon a man the powers and duties of a president, because we treat these rituals as authoritative; and this in turn implies that we participate in a complex, regulated practice in which certain patterns of behaviour count as acknowledging authority and others count as flouting it. No magic spell is cast, and no invisible thread is used to tie an infant and its name together. It is in virtue of the role that we accord these rituals in our subsequent behaviour that they possess their normative status. In these cases, power does not compel obedience: obedience is the source of power.

Similarly, if A's performance christens his sensation, it does so because thereafter he will call upon it if need be to bear authoritative witness that his use of the sign is correct. Stated without metaphor, the point is this: when A seems to recognize a sensation as the one he christened and says 'There's S again!' he must be able to justify his use of the sign – i.e., to confirm that he has used it correctly – by invoking the sensation that he christened. Otherwise, there will be no reason to regard the original performance as a definition. But since the sensation never existed beyond the confines of his mind, 'invoking the sensation' can only mean 'remembering what sensation he associated with the sign', and thus he would appear to be checking his memory against itself, or one memory of the sensation against another. But this is absurd: it is as if one tried to use a ruler to measure itself; or, as Wittgenstein said, 'as if someone were to buy several copies of the morning paper to assure himself that what it said was true'.[35]

Isn't it nevertheless possible that he is using the sign correctly? Granted, he cannot *confirm* that his present sensation is the one that he christened, but that alone doesn't show that it isn't. This objection misses the point. What concerns us is not whether A has the same sensation on both occasions, but whether 'S' has a meaning, i.e. whether A has defined the sign merely by uttering the sound and simultaneously concentrating his attention on the sensation. Even if we accept that on some later occasion he utters the same sound whilst concentrating his attention on the same sensation, this alone does not imply that 'S' actually means anything, and that what it means was determined by the original ceremony. 'Why can't my right hand give my left hand money?' asks Wittgenstein.

My right hand can put it into my left hand. My right hand can write a deed of gift and my left hand a receipt. – But the further practical consequences would not be those of a gift. When the left hand has taken money from the right, etc., we shall ask: 'Well, and what of it?'[36]

It is not enough that A should on two separate occasions make the same sound whilst concentrating his attention on the same sensation: his use of the sign must be determined by the ceremony, if the ceremony is to count as a definition of the sign. Otherwise, the ceremony will lack 'the further practical consequences' of a definition.

But why is it implausible that when he utters the sound whilst concentrating on the sensation for the second time, he does so precisely because of the original ceremony? Isn't this the most natural conclusion? Again, the objection is confused, for the ceremony will not count as a definition because it causes A to behave in a certain way. If I were to crash my car into a 'Stop' sign, would we call this 'following the rule'? As Wittgenstein once said, a key is not *anything* that opens a locked door! To use a sign in accordance with its definition is to treat the definition as authoritative: *this* is what it means for the use of the sign to be determined by its definition. But if the definition of the sign cannot be invoked to vindicate the sign's use, how can the definition be treated as authoritative? In short, whether or not A uses the sign 'S' consistently, the sign will be meaningless. He will, so to speak, be free to use it however he wishes. 'Whatever is going to seem right . . . is right. And that only means that here we can't talk about "right".'[37]

One may, of course, call a word such as 'pain', 'tickle' or 'itch' the name of a sensation. The conclusion of a philosophical argument is not an act of linguistic legislation. But if the argument is sound, then a word cannot be the name of a sensation in the same sense as the word 'chair' or the word 'table' is the name of a piece of furniture, because the meaning of a word such as 'pain' is not established by associating it with the corresponding sensation. One can point at a table and say that the word 'table' is the name of *this* piece of furniture; but one cannot point at a sensation and say that 'pain' is the name of *this* sensation; and as Wittgenstein showed, focusing one's attention on a sensation cannot serve here as a surrogate for the act of pointing. If we say that 'pain' is the name of a sensation, this simply means 'I am in pain' is the expression of a sensation, and 'He is in pain' is uttered on the grounds of his expressions of sensation.

How, then, do we learn to say 'That hurts!' or 'That tickles!'?

Here is one possibility: words are connected with the primitive, the natural, expressions of the sensation and used in their place. A child has hurt himself and he cries; and then adults talk to him and teach him exclamations and, later, sentences. They teach the child new pain-behaviour.[38]

The suggestion is not that, rather than describing the contents of the mind, avowals describe the natural expressive behaviour which betrays, for example, the fact that a child is in pain: on the contrary, 'the verbal expression of pain replaces crying and does not describe it'.[39] Hence the 'radical break' with the idea that language always functions in the same way. And it is because 'That hurts!' is an expression, a manifestation of pain that such an utterance has a privileged status. It cannot make sense to suppose that I am mistaken when I say that I am in pain. But this is not because I have an unerring ability to discern the contents of my mind: it is because I am not making a report, when I exclaim that I am in pain, but giving voice to my sensations.[40] Thus it is not my cognitive capacities, but the logical character of the utterance, its function in discourse, that excludes the possibility that I am mistaken. Avowals, such as 'My foot hurts!', cannot be mistaken in the sense in which questions cannot be false. If I say sincerely that I have a stabbing pain in my head, disagreement is literally nonsensical.

The purpose of the 'radical break' that Wittgenstein proposes is not merely to correct a grammatical misapprehension. Rather, Wittgenstein aims to show that an immensely influential conception of mental life and its relation to the physical world, a conception which permeates philosophical and psychological theories alike, is not a basic factual framework within which our psychological theories must be fitted, although that is how we generally treat it:

Being unable – when we surrender ourselves to philosophical thought – to help saying such-and-such; being irresistibly inclined to say it – does not mean being forced into an *assumption*, or having an immediate perception or knowledge of a state of affairs.[41]

If we conceive of mental life as an inner world – a world of sensations, images, thoughts and feelings – into which only one person can directly gaze, this is not an elementary, but inescapable, truth about human life; it is a picture: 'Not facts; but as it were illustrated turns of speech.'[42] And the picture will continue to captivate us for as long as we continue to misrepresent the grammar of this region of our language. But if we are able to grasp that the words we call names of sensations are not labels attached to psychological items, that we do not learn to use these words by associating them with the actors in an interior and private drama, and that they are not used to report who has appeared onstage and who has vanished into oblivion, then the temptation to conceive of the mind as a separate world to which a faculty of interior perception grants us access will be resistible.

If it is confused to conceive of sensation on the model of perception, it is doubly confused to conceive of perception on the model of sensation, thus misconceived. But this is precisely what the picture of an interior mental world invites, for sensations are, according to this picture, archetypal psychological entities, and their private apprehension is the paradigmatic psychological experience. If we are held captive by the picture of an interior mental world, then not only sensation, but perceptual experience also will appear in the guise of a private drama; not only words such as 'pain' and 'itch', but the names of colours, musical pitches and other perceptible qualities will also seem to be defined by forging a link in the imagination between a word and a psychological entity; and we shall regard these words as 'mere names for something that resides exclusively in our sensitive body'.[43]

This distortion of the logic of terms denoting perceptible qualities has been no less influential than the closely related, but dissimilar distortion of the logic of sensation-terms. For present purposes, however, we need not examine it in detail. It is sufficient to recognize that the idea that vision involves the introspection – or, to use the modern term, the 'monitoring' – of a private psychological experience is of a piece with the idea that sensations exist in a private mental world, into which only one person can directly gaze. If Wittgenstein's argument succeeds in demonstrating that the meaning of a sensation-term cannot conceivably be established by associating the word with a private experience, it follows that the meaning of a term denoting a perceptual quality cannot be determined in this way either, for exactly the same reasons. And it follows also that when a person tells us what he can see, or that he sees nothing, he is not describing – fallibly or infallibly – a private mental entity, any more than he is doing so when he says that he is in pain.

Neither is a perceptual report an expression or manifestation of visual experience, in the sense in which 'Ouch!' or 'It hurts!' are expression of pain, for it would be absurd to suggest that, e.g., reports of perceived colour are 'connected with the primitive, the natural, expressions' of visual experience, since there is no primitive or natural behaviour tied to the perception of colour. Of course, there are cases where a primitive pattern of behaviour is tied to the visual apprehension of a feature of the infant's environment. Nevertheless, perceptual reports are not taught as avowals of pain are taught. For example, infants are not taught to say 'I see a breast' instead of suckling. So, if perceptual reports are not descriptions of private experience, and do not replace primitive expressive behaviour, how *are* they used? The answer is straightforward: a man who tells us what he can see is, typically, telling us what visible features of his environment he can locate, identify and describe. And a man who says that he sees nothing is, typically, telling us that he cannot discern any visible features of his environment (because he has been blindfolded, for example, or because there is a thick mist, etc.).

A perceptual report may be used to justify the claim that things are thus or so ('How do you know?'; 'I see it!'), not because it offers the corroboration of a private psychological experience, but because it indicates the perceptual modality of knowledge, i.e. it identifies the circumstances in virtue of which one is in a position to say that things are thus and so: for example, there is sufficient light, one's view is unobstructed, etc. There are cases in which a claim that things are thus or so is corroborated by the avowal of a sensation or an experience. For example, if the sun is so bright that I cannot look at it, I might just blink at it, and report the progress of an eclipse by describing the shape of my after-image. If perceptual reports were descriptions of private experience, we should have to regard this as a normal exercise of the faculty of sight. But in fact there is no perceptual report here at all (normal or abnormal): I cannot see the partial eclipse of the sun, because the sun is too bright to look at; and neither do I see my after-image, for after-images are not visibilia: they cannot be illuminated or occluded.

IV

As the reader will recall, Weiskrantz argues that blindsight involves a dissociation 'between reacting and monitoring', between 'a visual discrimination and the commentary offered by the subject himself'.[44]

But what does Weiskrantz mean by monitoring? The answer is not straightforward, but the idea of a monitoring system clearly incorporates the principal features of the traditional philosophical picture of psychological experience that Wittgenstein attacked.

As we have seen, the traditional picture creates the illusion of an interior and private world. My conscious experiences – my perceptions and sensations, thoughts and desires – are private objects of introspective awareness: what Locke called 'internal sense'[45] makes me (and me alone) immediately aware of them. And when I say what I perceive and what I feel, I am describing these private objects.

Weiskrantz's idea of a monitoring system falls squarely in this tradition. Monitoring 'creates conscious experience' or 'awareness'; and awareness 'is a form of privileged access that allows further perceptual and cognitive manipulations to occur'.[46] The monitoring system is not merely intended as an *ad hoc* device to explain the difference between blindsight and normal sight: it 'constitutes consciousness'.[47] Not only perceptions, but sensations ('raw feelings'[48]) and presumably thoughts and desires too, can enter consciousness only as a result of monitoring. The inherent instability in the idea of an introspective faculty, which led Descartes to claim that the perception and its object are one and the same, recurs in the idea of a monitoring system. For although it 'constitutes consciousness', we are also told that it 'form[s] the corpus of material for the introspector of mental processes'.[49] Weiskrantz does not argue, in Cartesian style, that providing the subject-matter ('the corpus of material') for introspection and introspecting itself are one and the same and it is not always clear which of these tasks the monitoring system is supposed to perform. Finally, in the 1986 monograph Weiskrantz endorses the view that avowals are descriptions of private experience, which is, as we have seen, a corollary of the idea that consciousness is due to an interior, quasi-perceptual faculty.[50]

If the argument of the preceding pages is correct, we cannot explain D.B.'s condition in terms of the disconnection of a monitoring system, because the idea of a monitoring system incorporates the fatal defects of the traditional idea of an interior perceptual faculty. If the proposition that our awareness of our sensations and of what we see and hear is due to an interior monitoring system were true, then the very concept of sensation, and the concepts of perceptible qualities, would be unintelligible: for this proposition implies that 'pain', 'red', etc. are the names of private mental entities – which, as Wittgenstein showed, is self-defeating.

The idea of a monitoring system incorporates the defects of the traditional idea of an interior perceptual faculty, but they are not identical. For the traditional idea is basically the idea of a faculty or capacity, whereas Weiskrantz appears to have amalgamated this idea with the idea of a certain kind of neural organization.

The term 'monitoring' was at first used simply as part of the description of a clinical syndrome – the dissociation (in other words, the apparent inconsistency) between D.B.'s performance in the forced choice tasks and his commentary. The form that the experiments took (on the one hand, precisely defined discriminative tasks were repeated hundreds of times and assessed by the experimenters, and on the other, a regular commentary by the subject enabled them to monitor his actual awareness of visible stimuli) made it natural to describe this dissociation as being 'between reacting [sc. visual discrimination] and monitoring [sc. commentary]'. But the influence of the philosophical tradition encouraged psychologists from the outset to regard D.B.'s commentary as 'introspections'[51] and led Weiskrantz to use the term 'monitoring system' as the name of an interior perceptual faculty, which in D.B.'s case was no longer capable of monitoring the results of visual processing.

However, by 1987 Weiskrantz had come to use the term 'monitoring system' to denote a kind of neural organization:

> What I think has become disconnected [in blindsight] is a monitoring system, one that is not part of the serial information-processing task itself, but which can monitor what is going on. I think that is the kind of neural organization one is looking for in order to explain awareness.[52]

This state of affairs is reminiscent of a confusion concerning the use of the word 'shock' which hindered research during the 1940s, and which was spelt out in the general introduction to Grant and Reeve's MRC special report, 'Observations on the General Effects of Injury in Man':

> The word 'shock' is commonly used in two different senses to mean, on the one hand, a pathological state or process and, on the other, a clinical syndrome, often without any clear indication of which sense is intended. Sometimes it is used first in the one sense and then a little later in the other, apparently

without the user being aware of the change. Such a usage must inevitably cause confusion and contradiction.[53]

Just this sort of fluctuation occurs in Weiskrantz's 1987 article. Immediately after he has suggested that 'the brain structure involved in monitoring' may be situated several synapses beyond the striate cortex in each hemisphere, Weiskrantz asks how we could know 'whether the sort of "monitoring system" that I have suggested constitutes consciousness is connected or not in a non-verbal animal'. In spite of the curious use of the word 'constitutes', the context of this question clearly shows that it is a neurophysiological question. However, he answers it by describing 'an ingenious idea put forward by some Canadians' – a technique for 'investigating the distinction between a capacity or a skill [such as walking or washing] and a monitoring of that skill' in animals.[54]

> They have, in effect, allowed laboratory rats to do what they like and then asked them if they knew what they were doing. Actually they did not let them do quite anything they wished, but four things that rats do quite frequently and naturally without training: (1) facewashing; (2) rearing up; (3) walking; or (4) remaining immobile. So the animals had a choice of one of four things to do when they wished. But in order to get a food reward, after they performed any one of these acts they had to press one of four levers, so as to indicate what it was they had done. And the rats *could* do that. Now I do not know whether a sea slug or a crab could do that – I very much doubt it – or a frog, or a pigeon. I would be very surprised if a monkey could *not* do it. . . . So I think there may be a methodology which could be developed to ask animals to indicate what it is they know about their own behaviour.[55]

This quotation illustrates plainly the result of fluctuating between the use of the term 'monitoring' to denote a kind of neural organization, and its use to describe a clinical syndrome. For the experiment Weiskrantz describes (he adds certain refinements which need not concern us) may indeed enable psychologists to distinguish between an animal which can and one which cannot 'monitor' the exercise of a skill; but it does not provide any evidence at all for the existence of a particular kind of neural structure ('one that is not part of the serial information-processing chain itself', etc.).[56]

This alone shows that Grant and Reeve's warning bears repetition:

'Such a usage must inevitably cause confusion and contradiction.' But the promiscuous use of the terms 'monitor' and 'monitoring' also disguises the lack of any evidence that a rat's ability to press a green lever after washing its face depends upon a neural structure of the same kind as enables the normally sighted to describe their visible environment. Why should this far-fetched idea seem in the least plausible? I submit that in the absence of histological evidence, the idea is plausible only if we assume that both tasks depend on introspection, and that a particular neural structure enables us to introspect. This seems to be Weiskrantz's view. And it leads him to suggest that the difference between animals (such as monkeys) that have conscious experience and animals (such as crabs) that do not is the possession by the former of a faculty for introspection, which depends upon a neural structure 'that is not part of the information-processing chain itself'.

As we have seen, Weiskrantz's idea of a monitoring system is not straightforward. At first, the term 'monitoring' was used to refer to D.B.'s commentary. But it soon became involved in a tangle of confusion. For the idea of a monitoring system is the result of amalgamating the confused notion of an introspective faculty with the neural structure postulated in order to explain it, which is not unlike amalgamating the Cartesian soul and the pineal gland. (Except that the pineal gland actually exists, whereas Weiskrantz has simply postulated a neural mechanism to perform an imaginary function.) A monitoring system is thus an amalgam of a psychological capacity – or rather, *the* psychological capacity, upon which all conscious experience depends – and the corresponding neural structure, the structure that 'form[s] the corpus of material for the introspector of mental processes'.[57]

The idea of a neural monitoring system fares no better than the idea of a faculty for interior perception. And it follows that we cannot characterize D.B.'s condition in terms of the disconnection of a monitoring system. Are we then forced to concur with Campion and his co-authors, when they argue that 'the unconscious aspect of blindsight . . . is impossible to treat scientifically'? In other words, have we not simply recommended that scientists ignore D.B.'s private experience (or lack of it) and concentrate exclusively on 'establishing empirical relations between neural structures and behaviour'? On the contrary, the very idea that D.B.'s experience is inaccessible to the scientist is part and parcel of the picture of psychological experience that has proved to be incoherent. For it is precisely the view that

D.B.'s comments are descriptions of a private mental realm, and consequently that we cannot hope for an independent, rigorously scientific confirmation of their accuracy, that was shown to be untenable. And it follows that Campion's sharp distinction between D.B.'s comments and his behaviour is based on a misconception. For it is only if D.B.'s comments are regarded as reports which cannot be checked that we shall be tempted to classify them as something akin to hearsay in a court of law – useless as evidence and a distraction from the pursuit of truth. If, on the other hand, we see D.B.'s comments for what they are – verbal behaviour – the problem and the fascination of blindsight is thrown into sharp relief, and not buried by a dogmatic and confused methodology. For the problem is simply this: D.B.'s performance in the forced choice tasks is inescapable evidence that he sees; and his own comments are similarly inescapable evidence that he does not.

We are by no means forced to reject D.B.'s comments as unscientific and misleading; what we are forced to reject is the picture of D.B. as a man who is capable of responding to visual stimuli despite lacking any awareness of the private psychological experience which normally goes hand in hand with this capacity. The idea of a monitoring system (fallible or not) and Campion's behaviourist methodology are alike rooted in a conception of mental life as a private world to which only the subject of experience has direct, 'privileged' access.

V

Weiskrantz's third conclusion was that the phenomenon of blind-sight exemplifies Luciani's distinction between visual sensation and visual perception. As the reader will recall, Luciani argued that although the extirpation of the visual cortical centres permanently deprives monkeys of visual perception, 'when some time has elapsed after the extirpation, their visual sensations become perfect again'. And whereas the orthodoxy had been that human beings differ from monkeys in this respect (as a result of the encephalization of function), Weiskrantz argued that the phenomenon of blindsight proves otherwise.

What is surprising about this conclusion is that Weiskrantz was not more wary of interpreting the data on blindsight in terms of such a crude distinction. For in the light of the remarkably detailed studies of human beings and animals with occipital lobe damage, and the complex differentiation of the parameters of vision that the research has involved, the distinction between visual sensation and visual perception seems far too blunt an explanatory device. Indeed, the very idea of a visual sensation is far from perspicuous. For by the word 'sensation' we ordinarily mean aches, pains and itches, etc. Sensations are felt, and have bodily location. If my tooth aches, for example, I feel an ache in my tooth. It literally makes no sense to speak of an ache which I cannot feel, and it is no more intelligible to locate a toothache anywhere else in the body – in the foot, for example, or in the brain. But is a monkey supposed to *feel* its visual sensation of a lump of sugar, and if so where?

In fact, Luciani answers the second part of this question directly. The visual sensations, he writes, 'take place in the mesencephali ganglia, and more especially in the corpora quadrigemina'.[58] But what does this mean? It certainly does not mean that the animal feels a lump of sugar in its head. And presumably it does not mean that the animal feels the appearance of a lump of sugar in its head, for this would invite the question, what does the appearance of a lump of sugar feel like?[59] It will not improve matters to suggest that visual sensations are located in the brain, but not felt, for by 'the location of a sensation' we *mean* 'the place where the sensation is felt'. Moreover, if we side-step the question: what does a visual sensation feel like?, the question of where it is located is no more intelligible, for if I were to tell you that I can see a lump of sugar (or even that it seems to me that I can see a lump of sugar) and you asked me where I can see it, 'In my corpora quadrigemina!' would not be an accurate if uninformative answer, but sheer nonsense. If anything counts as a visual sensation, it is the blinding sensation caused by a bright light; and correspondingly, being deafened is the only obvious candidate for an auditory sensation. However, these sensations are in the eye and ear respectively, and not in the brain; and far from being the essential prerequisite of visual or auditory perception, they actually prevent us from seeing or hearing.

The distinction between visual sensation and visual perception does not elucidate the capacity which remains after occipital lobe damage. At best, it is a shorthand which carries an inconvenient baggage of philosophical confusion. But even viewed as such, the shorthand is quite inappropriate, for although it has been shown that, in respect of localization, acuity and the detection of movement and orientation, D.B.'s residual capacity is remarkably similar to the visual capacity of monkeys with confirmed destruction of the striate cortex, Luciani's grounds for describing monkeys after extirpation of the striate cortex as 'deficient of visual perception' lay in their agnosic behaviour, e.g. their incapacity to distinguish meat from sugar by sight alone, and (obviously) had nothing whatever to do with the dissociation of discriminative capacity and acknowledged sight. In fact, if we employ James's terminology (see above, p. 169), we shall be tempted to describe blindsight as the *inverse* of 'psychic blindness', so that D.B. will be regarded as deficient of visual sensation.

VI

The argument of this chapter has been mostly negative. I have examined the debate on blindsight, and discovered that on both sides conceptual confusion has been woven into the fabric of empirical research. And at root, the very same confusion, which is crystalized in the picture of a faculty for interior perception or a monitoring system, is at work. As a result, the exact characteristics of blindsight have been established by dint of painstaking research and remarkable ingenuity in experimental design, but the relationship between blindsight and normal vision has been seriously misrepresented. I would now like to suggest, very briefly, an alternative conception of this relationship, one which does not try to mitigate or escape the paradoxical character of blindsight.

In one of his lectures on the foundations of mathematics, Wittgenstein made the following remark:

> The use of the word 'understand' is based on the fact that in the vast majority of cases when we have applied certain tests, we are able to predict that a man will use the word in question in certain ways. If this were not the case, there would be no point in our using the word 'understand' at all.[60]

By the phrase 'when we have applied certain tests' Wittgenstein presumably meant such things as asking for and receiving an explanation of a word.

Wittgenstein's remark draws attention to the fact that there are many tests of understanding. The concept of understanding, like all psychological concepts, is defined in terms of the patterns of behaviour which license its use. If we wish to know whether somebody understands a word, we can ask him to explain the word's meaning, to use the word in a sentence, or to paraphrase a sentence in which the word occurs. Alternatively, we can use the word ourselves, and consider his response to what was said. These behavioural signs are not merely correlated with understanding, in the sense in which the symptoms of an illness, for example, may be correlated with the presence of a virus in the blood. For this would imply that the concept of understanding was fixed independently of, and prior to, its association with the behavioural signs, i.e. that something corresponds, in the case of understanding a word, to a blood test. In fact the concept of understanding is closely analogous to the concept of an ability or skill, an ability whose exercise consists in the correct explanation and use of the word, and an appropriate response to its use by others. In the vast majority of cases, as Wittgenstein says, these indices of understanding go hand in hand: a man who has passed one of the tests will generally be able to pass the others. It is very unusual to find a systematic dissociation between them. But this regularity of behaviour is a contingent feature of human life: it might have been otherwise. And Wittgenstein's point is that if the pattern of human behaviour were different, the concepts whose use is predicated upon the pattern that exists would no longer be useful ones.

Much the same can be said about the concept of vision, for a correct description of what is before one's eyes, the avowal that one can see it, an appropriate affective response to a visible threat, pointing, indicating whether it is light or dark, simply walking with confidence, are all criteria of visual perception. These indices of vision generally go hand in hand, and this background constancy of our interactions with the visible world is part of the framework within which perceptual verbs are used, and their use is challenged or confirmed; it is a prerequisite for the application of perceptual concepts. We teach and explain these concepts, and children learn their use, against this stable background. In the absence of such constancy we would not employ the perceptual concepts we do; not because they would be incorrect, but simply because the point of using them would be lost. If we did not cry out when hurt, and laugh and smile when amused, then our concepts of pain and amusement would have no grip on our lives.

It is never the facts themselves that are paradoxical, but our manner of representing them. Blindsight is paradoxical, not because

D.B.'s behaviour is absurd or contradictory, but because we are at a loss to describe it, except by resorting to paradoxical expressions, such as 'blindsight' or 'unconscious awareness'. Since the idea of a monitoring system and the distinction between visual sensations and visual perceptions have proved to be riddled with confusion, perhaps these notions too should be regarded as paradoxical contrivances, pieces of conceptual machinery which shunt the paradox out of sight, and so appear to ease the strain. We imagine that they are pieces of neurological machinery which explain D.B.'s behaviour, but in fact they are simply complex and fanciful expedients which ease our puzzlement by substituting a latent paradox for a patent one.

When we attempt to describe D.B., our perceptual vocabulary seizes up, because the very question that we feel irresistibly inclined to ask – namely, whether D.B. can see – is the one question we cannot ask. But the reason we cannot ask it is that the concept of vision cannot be used in his case, because the concatenation of skills and regularities of behaviour that the use of the concept presupposes has been disrupted. And the chief reason why we are tempted to dramatize this disruption of the pattern of human behaviour as a cessation of private visual sensation is that we are inclined to regard a perceptual avowal as a description of a psychological entity, an ethereal actor on a private, interior stage.

The term 'blindsight' is paradoxical, but the phenomenon is not. Rather, it exemplifies the disruption of the normal pattern of regularities of human behaviour which underlies our use of perceptual verbs. The importance of blindsight lies in the fact that this concatenation of skills and regularities of behaviour has not disintegrated, but is systematically ruptured: it exemplifies, as Weiskrantz says, a dissociation of dysfunctions. What it does not exemplify is a disruption of a process which begins with a peripheral stimulus and ends, in the normally sighted, with a private visual sensation; for this process is not an object of psychological study, but a philosophical fantasy, the product of conceptual confusion.

VII

Weiskrantz's experimental study of D. B. anatomized his capacity to detect and discriminate between visual stimuli within a scotoma. But as we have seen, Weiskrantz has also discussed at length the relationship between blindsight and normal sight, in order to explain what it is that we have and D. B. lacks. For his aim is not merely to establish what discriminative capacity survives a lesion of the right side of the primary visual cortex. And neither is it merely to show that the visual systems of humans and monkeys are not as different as was formerly supposed, although this is certainly an important result. Important as it is, the fundamental aim is to see what can be learned from cases of this sort about the neuropsychology of vision.

What can be learned, and how? I have already quoted Weiskrantz's remark, that 'inferences about normal processing stem less from the study of dysfunctions as such than from dissociations of dysfunctions'. Here is the context of that remark:

> One of the lessons of neuropsychology is that inferences about normal processing stem less from the study of dysfunction as such than from dissociations of dysfunctions. I have talked today about two quite different types of dissociation. The first is between dimensions of visual capacity, such as detection, form, spatial localisation, orientation and movement. . . . The second type of dissociation is of a different sort. It is between visual discrimination and the commentary offered by the subject himself. . . . The distinction lies not between verbal and non-verbal but in the type of question the subject is attempting to answer, and the type of decision he makes: it is between reacting and monitoring.[61]

My discussion of blindsight research has focused on the second type of dissociation, for three reasons. First, it is the principal source of the fascination with blindsight among experimental psychologists. As Weiskrantz wrote in the 1986 monograph:

> The problem that has captured the interest of blindsight researchers did not emerge from a mysterious vapourous mist, but directly from the study of the patients themselves and in their relation to behavioural and physiological evidence from animals. It was the disjunction between their verbal reports and their discriminative capacity that was surprising. The question now is what status (in 'scientific' terms) to attach to these verbal reports?[62]

Second, one of the principal issues dividing Weiskrantz and his critics is the issue of what status we should accord to D. B.'s 'verbal reports' or 'commentary'. The matter on which they are divided is not the *content* of these verbal reports: both sides agree that they should be construed as descriptions of private phenomenal experience.[63] What divides them is the question, what use science can make of these reports. Weiskrantz believes that it is foolish to exclude descriptions of private phenomenal experience from a scientific investigation into the neuropsychology of vision; that would be regressing to the arid methodology of the behaviourists. His critics disagree. That is why they have claimed that 'the unconscious aspect of blindsight ... is impossible to treat scientifically'.[64] In other words, what these critics balk at is precisely the scientific investigation of a syndrome which is defined in terms of the abrogation of 'privileged access',[65] because where access is privileged the objective standards of scientific research cannot be maintained.

The third reason why I have focused on the dissociation between visual discrimination and commentary is that the interpretation of D.B.'s verbal reports as descriptions of private phenomenal experience and the explanation of the difference between blindsight and normal vision to which this leads are fundamentally misguided. If we regard perceptual statements – statements like 'I see such-and-such' or 'I hear such-and-such' – as making 'verbal reference to phenomenal experience',[66] then we are held in the grip of an intellectual vice, in both senses of that word: an exceedingly powerful and irredeemably flawed philosophical picture of the human mind, of sensation, and of perception.

I have tried to substantiate this claim, in the following way. Following Wittgenstein, I have examined the link between two ideas: on the one hand, the idea that D. B.'s verbal commentaries – or indeed any expression of a person's thought, perceptual experience or sensations – are 'verbal references to phenomenal experience', i.e. descriptions of subjective experience, descriptions which are constructed out of names for phenomenal items; and on the other hand, the idea of an interior perceptual faculty which gives us 'privileged access', i.e. an exclusively intimate acquaintance, with an interior, hidden realm of phenomenal experience. These ideas are two sides of the same coin, two complementary aspects of the same distorted mythology. I have presented one of the many strands of argument that can be found in Wittgenstein's complex and fundamental challenge to this mythology, and the philosophical tradition that built and sustained it. And I have argued that the idea of a monitoring system is a variation on the theme of an interior perceptual faculty. Finally, I have offered an alternative account of the relationship between blindsight and normal vision, one which dispenses with the chimerical monitoring system.

Many experimental psychologists, faced with argument of this sort, are tempted to ask why anybody should suppose that a philosophical muddle is of vital importance in the investigation of residual capacity within a scotoma and its relation to normal vision. I addressed this worry in general terms in the introductory chapter. But the challenge implicit in the question assumes a particular form when it is raised in connection with a philosophical critique of a specific research project, because one can then ask, more tactfully, but with exactly the same purpose: what difference could any of this conceivably make to the next experiment?

The answer, of course, depends on what the next experiment is supposed to achieve. If, for example, the next experiment is intended to establish whether D.B.'s capacity to detect the orientation of a bar is affected if the bar is moving instead of stationary, then nothing that I have to say will have any bearing on it. Indeed, every one of Weiskrantz's experiments can be described, and its results interpreted, in a way that insulates it completely from any sort of philosophical criticism. But this safety is bought at a high price, because viewed in these terms the experiment contributes to the highly detailed picture of the discriminative capacity that has survived D. B.'s lesion, but it does not lend any support whatever to the apparently exciting discovery that a monitoring system is what enables the normally sighted to perceive visible features of their environment.

My criticisms of blindsight research do not concern its experimental aspect, which is ingenious, scrupulous, detailed and objective. Indeed my review of the controversy over blindsight was intended to show that the criticisms levelled against the research failed to hit their target. But I have also tried to show that the interpretation of experimental results has been influenced profoundly by an exceedingly powerful philosophical picture, one which has gripped the popular imagination for several hundred years and, in its different guises, has dominated both *a priori* and experimental psychology in the same period. Both the distinction between sensorial and perceptual processing (which Weiskrantz took over from Luciani) and the notion that blindsight exemplifies the disconnection of a monitoring system betray the influence of this picture.

The idea of a monitoring system is in essence a philosophical thesis in the guise of a neuropsychological hypothesis, the thesis that normal vision involves a subjective phenomenon to which each sighted person has privileged access; and for this reason I have tried to destroy its credibility. However, the overall purpose of this chapter is not destructive. It is now easy for us to acknowledge that despite their permanent contributions to the scientific study of vision, Alhazen, Kepler and Helmholtz were all, in their different ways, misled by the various philosophical views which they espoused, and which to a considerable extent moulded each man's view of his own achievement. And, of course, the vastly more sophisticated experimental method which guides research today cannot afford the least measure of protection against this sort of danger, for philosophical theories lie at the furthest remove from experimental confirmation or disconfirmation. They are infinitely accommodating to the facts, whatever the facts may be. The philosopher's job – as far as this sort of enquiry is concerned – is to remove the philosophical impurities which corrupt visual theory, so that the achievements of visual theorists can be seen in a truer light.

NOTES

I am very grateful to Prof. L. Weiskrantz for his comments on an earlier draft, and for several valuable discussions on these matters.

1 L. Weiskrantz, 'Evidence and Scotomata', *Behavioural and Brain Sciences* 6 (1983), 464–7.
2 L. Weiskrantz, 'Varieties of Residual Experience', *Quarterly Journal of Experimental Psychology* 32 (1980), 371.
3 These are summarized in L. Weiskrantz, *Blindsight* (Oxford: Oxford University Press, 1986), 140–3. More recently, Weiskrantz has developed a battery of techniques for studying residual capacity within a scotoma without requiring guessing responses: see L. Weiskrantz, 'Outlooks for Blindsight Explicit Methodologies for Implicit Processes', *Proc. R. Soc. Lond.* (1990), 1–32.
4 Weiskrantz, 'Varieties of Residual Experience', 374.
5 Ibid., 382.
6 Ibid., 383–4.
7 Weiskrantz, *Blindsight*, 169.
8 Ibid., 384.
9 Ibid., 384.
10 L. Luciani, 'On the Sensorial Localisations in the Cortex Cerebri', *Brain* 7 (1884), 145–60.
11 Luciani, op. cit., 153; quoted in Weiskrantz, 'Varieties of Residual Experience', 369.
12 Luciani, op. cit., 152–3.
13 Weiskrantz, 'Varieties of Residual Experience', 369.
14 Ibid., 384–5.

15 Luciani, op. cit., 148.
16 W. James, *Principles of Psychology* (London: Macmillan and Co., 1890), 49.
17 Ibid., 47.
18 Weiskrantz, 'Varieties of Residual Experience', 370.
19 J. Campion, R. Latto and Y. M. Smith, 'Is Blindsight an Effect of Scattered Light, Spared Cortex, and Near-threshold Vision?', *Behavioural and Brain Sciences* 6 (1983), 423–48 (peer review and reply, 449–86). Henceforth, references to this article and the accompanying material will be made by page numbers in parentheses.
20 Compare the remarks about shock, below, n. 60.
21 See Weiskrantz, *Blindsight*, 103–7.
22 In fact many of the tests were safe (ibid., 143–6).
23 This is amplified ibid., 103–7.
24 Ibid., 163.
25 Ibid., 148.
26 See ibid., 153.
27 See N. Malcolm, 'Consciousness and Causality', in D. M. Armstrong and N. Malcolm, *Consciousness and Causality* (Oxford: Basil Blackwell, 1984), 3–4, 30–1.
28 A rather different analogy has been proposed for the same purpose: '[In the case of blindsight,] the patient's reluctance to use his residual visual capacity is presumably because he has no record of its existence in self-awareness, and so he remains blind to the fact that he can see ... In an analogous way, we may suppose that some stimuli do not enter self-awareness even in intact brains . . . and we, like the blindsight patients, would be expected to deny vigorously their existence . . . [e.g.] the reputed influence of olfactory stimuli (pheromones) on human behaviour.' (D. A. Oakley and L. C. Eames, 'The Plurality of Consciousness', in D. A. Oakley (ed.), *Brain and Mind* (London: Methuen and Co., 1985), 223; for a similar argument and the same example, see J. Economos, in Campion, Latto and Smith, op. cit., 452.) This analogy, between pheromones and visual stimuli within D.B.'s field defect, fares no better than the other. To be sure, olfactory stimuli can influence human behaviour: the smell of a bakery in the early morning will have most passers-by sniffing the air like dogs. But pheromones cannot be called olfactory stimuli (which 'do not enter self-awareness') because however they may influence behaviour, they have no smell. Cocaine influences behaviour; but it is odourless for all that. In other words, to perceive something is not simply to be affected by it. (Nor is it to perceive its effect: gazing at a handsome suntan is not the same as perceiving the sun's intensity!) Rather, perception is typically a source of knowledge, for a perceptual capacity is a capacity to learn about certain (perceptible) features of the environment, either by touch or by the use of sense organs. Sight, for example, is the capacity to learn about the visible environment by using one's eyes; and to smell something is, at the very least, to learn how it smells – whether it is musty, acrid or alluring. It is true, of course, that psychological experiments have demonstrated that apparently unperceived auditory

stimuli may nevertheless influence my subsequent performance in, say, a verbal-recall task. But this fact does not show that the subject did, unknowingly, hear the words after all, for as we have seen, to perceive something is not merely to be affected by it – and this is the case regardless of whether the stimulus was perceptible (e.g. a sound) or not (e.g. pheromones). What the experiments show is that sounds may influence behaviour without being heard.

29 It would be a mistake to suppose that psychosomatic pains or the so-called phantom pains suffered by amputees disprove this principle. For psychosomatic pains are not non-existent, they are pains that are not caused by injury, disease, etc.; and it is neither the existence nor the phenomenological character of phantom pains that is problematic, but their physical location.

30 R. Descartes, 'Passions of the Soul', in E. S. Haldane and G. R. T. Ross (trans and eds), *The Philosophical Works of Descartes*, (Cambridge: Cambridge University Press, 1931), 329–429, at p. 340.

31 Quoted in James, op. cit., 179.

32 The most penetrating and painstaking guide to Wittgenstein's treatment of these issues is P.M.S. Hacker, *Wittgenstein: Meaning and Mind* (Oxford: Basil Blackwell, 1990).

33 See L. Wittgenstein, *Philosophical Investigations* (Oxford: Basil Blackwell, 1953), §292.

34 Ibid., §304.

35 Ibid., §265.

36 Ibid., §268.

37 Ibid., §258.

38 Ibid., §244.

39 Ibid., §244.

40 We can, of course, distinguish between an exclamation of pain and what may properly be called a report, such as one gives to a doctor. But the report is not based on introspection either. The analogy with statements of intention is useful: one may exclaim 'I'm leaving!' or else give a careful account of where one intends to go. In both cases on is announcing an intention; in neither case is one describing a private psychological entity.

41 Wittgenstein, op. cit., §299.

42 Ibid., §295.

43 Galileo, *The Assayer*, quoted in P. M. S. Hacker, *Appearance and Reality* (Oxford: Basil Blackwell, 1987), 3.

44 Weiskrantz, 'Varieties of Residual Experience', 383.

45 Locke, *An Essay Concerning Human Understanding*, II, ch. i, sect. 4.

46 L. Weiskrantz, 'Neuropsychology and Consciousness', in C. Blakemore and S. Greenfield (eds), *Mindwaves* (Oxford: Basil Blackwell, 1987), 319; Weiskrantz, *Blindsight*, 169.

47 Weiskrantz, 'Neuropsychology and Consciousness', 317.

48 Weiskrantz, *Blindsight*, 166.

49 L. Weiskrantz, 'Brain Function and Awareness', in R. L. Gregory (ed.), *The Oxford Companion to the Mind* (Oxford: Oxford University Press, 1987), 112.

50 Weiskrantz, *Blindsight*, 164.
51 Weiskrantz, 'Varieties of Residual Experience', 374.
52 Weiskrantz, 'Neuropsychology and Consciousness', 316.
53 Series 227 (1951), 1.
54 Weiskrantz, 'Neuropsychology and Consciousness', 317; ibid., 318–19.
55 Ibid., 317.
56 Weiskrantz, 'Neuropsychology and Consciousness', 316.
57 See n. 49.
58 Luciani, op. cit., 153.
59 The answer is not: white and granular. This would imply that visual sensations are seen rather than felt. But it is certainly the lump of sugar, rather than a putative sensation, that the animal sees, if it sees anything. For visual sensations, if there are such things, cannot be visibilia. If they were, they could be illuminated or photographed.
60 L. Wittgenstein, *Lectures on the Foundations of Mathematics: Cambridge 1939*, ed. C. Diamond (Hassocks: Harvester Press, 1976), 23.
61 Weiskrantz, 'Varieties of Residual Experience', 382–4.
62 Weiskrantz, *Blindsight*, 163.
63 'The examiner, like all of us in our daily interactions, assumes that the verbal response *does* have content and reference. ... We shall assume here that such a verbal reference is usually to phenomenal experience (only "usually", because verbal reports can themselves be automatic and devoid of any corresponding experience as a referent.)' Weiskrantz, *Blindsight*, 164.
64 J. Campion et al., 'Is Blindsight an Effect of Scattered Light', 427.
65 Weiskrantz, *Blindsight*, 169.
66 See n. 63.

INDEX